The Inexorable Evolution of Financialisation

The Inexorable Evolution of Financialisation

Financial Crises in Emerging Markets

Domna M. Michailidou

Economic Consultant, Department of Country Studies, OECD, Paris, France and Research Fellow, Judge Business School, University of Cambridge, UK

First published 2016 by
PALGRAVE MACMILLAN

Palgrave Macmillan in the UK is an imprint of Macmillan Publishers Limited, registered in England, company number785998, of Houndmills, Basingstoke, Hampshire RG21 6XS.

Palgrave Macmillan in the US is a division of St Martin's Press LLC, 175 Fifth Avenue, New York, NY 10010.

Palgrave Macmillan is the global academic imprint of the above companies and has companies and representatives throughout the world.

Palgrave® and Macmillan® are registered trademarks in the United States, the United Kingdom, Europe and other countries.

ISBN 978–1–137–55363–8

This book is printed on paper suitable for recycling and made from fully managed and sustained forest sources. Logging, pulping and manufacturing processes are expected to conform to the environmental regulations of the country of origin.

A catalogue record for this book is available from the British Library.

Library of Congress Cataloging-in-Publication Data
Michailidou, Domna, 1987–
The inexorable evolution of financialisation : financial crises in emerging markets / Domna Michailidou, Teaching Fellow,School of Public Policy, University College London, UK.
pages cm
ISBN 978–1–137–55363–8 (hardback)
1. Developing countries—Economic conditions.   2. Debts, Public—Developing countries.   3. Financial crises—Developing countries.   4. International finance.   I. Title.
HC59.7.M488   2015
338.5'42091724—dc23   2015023407

Typeset by MPS Limited, Chennai, India.

Στον Άρη και τη Μάρτζυ, Τον ουρανό στο κεφάλι μας –
μόνο αυτό να φοβόμαστε

A small contribution

to the inexorable quest

for understanding

financial markets

ΔOMNA MICHAILIDOU

JULY 2017

Contents

List of Figures and Tables		viii
Foreword by G. C. Harcourt		x
Preface		xi
Acknowledgements		xiv
1	Introduction: Financial Crises – An Inter-Temporal, Inter-National and Endogenous Capitalist Problem	1
2	A Keynesian and Post-Keynesian Theoretical Brief: Selected Concepts	15
3	Post-1980 Global Liquidity Data: Exponential Flows	38
4	Supply-Push: The Western-Induced Endogenous Generation and Proliferation of Liquidity	47
5	Demand-Pull: The Internally Induced Attractiveness of Emerging Markets	56
6	Mexico: The Laissez Faire Paragon Gone Wrong	64
7	Brazil: The Anti-Mexican Public Debt Failure	84
8	South Korea: The Private Debt Story	105
9	Deregulation and Volatility: Where the Three Economies Meet	121
10	An Endogenous Conclusion	152
Appendix		169
Notes		171
References		182
Index		194

List of Figures and Tables

Figures

1.1	The "3 routes to crisis" and their early manifestations	7
3.1	The stock of global financial assets, 1980–2007	39
3.2	Gross Portfolio inflows in Latin America, 1950–2010	42
4.1	Evolution of financial assets, USA – deflated to 2010 US$	48
4.2a	Real interest rates, USA	53
4.2b	Short-term interest rates, USA	53
4.3	Ratings of foreign currency sovereign debt	54
6.1a	US dollar LIBOR interest rate (six-month)	65
6.1b	Immediate interest rates, USA	65
6.2	Mexico's contribution to emerging economies' GDP and asymmetrical share of capital flows	69
6.3	Mexico's private debt, US$ (2012)	71
6.4	Stock of net foreign exchange reserves in 1994 ($US mn)	75
6.5	Mexico's reserves position, US$ (2010)	76
6.6	Mexico's real effective exchange rate	78
6.7	Mexico's current account balance, percentage of GDP	78
6.8	Mexico's public debt, PPG, percentage of GDP	79
6.9	Yields on Mexican and US Government securities, January 1994–January 1997 (in percent)	81
7.1	Brazil's inflation, GDP deflator (annual percentage)	85
7.2	Brazil's current account balance, percentage of GDP	88
7.3	Composition of capital flows, US$ (2012)	89
7.4	Brazil's real effective exchange rate (REER) (1994=100)	95
7.5	Brazil's public debt, percentage of GDP	98
7.6	Brazil's private debt, US$ (2012)	99
7.7	Brazil's reserves position, US$ (2010)	100
8.1	Japan's real effective exchange rate (2005=100)	106

8.2   Korea's current account balance, percentage of GDP   111

8.3   Korea's trade balance, percentage of GDP   112

8.4   Korea's public debt, percentage of GDP   114

8.5   Korea's reserve position, US$ (2010)   118

8.6   Korea's external debt, percentage of GDP   118

9.1   Mexico's stock market capitalisation, US$ (2012)   123

9.2   Brazil's stock market capitalisation, US$ (2012)   124

9.3   Korea's stock market capitalisation, US$ (2012)   124

9.4   Public bonds Latin America, US$ (2012)   126

9.5   Public debt dynamics: Central Government debt, percentage of GDP   126

9.6   Private bonds Latin America, US$ (2012)   128

9.7   Shortening of debt maturities and crises in developing countries   130

9.8   Ratio of short-term debt to reserves   132

9.9   Reversal of private flows in times of crisis, US$ bn   132

9.10   Foreign exchange reserves Latin America, US$ (2012)   135

9.11   Foreign exchange reserves East Asia, US$ (2012)   136

9.12   Interest rate differentials, the US and the three economies   142

9.13   Kindleberger and data – pro-cyclical flows, Latin America   145

9.14   Consumption levels, Mexico and Korea, percentage of GDP   149

Tables

5.1   Latin America stock exchange prices, 1990–1998   58

6.1   Government bond investments   73

7.1   Inflationary revenue contributions in the early 1990s   91

7.2   Real interest rates (average annual rates)   100

7.3   Outstanding government debt, bn of Reais   101

7.4   Total and non-performing loans to the private sector, mn of Reais   101

8.1   Short-term and total debt in East Asia   107

9.1   Growth of short-term debt to developing countries in the 1990s   131

Foreword

I had the privilege of examining the dissertation from which this book idea arose. Now I have the pleasure of writing a foreword to it. That dissertation and this volume are role models of how an applied topic should be tackled and brought to completion. Dr Michailidou wanted to know the impact of freeing up capital markets on relatively small middle-income open economies. Her case studies are three very different economies – Mexico, Brazil and Korea. She examines how the role of greatly increased liquidity due to the freeing up of capital markets combined with globalisation interacted with the processes at work in the economies to lead all three by different detailed routes to financial crisis.

For her theoretical framework, she draws on the writings of three great economists: John Maynard Keynes, Charles Kindleberger and Hyman Minsky. Her theoretical structure is an amalgamation of their insights. She uses it to make sense of the very careful empirical narratives she has written concerning the experiences of the three economies from the 1970s to the early 2000s. She concludes with some implications for policies that may help governments to tackle future episodes of this sort occurring and having such drastic social and economic effects on similar and other economies. An especially acute insight concerns the negative economic and social consequences of finance rather than manufacturing being the epicentre of the principal processes at work in economies.

Her approach is much influenced by Gabriel Palma, her supervisor and mentor. Palma and now Michailidou continue in the tradition of the best Cambridge economists who come under the rubric of post-Keynesianism, especially Nicholas Kaldor. Her use of simple and revealing figures and tables, a hallmark of Palma's work, is just the way good applied work should be done.

I recommend her book for all these virtues and ask you, dear reader, to now read on.

G. C. Harcourt
School of Economics, UNSW Australia

Preface

The 2007 financial crisis is the most recent reminder that economists are a long way from understanding public finances, private debt dynamics, the operation of the banking system and finance as a whole.

What has become clear is that mainstream economic theory could not provide answers and certainly did not avert such a financial meltdown. We should thus look beyond mainstream theory in order to understand what different explanations have to offer with regard to the causes of financial instability. In order to create a holistic understanding of the emergence of unstable financial markets and consequently to devise policy recommendations to avoid such a formation in the future, different fragments of financial history need to be combined. It is important that insights from mainstream economists are not totally overlooked as they have been paramount to the evolution of capitalism and financial markets in particular. The persistence of the two dynamics described below can lead to equally myopic understandings of capitalist financial systems: first, the lack of Keynesian theory in the understanding of financial markets and, second, the omission of mainstream thinking in the understanding of the evolution of capitalism. The first has already resulted in the recurrence of un-averted financial crises, while the second can result in parochial conclusions that overlook actual developments and market behaviours. A framework that draws on theoretical insights of different, even polar opposite, parts of economic literature needs to be developed in order to facilitate the design of new financial and regulatory policy to tackle instability and use finance as a tool to enhance the real economy rather than being the core of economic activity itself.

The above implies, and will hopefully result, in a more detailed understanding of the dialectic relationship between liberalisation and capital inflows, or else deregulation and debt, or, even better, supply and the corresponding ever-clearing levels of demand – where demand for finance will permanently match any increases in the supply of finance, whereas the opposite formulation does not hold.

This book attempts to provide an understanding of this dialectic relationship in the intrinsic clearing balance of financial markets through addressing a fundamental question in financial and development economics: Does financial liberalisation, when concurring with high levels of international capital movement and little or no capital controls, lead inexorably to financial crises? In doing so, the book will examine the origins of and responses to financial crises in the context of three very different middle-income economies in the 1990s: Mexico, Brazil and South Korea.

The aim is to understand the causes of the abrupt increase in the stocks and flows of financial capital, the reasons behind their direction towards new outlets and the strategies pursued in the recipient countries to deal with the inflows. In the 1990s Mexico, Brazil and South Korea were all recipients of large flows of international liquidity but had very different economic characteristics, and adopted different structural reforms and liberalisation policies. They are examples of three possible routes to financial crisis. Mexico is an example of an economy with a mostly *laissez faire* policy *vis-à-vis* the surge of inflows. Brazil comprises an economy which instead adopted a nearly full sterilisation policy at the same time as embracing full liberalisation. In Korea the additional finance created by inflows was used productively by the corporate sector, but the economy still experienced a severe crisis as a result of an unsustainable increase in its corporate debt. The book demonstrates that three countries with radically different economic policies *vis-à-vis* surges in inflows all suffered from financial crises as an unavoidable outcome of their capital account liberalisation given the magnitude of global liquidity stocks and flows.

The book aims to contribute towards a better understanding of financial crises in middle-income developing countries in general, as well as Mexico, Brazil and South Korea in particular. One of the main propositions found in the work of John Maynard Keynes – the endogeneity of disturbances to the financial system and the intractable uncertainty of financing and investment decisions – is explored. It will be argued that Keynesian and post-Keynesian theories of Minsky and Kindleberger provide a fruitful framework for explaining the relationship between capital account liberalisation and financial crises in each case. In addition, the analysis will attempt to demonstrate the problems and limitations with mainstream economists' analyses with regard to two main channels. First, while mainstream economic discourse tends to stress the role of unsuccessful domestic policies on the evolution of financial crises, this analysis will demonstrate that capital account liberalisation led to financial crisis regardless of the domestic policy pursued. Second, the analysis will illustrate how economic reality is much more complex than assumed by the Efficient Market Hypothesis (EMH) that undergirds policies of financial liberalisation that are commonly recommended by international organisations to emerging economies.

There are potential important policy implications that can result from this body of research. The book aims to understand the mechanisms behind the occurrence of systemic financial crises and, in particular, whether capital control devices can be fine-tuned to avoid financial crises. A major thesis that will be emphasised is the need to recognise the benefits afforded by the control of capital inflows and the pursuit of engineered financial policies in order to prevent financial instability. This challenges the much celebrated virtues of open capital accounts and liberalised liquidity flows.

Acknowledgements

My inexorable interest in the idiosyncratic function of financial markets is a direct result of the presence, absence (!) and influence of Gabriel Palma. It was an honour being his student, an intellectual challenge being his discussant and a source of wisdom and family warmth getting close to him. Apart from a supportive and understanding PhD supervisor, I was incredibly lucky to have by my side an incredibly knowledgeable academic, loving individual, unique thinker and a great teacher who set the standard for critical thinking formidably high. Hours upon hours of discussion in his infamous 'office', lengthy midnight calls and nights (if not mornings) of afterthought following them will be among the strongest memories of my years in Cambridge.

This book would not have been possible without the advice and support of Geoffrey Harcourt. It was as a result of his encouragement that I submitted this manuscript for publication. I could not have hoped for a more knowledgeable and quick-witted critic and supporter at the same time. I am also extremely thankful to Ha-Joon Chang. It has been an incredible fortune being close to a remarkable teacher with the perspective of a global thinker who has been open to discussion, willing to critically evaluate my work and always available in times of need.

I will always be thankful to two individuals who shaped my path not only as remarkable academics but mostly as devoted, stimulating and motivating individuals: Sue Bowden and Alvaro Pereira. They were both an unlimited source of inspiration and enthusiasm in an otherwise wearisome field. Sue is a truly moving teacher – second to no one I have met so far. Alvaro is the most extraordinarily personable and charismatic academic I have ever met. He injected enthusiasm and interest in the least imagined areas of my undergraduate years. Life has it that he is currently injecting equal enthusiasm in my post-doctorate years as my boss, this time in the OECD!

At Cambridge, I must thank the Cambridge Commonwealth, European and International Trust, the Vergotis Foundation and Newnham College for funding my research. In the Centre of Development Studies, Shailaja Fennel, Ajit Singh and Robert Rowthorn from Economics provided me several times with helpful advice but most importantly fuelled me with interest for my research and field of study. In the real world I would like to say a big thank you to Palgrave Macmillan for their support and encouragement. My editor, Laura Pacey, has been incredibly helpful in facilitating the efficient production of this manuscript.

I should also thank the Centre of Development Studies, the Department of Economics and the Judge Business School for giving me the opportunity to lecture, supervise and engage with a pool of very different students in various economic subjects. It was most often the happiness brought about by the challenges of teaching that kept me company, but also the in-class discussions that often initiated questions that encouraged my further research. Understanding the difference – and most importantly progressing – from a state of conveying concepts to ensuring your audience is actually stimulated by them has been the most creative challenge of my years in Cambridge. On this, I should thank all of my students for their involvement, enthusiasm and patience with me, but I should also thank a person who indirectly, and most likely involuntarily, cultivated my excitement for teaching in the last 27 years. My aunt Athena has been a limitless source of energy and zeal for education. Her courage and endurance to achieve it are nowhere to be found nowhere else.

On a personal level I would like to thank Pavlos Efthymiou, Alexander Kentikelenis, Ali Khan, David Matathias, Igor Rocha, Todd Tucker, Kim Wagenaar, Javier Gonzalez and Catalina Droppelmann. Their ideas, feedback, company and good humour have certainly contributed to the fondest of my memories. The sudden arrival of Santiago undeniably added happiness and hope to many grey Cambridge days. There are two people I cannot fail to thank, Natalya and Jon. Natalya Naqvi has become family to me in the last years. Her sparkle, energy for life, genuine critical eye and patience with me have been invaluable. Jonathan Kennedy has proved a very loving and unswerving companion. Supportive in bleakness, enduring in madness, affectionate in tranquility and still loving of my energy and feelings. Jon achieved and even optimised the unoptimisable: being patient, with my work and myself while at the same time being the most critical, creative and above all loving connoisseur of my work. Thank you – genuinely, deeply and wholeheartedly.

Lastly, I would like to thank above everyone else my parents. My father's critical spirit, thirst for knowledge and continuous urge to see the structural and holistic picture have guided me in life decisions. The affection, sweetness and care of my mother have kept me company and have flooded the deepest of my being with love. Individually, they have been tender and giving to me on a level I could have never asked for, but it has been their unity that has taught me the real power of human love, sentiments and feelings. This book is dedicated to them, Aris and Martzy.

1
Introduction: Financial Crises – An Inter-Temporal, Inter-National and Endogenous Capitalist Problem

The incidents of financial crises in emerging economies of the 1990s are numerous and of great interest for macroeconomists. The subject provides substantial material for the study of emerging economies, financial markets, liquidity movements, public and private debt dynamics, as well as macroeconomic policy design and application. This book presents a persuasive argument showing that high levels of financial flows together with low, if not absent, levels of capital controls are key in the generation of financial crises in newly liberalised economies.

A key question in development and financial economics is addressed: Does financial liberalisation when concurring along with high levels of international capital movement and little or no capital controls lead almost inescapably to financial crises? Concentrating on middle-income economies, and especially choosing three very different economies that all experienced financial crises in the 1990s, this book concludes that there are clear lessons to be learnt regarding financial fragility, volatility and failure given capital markets' liberalisation.

One of the main propositions found in the work of John Maynard Keynes regarding the capitalist financial system being inherently unstable is examined throughout the book and applied to middle-income developing countries. This proposition has divided economists for several decades and has produced a large debate on the necessity, nature and appropriate extent of government regulation in financial markets and capital accounts. The book adopts a novel approach in applied economics with regard to the understanding of systemic causes of financial crises. Rather than investigate specific geographical regions or common policy patterns leading to crises, this research builds a wide array of all possible domestic policy scenarios that independently lead to crises in order to provide a holistic understanding of the crises' intrinsic nature to the capitalist system of finance.

Through the analysis of three different economies in the context of domestic and international market liberalisation, this book explores the nature of systemic fragility in financial markets in middle-income countries with open capital accounts. Specifically, it investigates the relationship between sudden surges of capital inflows and financial crises in a group of middle-income developing countries with recently liberalised capital accounts.

An inter-temporal capitalist issue

Given the current financial turbulence and the on-going discussion on the causes of the present crisis, this book re-introduces Keynes' proposition regarding the endogeneity of disturbances to the financial system and intractable uncertainty of financing and investment decisions in the context of middle-income developing countries. This is achieved through an analysis of the validity of the above-mentioned proposition in the framework of three earlier crises (those of Brazil, Mexico and South Korea) which mainstream economic analysis has hitherto studied mostly in terms of misdirected, inadequate and unsuccessful domestic policies. The book investigates how the occurrence of a crisis is shaped by the interplay between exogenous surges in liquidity and the pursuit of domestic economic policies. To draw these investigations into broader focus, the susceptibility of the capitalist system to financial disturbances and crises in a broader economic climate of high international liquidity is explored, along with the impact of domestic policies which seek to liberalise the three economies' capital accounts. This is delivered through an examination of the direction, character and volatility of international liquidity at the time. Though all three countries examined followed radically different routes to crises, all of them were preceded by policies of rapid financial deepening, liberalisation and deregulation.

The on-going world recession and continuously deepening Eurozone debt crisis bring to the forefront of discussion the need for economic policy designed to tackle financial instability. The question thus addressed in this book is essential for the identification of the nature and volume of intervention needed in financial markets. The hazard of financial instability has become central in development economics, and increasingly there has been discussion on the nature of required policy design and intervention. Creating a framework inimical to systemic financial crises has been historically a major concern of policymakers, but now more than ever this development is in need of urgent realisation. Understanding the mechanisms behind the occurrence of systemic financial crises and averting their incidence could be an important first step for policy towards this direction. It is exactly to this field that this research attempts to make a contribution.

To understand how capital flows can induce volatility in financial markets, and consequently to the whole of the economy, the book investigates a series of specific and inter-connected developments which, given the economies' macroeconomic fundamentals, contributed to the crises that occurred. These are the causes of the abrupt increase in the stocks and flows of financial capital, the reasons behind their direction towards new outlets – specifically emerging economies – and the policies pursued in the recipient countries to deal with the inflows and the type and maturity-horizons assigned to the inflows. With regard to the factors causing the abrupt jumps in the generation and circulation of flows, we identify external and internal factors contributing to the changes and shaping the levels of financial capital in the emerging world. Following the work of distinguished scholars, a distinction is drawn between supply-push and demand-pull factors related to the jumps of capital flows (see Palma, 2003a, 2011a). The first are specific to the generation of liquidity through deregulation, financial engineering and lower profit opportunities manifested in the lower returns of US Treasury bonds and the overall slowdown of economic growth in the Western markets. The second are specific to changes applied to the overall economic policies and financial markets of emerging economies. This is delivered to set the background against the attraction of all capital inflows which when combined with an analysis of their type and maturity allows us to shape conclusions on the real causes of the crises.

The aim of the book

The book aims to assess the following two questions: how are injections of international liquidity absorbed in middle-income developing countries and do they contribute to the genesis of financial crises? And how do policies of capital account liberalisation are associated to financial fragility? These questions are addressed in reverse order. The first question is approached through the breakdown of the stock of financial assets in these countries (into bank deposits, stock market capitalisation figures, public and private bonds) and the analysis of the significance and implications of the evolution of each form of liquidity in each country. The second question is addressed through investigating the reasons for the post-1980s' rapid increase in international liquidity levels through an overall political economy framework and through exploring the economic policies of each country in the context of their general performance. The outcome of this analysis will be used to determine the reasons behind liquidity inflows in the countries studied and, more broadly, the implications of unrestrained liquidity injections with regard to the fuelling of financial booms. Through determining these two elements, it will be possible to establish the impact of one more critical Keynesian concept, that of expectations.

The questions, set out above, raise the following additional avenues of investigation that contribute to a more rounded understanding of the research question.

- Why has the world economy experienced such an increase in international liquidity since the 1980s?
- Why did middle-income developing countries suddenly become attractive as an outlet for this liquidity in the late 1980s and early 1990s?
- Why did a sudden surge in inflows create so much domestic havoc in middle-income developing countries?
- How does the study of three different middle-income developing economies, which have all suffered from financial crises, illustrate the problems brought about by abrupt liquidity injections following capital account liberalisation policies?
- What kind of theoretical and policy lessons result from such a study?

The book examines whether nations with radically different economic policies *vis-à-vis* surges in inflows all suffered from financial crises as an unavoidable outcome of their capital account liberalisation given the magnitude of global liquidity stocks and flows. The answers to the questions set out above can provide a useful background when investigating the causes of the current crisis and most importantly when designing a set of policies targeted at curtailing the impact of any crisis re-emergence.

The structure of the book

The book consists of this introduction and nine additional main chapters. The second chapter presents an overview of Keynesian and post-Keynesian theoretical concepts that are relevant to financial markets' behaviour, volatility and vulnerability – as well the neo-classical concepts that they are opposed to. This chapter is key for the understanding of the book's discussion but optional to readers with a good knowledge of post-Keynesian economic principles. The third chapter provides a brief analysis of global liquidity data since 1980 in order to investigate the causes behind their exponential growth. The fourth examines the structural causes of liquidity generation in the financial centres of the world and the endogenous causes behind the external direction of financial liquidity. The fifth chapter analyses the historical evolution of emerging financial markets and examines the causes of liquidity movements from the financial centres of the world towards the emerging markets that were exogenous to developments in the former. The sixth, seventh and eighth chapters study the three different routes to financial crisis followed by each of Mexico, Brazil and South Korea, respectively. What features can we extrapolate from the three different routes to financial crises? The ninth and the last chapters of the book place all data and case studies together and draw conclusions on the veracity and potential consequences of the asserted relationship between high levels of financial mobility, absence of capital controls and emergence of financial crises. Throughout the book a Keynesian and post-Keynesian analytical framework is adopted and tested as the best fit to theoretically frame the postulated relation.

Post-1980 liquidity study

The third, fourth and fifth chapters of the book explore the reasons behind the rapid increase of global financial liquidity after 1980. These chapters attempt to determine the reasons for the change in the relationship between global financial assets and global output post-1980. The overall international financial background of increased capital transactions is initially presented, and two major influences are then discussed – each one of these two influences is presented in a separate chapter. These were the dimensions and development of the economic deregulation policies and the generation of new liquidity flows via, among others, the establishment and expansion of complex structured financial instruments in the Western economies first and the world's emerging markets second. The fourth chapter sets out the variables related to the jumps in the generation and circulation of financial liquidity in the West. It includes an investigation of how the direction of liquidity shifted from productive investment to the trading of financial instruments as a result of these developments and also suggests that the innovation of new financial products produced, by itself, its own liquidity. The fifth chapter outlines the reasons behind developing countries appearing to be highly attractive to surges of global liquidity flows after the 1980s. In this chapter Palma's proposition that developing countries provided a market of last resort for international liquidity flows will be investigated (Palma, 1998, 2003a). This proposition suggests that the rapid drainage of highly profitable activities in the developed world directed liquidity into developing economies in the pursuit of higher returns. The timing and direction of liquidity shifts to the developing world is examined together with the overall economic and political background of the recipient economies. This will be delivered in order to understand the reasons underpinning the purported attractiveness of developing economies.

The "three routes"– Chapters 6, 7 and 8

The sixth, seventh and eighth chapters of the book explore the way in which three different middle-income developing economies – those of Mexico, Brazil and South Korea – drove themselves to financial crises in the 1990s. These three economies have been specifically chosen as characteristic examples of different economic policy-making developed, systematically or intrinsically, to deal with the problem of the absorption of foreign flow surges. Palma's concept of the "Three Routes" to financial crises (Palma, 2000, 2002a, 2003a) is adopted throughout this book to refer to the distinctive domestic economic policies followed in the three economies studied, all of which manifested themselves in financial crises. All three economies implemented structural reforms and liberalisation policies in the same decade, but with different paths and intensities. The routes followed by Mexico and Brazil are considered as the two extreme case studies in the analysis. Mexico followed a policy of absolute financial liberalisation while Brazil, in order to purposefully avoid a Mexican-type crisis, fully sterilised capital inflows. The Korean case was at neither extreme as it followed a policy of freely allowing capital inflows while channelling them into an ever-increasing private-debt business sector. Figure 1.1 provides a brief overview of the "three routes argument" by portraying each economy's domestic policy and consequent economic problems. Large "big bang" style liberalisation reforms were implemented in all three economies, with the Latin American ones being the most resolute followers of the neoliberal doctrine of full deregulation of the capital account and the domestic financial markets, and South Korea following quite an idiosyncratic

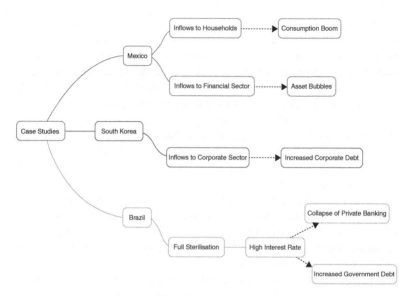

Figure 1.1 The "3 routes to crisis" and their early manifestations

Asian interpretation of the WC. Chapter 6 portrays the case of Mexico as a characteristic example of an economy with a mostly *laissez faire* policy *vis-à-vis* the surge of inflows. The non-interventionist policy implemented by its central bank resulted in asset bubbles (both in the stock market and real estate) and a consumption boom that eventually induced a vast increase in non-performing household debt (Palma, 2011a). Brazil is then analysed in Chapter 7 as an economy adopting instead a nearly full sterilisation policy and at the same time embracing full liberalisation and an opening of its capital accounts. It is selected as a characteristic example of an economy whose central bank sold government bonds to withdraw the increased liquidity created by foreign exchange inflows. Brazil, trying to avoid a Mexican-type downturn, engaged in the policy of costly sterilisation that eventually led to public sector Ponzi finance. The full sterilisation policy that followed was attached to financial instability through the high interest rate required for its operation. This eventually led to the collapse of the domestic private banking system due to an increase in non-performing debt, and to a further increase in public debt resulting, among other things, from the government's rescue plan for these failing banks. Lastly, Chapter

8 examines South Korea as an example of an economy where even though the additional finance created by inflows was used productively by the corporate sector (and, as a result, no asset bubble or consumer booms were immediately generated), the economy still experienced a severe crisis, this time via an excessive increase in corporate debt. In South Korea, the collapse of profitability in the corporate sector (mainly due to falling micro-electronic prices) meant that corporations required the additional finance for investment. An additional problem of the economy finally precipitating the negative developments was that the Korean central bank was caught at the apex of the crisis with low levels of reserves (Palma, 2000).

The rationale behind choosing such contrasting economies in terms of the ways in which they formulated policies to deal with surges of inflows, is to emphasise the difficulties of dealing with such large surges of inflows once an open capital account has allowed entry. These chapters explore the domestic policy changes in each of the three economies prior to the crises with regard to the elements relevant to the absorption, structuring and distribution of liquidity inflows.

Theory, policies and data: putting everything together – Chapters 9 and 10

Chapter 9 combines the policy changes pursued and the financial data explored in all three cases with selective parts of post-Keynesian theory. Analytically, it discusses whether the initial proposition – that open capital accounts at times of high international liquidity can lead to surges in capital inflows that tend to create unsustainable macro-economic imbalances irrespective of domestic policies devised for their absorption – can be validated by the three cases studied. All three crises studied are analysed in the framework of finance and trade liberalisation preceding their occurrence. In each economy the sudden increase in capital flows and the simultaneous jump in private and public indebtedness were followed by a sharp reversal in the flow of capital. The domestic and international insights regarding the importance of the economies' 1990s' structural reform and stabilisation plans are challenged here via the analysis of the boom and bust cycles that the economies experienced. This establishes a thorough reassessment of their development strategies. The penultimate chapter therefore summarises and formalises the results of the entire research and affirms that the surge of inflows has been found to make the three economies in question susceptible to financial crises as a result of the policy of opening their capital accounts.

Within the chapter there is a more detailed association between the Keynesian tradition studied and the developments in each of the three economies examined. The degree to which the trajectories of the crises in the economies studied follow some of Keynes', Minsky's and Kindleberger's analyses is examined with regard to specific developments in the economies' financial markets and associated macroeconomic fundamentals. Key financial indicators for all Mexico, Brazil and Korea are combined here with already existing literature on the causes and experiences of financial crises and with the actual policy changes pursued in order to understand whether the theory studied can be validated by a set of three very different markets with very similar underlying frameworks. It becomes evident, through the coherence and severity of all three cases of finance deregulation and subsequent financial crises, that the costs in terms of economic growth and development were severe. The crises in all three economies affected not only borrowers and lenders but also individuals with little or minimal involvement in capital market developments, who experienced not only the fall of their incomes but also the inability of their welfare states to shield them at these times of crisis.

The last chapter of the book (Chapter 10) provides a short summary of the findings discussed in Chapter 9 of the book combined with possible contemporary interpretation and policy implications. As a concluding remark a discussion of the contemporary practical relevance of the findings and resulting policy implications is included. The conclusions applicable to middle-income developing countries, their situation within the current global economic crisis and the relevance of excess liquidity-generated crises with the current Eurozone debt crises are afforded particular attention here. The study of the relationship between the occurrence of crises and financial liberalisation is understood, in all three case studies, through the set of fiscal and monetary stabilisation measures adopted by each government. This study asserts that the nature, structure and methods of all economic reform packages implemented in each of the three economies were, in a unique way for each one, critical to the development of an inherently unstable micro- and macroeconomic framework. We conclude by suggesting the need for the reintroduction of capital controls as a mechanism to prevent surges in inflows and the resulting financial instability. It is suggested that a realignment of priorities needs to take place in mainstream economic theory and practice. Instead of celebrating the virtue of open capital accounts and liberalised liquidity flows, recognition should be given to the benefits afforded by control over capital inflows and the pursuit of engineered financial policies primarily in the context of emerging economies. The research attempts to contribute towards a better understanding of financial crises in middle-income developing countries in general, as well as Mexico, Brazil and South Korea in particular. It seeks to determine whether capital control devices can be finely tuned to avoid financial crises. This could result in a change in the mainstream perception of the economic effects of liberalised financial flows, open capital accounts and over-liquid economies.

Some notes on data

In order to adequately address the questions set out above, we compiled a database covering the period of capital market liberalisation and its immediate aftermath in the late 1980s and 1990s for all three economies studied and their respective regions. Data on certain variables have been collected from the early 1980s. The analysis primarily relies on two main types of data: data describing financial flows and stocks, and data on the countries' macroeconomic indicators. We have collected these on a timely and regular basis not only for the three economies studied but also for other developing countries of their region to facilitate further comparative analysis and as a result to be able to reach more generic conclusions.

Throughout the book we follow the heterodox economics tradition of using a vast amount of descriptive statistics to emphasise real-world trends and understand the political economy of developments. This is delivered in order to emphasise the macroeconomic picture of the developments and effects of liquidity flows rather than conducting some econometric analysis, which would isolate their specific influence on one or a defined set of indicators.

The detailed statistical analysis ranges from the beginning of financial liberalisation to the year of the financial collapse of each economy. The findings contribute greatly towards identifying the causes of the economies' busting – and more specifically the similarity of their nature. On this point it is important to acknowledge early on in the book two possible limitations of data analysis and collection. The first refers to the researcher's inability to fully and flawlessly isolate the effects of international capital flows on domestic prices. Macroeconomic variables such as fluctuations in exchange rates, interest rates and the rate of inflation unavoidably obscure the nature and magnitude of external liquidity effects on prices. The second limitation is attached to the quality of data available confining the researcher's ability to identify the exact quantitative variables affecting the results of the research. These challenges, which are instigated by the irregularity of observations, diversity of sources, confidentiality of the relevant information and consequent need to scrutinise their coherency, seem unavoidable when trying to obtain a complete image of the area studied.

Overall, we aim to contribute to the heterodox tradition by showing that quantitative analysis, descriptive statistics, and a detailed study of the individual markets and the international political economy of the time provide a valuable inter-temporal tool to address the book's fundamental question – this of instability being an inherent characteristic of capitalist financial markets.

Some notes on the analytical framework

Financial theory – the norm and alternatives

Financial theory from the perspective of Keynes, Minsky and Kindleberger, accorded little importance by the currently dominant school of mainstream economics, is adopted as the main analytical tool throughout this book. By exploring the interpretive possibilities offered by non-mainstream economic theory, the book emphasises the deficiencies in the mainstream assumption that open capital accounts do not produce financial disturbances unless disturbed by external factors. Analytical concepts, such as Keynes' assertion that excessive growth in the financial sector and circulating liquidity cause conditions of instability, are tested and adopted through the entity of the book. These are opposed to mainstream economists' proposed benefits of seemingly unlimited financial deepening.

Throughout the book a Keynesian perspective is adopted. Some Keynesian and post-Keynesian concepts become central to the understanding of the key arguments. To understand the specificity of each of the three crises, the manner in which they correlate with the Keynesian tradition is analysed, and a description of the key Keynesian topics is presented. Critiques arising from the Keynesian tradition but also, further from within the neoclassical school are also considered when exposing relevant "truth-claims" of mainstream economic proposals. The concept of symmetric information has been convincingly discredited (notably by Stiglitz, see Stiglitz and Weiss, 1981), and market failures like this are emphasised throughout the book when exploring the generation, direction and volume of financial flows to the economies studied. Inefficiencies and market disturbances such as asymmetric information and principal-agent problems were prevalent in the direction of excessive flows from Wall Street to Mexico, Brazil and South Korea. Additional criticisms of the Keynesian tradition to neoclassical assumptions on the benefits of liberalised markets are included throughout the body of the book. Other than the non-efficient and information-asymmetric allocation of financial flows to all three economies, the Keynesian challenge to loanable funds theory will be examined and eventually adopted in the study of specifically Latin American countries, where the availability of cheap domestic finance did not create an incentive for investment.

Keynes, Minsky and Kindleberger

The theoretical background employed in this book focuses on the work of three key economists, Keynes, Minsky and Kindleberger, on the causes of financial crises, the effects of liquidity movements, the overall structure of financial systems and the character of money. Through focusing on this literature we directly explore the question – which is not appropriately addressed by mainstream economics – on the existence of a direct association between financial instability and liquidity injections.

The choice to focus on these three authors results from the aforementioned internal (i.e., market failures) and external (i.e., theory omissions of inherent financial instability to the markets) shortcomings of orthodox economic theory and policy. These shortcomings are typically ignored in times of economic euphoria and somehow miraculously rediscovered in times of financial turmoil. The economies studied, along with most economies of their regions, all embraced the free market ideology in the late 1980s and 1990s. This was predominantly manifested via the adoption of the Washington Consensus (WC) principles focusing on what was known as "first generation reforms", the implementation of which was thought to generate efficiency, growth and investment gains for all agents involved. The WC principles were described by Williamson as "worldwide intellectual trends" mostly expressed in the case of Latin America and the transition economies, and were viewed as prerequisites for economic growth by both the IMF and World Bank. International confidence in the reforms was such that it was suggested that even the NICs should adopt Williamson's "outward orientation, free-market capitalism and prudent macroeconomic policy reforms" as the main body of their economies' *modus operandi*. Suggestions by economists like Balassa identified the urgent need for a reversal in several "repressive" regulations in Latin America. Such 'repressive regulation' in need of reversal included restrictions on capital flows and directed credit – regulation both of which were thought to be constraining the economies' levels of efficiency and productivity (Balassa, 1989). The resulting market-oriented strategy of most "transition" economies was designed as a universal and a-historic blueprint applicable to any developing country (see Taylor, 1999) but nowhere applied with such fervour as in Latin America (see Palma, 2003b).

The work of Keynes, Minsky and Kindleberger is particularly important to the understanding of the challenges, complexities and problems initiated not only by the very nature of the liberalisation policies pursued but also from the speed and audacity of the reforms. In all economies – and again even more fervently so in the Latin American ones – the neoliberal reforms were applied not only as a universal blueprint but as a "shock therapy". The speed and incautiousness of the reforms was such that little attention was paid to various complementing but necessary social arrangements and institutions predominately related with establishing a regulatory and supervisory infrastructure system. It soon became apparent that economic growth did not follow the anticipated convergence route, while income and wealth inequalities established an ever-increasing pattern of escalation.

The findings of Keynes and Minsky are thus essential when analysing the systemic characteristics of liquidity, financial instability and structural challenges of the neoliberal WC reforms, whereas the work of Kindleberger is critical when examining the consequences of liquidity shocks and the abrupt fashion in which the WC was adopted, applied and developed. The literature included provides a discussion on economic fragility being endogenous to the financial system, the implications of high levels of liquidity, the formation of expectations, the role of expectations in shaping irrational decisions, the function of speculation and uncertainty, and the rejection of some relevant neoclassical axioms and assumptions. Keynes together with Minsky and Kindleberger have been chosen as great sources in the understanding and explanation of the economic and financial disaster that can be caused by abrupt liquidity injections. The literature examined is essential for the understanding of the problems created in the three economies examined, as it builds a theoretical framework for the analysis of liquidity-induced financial imbalances.

It should be noted however that the specific brand of financial crises studied here refers to middle-income countries that have been "shocked" by a sudden surge of foreign inflows. As a result, the emphasis in the analysis will not be explicitly directed to, but could pertain to, financial fragilities in mature capitalist economies or to developing countries with relatively closed capital accounts.

The following chapter outlines some of the key Keynesian and post-Keynesian concepts in my analysis. These are essential for the understanding of the discussion and conclusions of the book. Readers with an in-depth knowledge of Keynesian and post-Keynesian economics may want to continue straight to Chapter 3.

2
A Keynesian and Post-Keynesian Theoretical Brief: Selected Concepts

This chapter includes a review of the theories of Keynes, Minsky and Kindleberger regarding financial crises, the role of liquidity, the function of expectations and the implications of speculation encompassed by several controversial assumptions of conventional monetary theory. Part of the three authors' work is analysed and presented here as essential to the understanding of the inherent and systemic characteristics of over-liquid markets in capitalist societies. Along with the selected Keynesian and post-Keynesian concepts, part of neoclassical literature on efficient markets will be presented in order to point out some of its inherent contradictions. This is delivered in order to establish an overall framework that will then be used to evaluate the proximity of the book's findings to theoretical underpinnings. This chapter sets the framework for the later investigation and comprehension of the function and consequences of high monetary circulation in newly emerging capital markets. As mentioned in the introduction, if the reader feels comfortable with this literature they may continue directly to the empirical investigation starting in the next chapter.

A review of Keynes will be first set out as it is considered to have laid the foundations for the understanding of the operation of capitalist financial markets, the role of banking and the character of money and liquidity. This review will then be complemented and expanded by an overview of Minsky's theoretical developments, particularly with regard to his emphasis on the inherent instability of the capitalist financial system and the ways in which the composition of cash flows in an economy and its structure of finance can contribute to the enhanced vulnerability of the system. Finally, a summary of Kindleberger's analysis of the mechanics of crises' development and the importance of market expectations in turning economic euphoria into distress will be given.

Keynes on crises, liquidity, expectations and uncertainty

> It is an essential characteristic of the boom that investments which yield in fact, say, 2% in conditions of full employment are made in the expectation of a yield, say, 6% and are valued accordingly. When the disillusion comes, this expectation is replaced by a contrary 'error of pessimism', with the result that the investments, which would in fact yield 2% in conditions of full employment, are expected to yield less than nothing; and the resulting collapse of new investment leads to a state of unemployment in which the investments, which would have yielded 2% in conditions of full employment, in fact yield less than nothing.
>
> (Keynes, 1936, pp. 321–22)

Keynesian criticisms on monetary theory relevant to the study are the rejections of:

1. Money neutrality
2. Ergodic axiom
3. Loanable funds theory

Money neutrality

Keynes rejects the widely accepted notion that barter transactions are the essence of our economy and money simply exists as a neutral tool to facilitate them. Instead, he proposes that money is of critical importance both in the short and long run as money and the possession of liquidity ultimately affect output and employment outcomes through regular decision-making. Keynes asserts the view that money plays a role of its own and directly affects decisions in a way that the future development of events in both short and long run cannot be predicted without prior knowledge of money behaviour.

The neutral money axiom, a universal tenet of classical economics is based on the conviction that employment and output are determined in the long run by non-monetary factors, and therefore, any changes in the quantity of money do not produce effects on the level of employment and overall production. Keynes proposes that this economic understanding, however, does not allow any space for the emergence of 'peculiar events' such as booms and depressions (Keynes, 1939a).

Money neutrality refers to a state where in the long run all 'mistakes' endogenously and naturally wither out, and therefore, central bankers do not need to assume the role of economic 'stabilisers'. Long-run money neutrality would mean that the quantity of money is capable of solely determining the price level, and therefore, the role of monetary policy can be reduced to acting as a 'nominal anchor' (Friedman and Kuttner, 1996). It is only when money is understood as having real effects (i.e., it is not neutral) that central bankers are expected to take an active role in policy-making. It is thus in this framework, of rejecting monetary neutrality, that this book focuses on financial developments, economic policy changes and overall market swings.

> Money plays a part of its own and affects motives and decisions and is in short one of the operating factors in the situation, so that the course of events cannot be predicted either in the long period or in the short, without a knowledge of the behaviour of money between the first state and the last. And it is this which we ought to mean when we speak of a monetary economy ... booms and depressions are peculiar to an economy in which ... money is not neutral.
>
> (Keynes, 1933, pp. 408–09)

Ergodic axiom

The ergodic axiom suggests that present data and samples drawn from past are equivalent to drawing a sample from the future so that the outcome at any future date comprises the statistical shadow of past and current market data (Bibow, 2009). This axiom is responsible for the belief that one can convert uncertainty into calculable risk – as it proposes that any future outcome can be predicted with a high degree of statistical accuracy on the basis of samples drawn from the past and the present.

Friedman asserted that even if rational agents cannot precisely calculate the probability assigned to future outcomes in the long run, they are proved to be economically successful as if they had initially drawn a reliable sample from the future (Friedman, 1998). In an ergodic perception of reality, a process equivalent to the Darwinian notion of natural selection and survival of the fittest takes place because in the long run only agents with less systematic forecasting errors survive. This is understood to be the reason why the financial systems that tend to survive are the ones where no major misalignments take place.

For Keynes the uncertainty of the long run is strongly associated with the non-ergodic nature of reality. The distinction between uncertainty and probabilistic risk is clearly drawn by Keynes. He rejects the assumption that it is possible to calculate uncertainty on the basis of historical data and use this as a reliable guide to future performance. Solow, following a Keynesian logic, asserts that:

> Unfortunately economics is a social science. To express the point more formally, much of what we observe cannot be treated as the realisation of a stationary stochastic process without straining credulity ... the end product of economic analysis ... is contingent on society's circumstances – on historical context ... for better or worse however, economics has gone down a different path.
>
> (Solow, 1985, p. 328)

Keynes' rejection of the ergodic axiom is adopted and applied throughout this book. In fact this rejection is further validated through the realisation that the market optimism and euphoria taking place prior to each crisis were not – in an efficient market hypothesis prediction – foretellers of the financial bust following.

Loanable funds theory

The loanable funds theory assumes that savings is the main constraint to investment. This idea is rejected in Keynes' finance motive debate. Keynes instead proposes that liquidity can be a constraint on the accumulation of capital.

> In general the banking system holds the key position in the transition from a lower to a higher level of activity.
>
> (Keynes, 1939b, p. 222)

The concept that money and banks – rather than savings – have a guiding role in enabling capitalist accumulation is central to Keynes' work. Keynes denies the propositions of loanable funds theory that saving is the source of investment and that the decision to save determines the rate of interest. Hence, Keynes suggests that the mere availability of more savings does not necessarily lead to an increase in investment, nor does an increase in thrift directly and immediately lower interest rates.

> Increased investment will always be accompanied by increased saving, but it can never be preceded by it. Dishoarding and credit expansion provides not an alternative to increased savings, but a necessary preparation for it. It is the parent, not the twin, of increased saving.
>
> (Keynes, 1939a, p. 281)

> The Investment market can become congested through shortage of cash. It can never become congested through shortage of saving. This is the most fundamental of my conclusions within this field.
>
> (Keynes, 1939b, p. 222)

One example of 'loanable funds thinking' can be summarised by Bernanke's view on the current crisis as outlined below.

> The increase in global savings (mainly arising from developing countries being transformed from net importers to net exporters of savings–mostly in the case of Asian countries) provided additional liquidity to capital markets. This was achieved via the channelling of these savings into the purchase of foreign financial assets through the issuance of domestic debt and thus the acquisition of American bonds. This increase in the demand for federal bonds helped interest rates in the US to remain low and ultimately gave rise to corporate and household investment.
>
> (Described in Bibow, 2009)

For Keynes the essence of the finance problem lies not in savings but in liquidity. He proposes that for finance not to disturb the growth of real activity, an amount of money has to be reserved to facilitate the current level of activity. If, however, additional financing is required, it is the role of banks to provide it prior to the emergence of additional investment or savings. According to Keynes, the pace of capital accumulation is determined by the coordination of:

- The willingness of entrepreneurial investors to instigate capital projects given their uncertainty on future yields; and
- The willingness of financiers to part with liquidity.

In more simplified terms Keynes rejected the loanable funds theory on the basis that an increased propensity to save together with a decreased propensity to consume, *ceteris paribus*, will depress current demand for industrial goods and consequently slow down the overall level of real economic activity while repressing employment. As long as an economy is locked below its full employment potential, any increase in the propensity to consume will be followed by an increase in employment and output and consequently economic performance.

> If there is no change in liquidity position: public can ex ante save, and ex post and ex anything else until they are blue in face....
>
> (Keynes, 1939b, p. 223)

The rejection of the loanable funds theory and its implications on the role of finance-generated liquidity are key to the study of Mexico, Brazil and Korea. Keynes' acknowledgment of the key position that the general banking system – and the later developed para-banking and shadow-banking systems – holds in the overall generation of market activity is crucial to our study. The quote of Keynes above emphasises banking as key in enabling a higher scale of activity. If the supply of money remains unchanged, Keynes assumes that a 'congestion' in the market of loans will be created by any exogenous increase in planned spending (Keynes, 1939b, and see also Davidson, 2007). It is through this perspective that the generation of liquidity and extraordinary levels of financial trading took place in the majority of middle-income economies in the 1990s rather than higher actual investments and domestic savings.

Keynes and liquidity

In relation to loanable funds theory analysed above, Keynes supports the notion that changes in interest rates can result in changes in liquidity demand caused by the tendency of financiers to try and prevent a profit shortfall by expanding their activities. Interest rates might therefore change in desired directions as a result of income falls induced by spending shortfalls rather than increases in thrift itself (see Chapter 10 in Keynes, 1936).

Keynes regarded the rate of interest as a variable determined by the interplay between the terms in which the public desires to become more or less liquid and the terms on which the banking system is willing to become more or less illiquid (Bibow, 2009).

> The rate of interest is the price which equilibrates the desire to hold wealth in the form of cash with the available quantity of cash ... This is where and how, the quantity of money enters into the economic scheme.
>
> (Keynes, 1936, pp. 167–68)

Liquidity was viewed by Keynes as the survival tool in a money-using and entrepreneur-managed market economy where attention has to be paid not to the uncertain future but to the future availability of liquidity allowing contractual payments to be met. Liquidity is consequently needed to meet contractual money obligations and, as a consequence, investment will not be constrained by their income as long as unemployed resources are available. Liquidity demand is considered as a primary cause of involuntary unemployment as it presumes a desire to save and therefore not consume or utilise resources.

Investment is conceptualised by Keynes as an exogenous spending flow only constrained by expected future money inflows upon which financial institutions will be willing to grant loans.

> In a world where money is created primarily only if someone increases their indebtedness to banks in order to purchase newly produced goods, real investment spending will be undertaken as long as the purchase of newly produced capital goods are expected to generate a future of dated cash inflows whose discounted present value equals or exceeds the money cash outflow.
>
> (Davidson, 2007, p. 89)

In Keynes' analysis the primary function of the financial markets is to provide liquidity (rather than efficiency) and this – the point where a market can suffer collapse – is at the core of this research. In liquid markets, participants believe that financial markets will indefinitely be able to provide liquidity, given that financial assets can be easily and rapidly sold – *in this research we see the relevance of Keynes' rejection of the ergodic axiom when looking at excessively liquid markets.* However, this environment automatically induces investors to believe in the everlasting existence of a fast exit mechanism in times of dissatisfaction, which ultimately may lead to the crash of the entire system.

To understand better the liquidity preference theory, one has to look to the exogenous nature of money. Keynes described money exogeneity in the sense that money is not fully under direct control of the monetary authority but rather is dependent upon the behaviour of banks. In his *General Theory*, the exogeneity in money supply assumes that any changes in the supply of money normally take place at the discretion of monetary authorities or banks independently of any changes in money demand. For Keynes, therefore, money becomes an endogenous variable only to the extent that money supply changes are caused by money demand changes.[1]

Keynes on uncertainty and expectations

Minsky proposes that Keynes' *General Theory* is not about a stable well-behaved system sporadically shocked by short-lived interruptions but rather about the inherent instability of the capitalist system of production which, unless tamed by appropriate government policies, is prone to severe financial crises (Minsky, 1982b).

The existence of inherent uncertainty within the system and the consequent inability to transform it into calculable risk has made the role of expectations critical to the operation of the entire system. In the *General Theory* expectations are treated as having a substantial role in investment decisions, thereby determining all business decisions. Equivalently, liquidity preference – in terms of the way in which individuals, households and investors decide upon holding particular forms of wealth (see Crotty, 1994) – is generated by market agents' expectations regarding future developments. This is referred to as the speculative motive. In this way expectations influence the decomposition of the speculative motive for holding money in terms of different forecasts on future values.

Keynesian and classical economic theories treat uncertainty in completely different ways.[2] Keynes recognised the existence of uncertainty within markets and emphasised the prudence of demanding and holding money over and above the amount of existing contractual payment obligations. The origins of Keynesian uncertainty are rooted in and inherent to the function and behaviour of financial markets. This Keynesian uncertainty is fundamentally different to the neoliberal uncertainty – the latter being primarily expressed as the market failure of asymmetric information. Keynes therefore treated the holding of liquidity as a safety blanket over the possibility of future financial exposure. The classical theorists, conversely, do not espouse money for liquidity purposes given the fundamental assumption of future certainty and 'liquidity obsession' having no impact in the aggregate level of employment and output in an economy (Davidson, 2007).

For Keynes, expectations are so deeply important for the function of capitalist systems that they directly determine two of the three major functions of aggregate demand.[3] According to his thinking expectations are central in the investment and liquidity preference functions of aggregate demand:

1. The investment schedule depends on the comparison between the market rate of interest and the marginal efficiency of capital (thereby the discount rate under which expected future revenues and the current supply of capital goods are equalised);
2. The liquidity preference function, depends upon individuals' expectations upon changes in the rate of interest – with the consequent expected capital gains/losses and preference for bonds/money.

In the investment schedule it is often the case that in the short run businesses invest more when they hold more cash, but in the long run their propensity to invest is directly determined by the expected profitability of investment (depending upon the expected demand for output for which additional capital and productive capacity is needed) rather than the current rate of profits (Eisner, 1997). Equivalently, the marginal efficiency of capital also relates to the expectations regarding the future net returns of investment to the extent that they will exceed the prevailing rate of interest.

Generally, effective demand is shaped by expectations – and changes thereto. Demand for goods leads to new orders for capital investment goods by entrepreneurial investors facing uncertainty, a process that can develop as the outcome of financial volatility. Furthermore, the level of employment is not principally determined in labour markets but instead is based on producers' assessments of expected sales relative to the current supply conditions.

Keynes' concept of uncertainty is closely tied to his rejection of the ergodic axiom. The capitalist system he describes is always moving from an irrevocable past to an unpredictable future and is therefore fundamentally incompatible with the proposal that it is possible to predict future outcomes from conclusions drawn from past performance. It is in this line of thinking that this book investigates and analyses the sudden and rapid growth patterns of all Mexico, Brazil and South Korea and their dramatic turnarounds.

Minksy on financial crises

Minsky's main contribution to the economic analysis of financial crises lies in his *Financial Instability Hypothesis* (the 'FIH'), a theory of how a capitalist economy endogenously generates financial structures susceptible to crises and how the normal functioning of markets in a booming economy triggers financial crises. The FIH is an attempt to build a theory to illustrate why financially sophisticated capitalist economies are inherently unstable.

Minsky proposes that systemic fragility is a persistent characteristic of the capitalist financial structure which explains its tendency towards financial crises. He argues that the fragility of the financial structure comprises an endogenous precondition for financial crises, which is systemic. This means that financial crisis results from the normal functioning of the economy, and thus, the susceptibility of the economy to disruption is not necessarily due to accidents or policy errors. Minsky traces an economy's susceptibility to disruption through an analysis of its dominant cash flows and payment commitments. This is manifested in Minsky's identification of differences between actual and projected cash flows and the debt commitments that these can be attached to. These debt commitments are inevitably reflected on the liabilities side of the economies' balance sheets and have an immediate impact on the economies' business cycle.

The financial instability hypothesis

The FIH was developed as an alternative to the prevalent neoclassical theory that views output and employment fluctuations as anomalies of the economic system. The FIH was built as an extension of Keynes' *General Theory* explaining why employment and output are endogenously prone to fluctuations. Minsky stressed that the main propositions of the *General Theory* lie in the identification of disequilibrating forces operating in financial markets which have a direct impact on the valuation of capital assets relative to the price of current output and, therefore, together with changes in financial markets conditions, lead to changes in investment activity. It is thus Keynes that influences Minksy in placing investment and its finance at the core of aggregate economic activity. The FIH is a theory built to explain the procyclical behaviour of capitalist economies; it is 'an investment theory of business cycle and a financial theory of investment' (Minsky, 1982a, p. 95).

The demand for investment is described as a function of the valuation of stock assets, the availability of finance from internal funds and financial markets, and the supply price of investment output. Minsky argues that the investment demand function effectively illustrates how agents involved in debt-enhancing finance will lead to an eventual collapse in the overall level of investment. The logic of this argument is that a collapse in asset values will lead to a collapse in investment which will, in turn, decrease the profit generated by capital assets, increasing the difficulties to service any kind of financial commitments.

The fundamental proposition of the neoclassical synthesis, that unless disturbed from outside, a decentralised market structure will yield a self-sustaining, stable price, full employment equilibrium, is in sharp contrast with the FIH. The FIH emphasises that extreme business cycles' fluctuations are due to financial attributes that are integral to capitalist operations and that the capitalist market mechanisms cannot lead to a self-sustaining, stable price, full employment equilibrium.

Under the FIH 'the fundamental instability of a capitalist economy – is a tendency to explode – to enter into a boom or euphoric state' (Minsky, 1982b, p. 118). It is therefore important to make a clear distinction between a booming phase of the economy and a steadily growing one. Minsky identifies that in a booming/euphoric economy, a high willingness to invest and acquire liabilities will create demand conditions that lead to tight money markets. 'Financial structures and financial interactions are the phenomena in a capitalist economy that make the development of those long-term expectations that lead to a collapse of investment an endogenous phenomenon in the particular circumstances that in fact arise after the aftermath of a sustained expansion' (Minsky, 1982a, p. 102).

Minsky argues that, as the euphoric period of the economy lengthens, existing debts are easily serviced, heavily indebted units can prosper and, most importantly, views about the acceptable debt burden change to being intrinsically elastic. As an outcome of this, the weight of debt finance, the price of capital assets and the level of speculative investment all increase. As this process continues the economy is transformed into a booming economy. Thus, the fundamental instability of the capitalist economy is an upward one; it is specifically its tendency to transform doing well into a speculative investment boom. In this book we find that all economies analysed developed equivalent stages of booming economies as a result of higher prosperity and associated increased levels of acceptable debt burdens. To decompose this statement one has to understand that each new type of money generated in a euphoric period results in the financing of additional demand for capital assets or investment. In turn, this causes increases in: asset prices; the demand price for current investment; the overall level of investment finance and, consequently, capital gains and profits. The economy will therefore expand beyond any stable full employment level as 'any full employment equilibrium leads to an expansion of debt financing – weak at first because of the memories of financial difficulties – that moves the economy to expand beyond full employment' (Minsky, 1986, p. 178).

Any transitionary liquidity state of the economy is considered to be translated into an investment boom which will inevitably strip the units of liquidity and increase the debt-equity ratios for financial institutions. Minsky notes that if the conventional liability structures for financing positions in some capital assets change (so that more debt becomes acceptable), the firms that financed their positions by conforming to the previous conventions acquire additional borrowing power. These firms therefore are able to acquire more cash by issuing more debt with the same capital assets as before. Minsky proposes that the 'margins of safety are eroded even as success leads to a belief that the prior and even the present margins are too large' (Minsky, 1986, p. 220), and thus, the debt to equity ratio should be further increased. Whether the break in the investment boom will lead to a non-traumatic recession, a financial crisis, a debt deflation or a deep depression depends on the overall levels of liquidity, the relative size of the government sector and the existence of a lender of last resort.

Instability

The stability in the financial system is assumed to be endogenously determined and, as outlined above, decreasing in periods of sustained boom. The structural characteristics of the system change in periods of sustained euphoria and lead to declining levels of overall stability which can trigger sharp financial reactions inevitably revealing any institutional deficiencies and lowering the effective floor to income. This can be achieved by the euphoric feedback inducing sectorial financial difficulties that can escalate to general panic leading to moves such as reconsiderations of portfolio composition.

The disruption of any full employment equilibrium is a critical concept in Minsky's analysis of markets' operation. 'In a capitalist economy hospitable to financial innovation, full employment with stable prices cannot be sustained, for within any full employment situation there are endogenous disequilibrating forces at work that assure the disruption of tranquility' (Minsky, 1986, p. 178). Minsky argues that within capitalism the overall level of instability might be decreased by public policy inducing changes in investment, wages and the government budget, but cannot be fully eradicated. On this exact point of possible instability eradication, this study demonstrates the absence of such public policy interventions in the economies studied – in fact it demonstrates that policy mediation can accomplish the opposite.

The principal manifestation of uncertainty can be found in market agents' investment decisions and in their willingness to lever or debt finance positions in inherited capital assets, financial assets and newly produced capital assets. Through analysing the composition of an economy's cash flows (and therefore investment composition), Minsky determines its susceptibility to financial disruption.

Minsky distinguishes three major types of cash flows: income, balance sheet and portfolio.

- **Income** cash flows include wages and salaries and can generally be defined as payments from one stage of production and trade to another.
- **Balance sheet** cash flows are the cash flows mandated by existing/inherited liabilities and can be determined by contracts that are debt instruments.
- **Portfolio** cash flows are the result of capital and financial asset change of hands, the outcome of decisions to trade assets and could also be the result of past financial commitments.

Minsky argues that 'financial instability is linked to the relative importance of income, balance sheet and portfolio cash flows in an economy' (Minsky, 1986, p. 203) as, in theory, income cash flows are the foundations upon which balance sheet and portfolio cash flows rest. In practice, however, there can be asymmetries between different cash flows, so that balance sheet flows are often much larger than the expected income receipts. Accordingly, an economy where income cash flows are dominant in meeting balance sheet commitments is financially robust and relatively immune to crises. On the contrary, an economy in which portfolio transactions are used as the means to obtain balance sheet payments is financially fragile and crisis-prone.

In addition to the distinction between different cash flows, Minsky develops a useful distinction between different financing positions (Minsky, 1986). This is characterised by differences in cash payment commitments on debts and expected cash receipts from quasi rents yielded by capital assets or debtor commitments on owned financial instruments. The financing positions that Minsky identifies are as follows:

- **Hedge finance:** A financing position where the cash flow commitments on debts are such that over each significant period the cash receipts are expected to exceed the cash payments. Hedge units therefore cannot have large volumes of demand debt and contingent debts cannot comprise a large part of the unit's liabilities.
- **Speculative finance:** A position where cash flows to the unit from the operating assets are expected to be less than the cash payment commitments in some, mainly near-term, periods. A speculative financing unit has a positive net worth, even though, in some near-term periods, cash payment commitments exceed the cash flow from operations. Borrowers and lenders expect that the debtor will be able to refinance his position. New debts will be issued to raise funds to pay maturing debts. Speculative units usually involve short financing of long positions.
- **Ponzi finance:** A speculative financing unit for which the interest portion of its cash payment commitments exceeds its net income cash receipts. Such a unit has to increase its debt in order to meet commitments on outstanding instruments. Ponzi units are similar to speculative ones in that for short periods cash payment commitments exceed expected cash receipts. However, in Ponzi finance financing costs in short periods increase outstanding debt such that Ponzi units capitalise interest rates into their liability structure.

This categorisation of financing positions can be quite revealing for the susceptibility of the economy to financial distress as the dominance of each of the three types described can yield very different economic performance results.

If dominant, hedge finance arrangements are such that contractual commitments will always be fulfilled unless the quasi rents earned by capital assets fall below the expected levels. Hedge units, therefore, are only vulnerable to uncertain futures and unexpected price changes – such as unanticipated interest rate increases. Speculative units will need to gather funds from various markets in order to fulfil payment commitments on outstanding debt. Therefore, speculative units will be vulnerable not only to product market developments but also to financial market ones. At the same time, Ponzi units are vulnerable to developments that would affect speculative units but also to factors such as income shortfalls or interest rate escalations, which will effectively increase the units' financial commitments and can lead to widespread default or bankruptcy. Moral hazard is often prevalent when market agents engage into Ponzi finance as they behave in such a destabilising manner out of expectation that they will be eventually rescued. As it will be demonstrated later on in the book, the economy of Brazil fell into a public sector Ponzi scheme. Accordingly, the developments in international financial markets and specifically the design of monetary policy and interest rates pushed the local authorities in continuous debt-generating activities to support and service the increasing amounts of public debt resulting from the full sterilisation policy and the state rescue of private banks.

Whereas the money supply rule may be a valid guide to policy formation in a regime dominated by hedge finance, such a rule loses its validity as the proportion of speculative finance increases. Units that engage in speculative finance are vulnerable on three fronts:

- They must meet the market changes as they refinance debt. A rise in interest rates can cause an increase in their cash payment commitments relative to cash receipts;
- As their assets are of longer maturity than their liabilities, a rise in both short-term and long-term interest rates will lead to a greater fall in the market value of their assets relative to their liabilities – thus, the market value of their assets can become smaller than the value of their debts;
- The views as to acceptable liability structures are subjective and a shortfall of cash receipts relative to cash payment commitments anywhere in the economy can lead to quick and wide-ranging revaluations of desired and acceptable financial structures.

Minsky argues that the mixture of hedge, speculative and Ponzi finance in an economy is a major determinant of its stability.

> Financial commitments and practices are linked to the real resource commitments made in capital asset ownership and investment production. In aggregate the prospects of financial assets in an economy can be no better than the financial prospects of their underlying units. However, the critical debt-financing is linked to the ownership and creation through investment of capital assets.
>
> (Minsky, 1986, p. 209)

Minsky suggests that an economy dominated by speculative and Ponzi units of finance will have substantially lower margins of safety and a highly fragile financial structure which, as history has confirmed, is a prerequisite of financial crises. The importance of Minsky's argument, however, does not simply lie in identifying the mechanics of finance which lead to speculative and even Ponzi units but in its proposition that capitalism itself ('a regime in which capital gains are being earned and are expected is a favourable environment for engaging in speculative and Ponzi finance' – Minsky, 1986, p. 210) is a favourable environment for the dominance of such financing units.

In more general terms the main determinants of stability are: the adequacy of cash flows from income relative to debt, the adequacy of refinancing possibilities relative to position and the ratio of unprotected to protected financial assets. 'The trend or evolution of the likelihood of financial instability depends upon the trend or evolution of the determinants of financial instability' (Minsky, 1982b, p. 128). The FIH is constructed to explain how financial instability is not an anomaly of financial markets but instead a normal aspect of its functioning, an internally generated result of the natural behaviour of a capitalist economy.

Kindleberger on financial crises

The core of Kindleberger's understanding of financial crises can be summarised as the proposition that every financial crisis is a supply-side crisis of finance with a sudden surge in liquidity at its centre.[4] Kindleberger insists that an endogenous reinforcing relationship exists between liquidity and crises, given that liquidity supply continuously creates its own demand. This proposition has been adopted throughout the book as the set of middle-income countries that are analysed is found to validate it. In this liquidity-supply-generated demand it has frequently been the case that when an agent is willing to lend, a recipient is readily available. On the contrary, there have been plenty of cases where liquidity supply does not meet high levels of liquidity demand and agents who are willing to borrow are denied the funds.

Kindleberger's focus on supply is such that he argues that nothing wakes animal spirits more than easy and cheap access to liquidity as it drastically increases expectations for the future. These increased expectations for the future are associated with financial euphoria and a booming section of the financial cycle. Increased spending and investment follow and, as a consequence, the rates of overall economic growth accelerate. High growth rates enhance positive speculation and can result in spending and investment manias. This study outlines the reasons behind the sudden rise in the supply of liquidity. Then, we investigate how this rise developed self-sustaining expectations, regarding the future prosperity of emerging financial markets creating their own financial, rather than productive, investment manias.

The endogenous character of monetary expansion is one of the key points in Kindleberger's analysis. The mutually reinforcing relation between liquidity and demand results in a 'systemic and endogenous rather than a random and exogenous process of monetary expansion' (Kindleberger and Aliber, 2005, p. 57). The mere fact that people have access to a lot of finance at a low price with low transaction costs generates a perpetual cycle of liquidity-bred demand where nothing increases expectations on future capacity to pay more than increased access to credit.

The pro-cyclical changes in the supply of credit are considered to be the cause of a cycle of financial manias and panics. Credit supply rapidly increases in times of economic euphoria, while credit growth rates quickly decline when economic growth slows. Manias are associated with the euphoric side of the cycle as they involve current or near future increases in stocks, real estate, currency or commodity prices which are inconsistent with the equivalent distant future prices (Kindleberger, 2000). The characteristics described above were all apparent in each of the three economies studied in this book.

Manias

Manias have been associated with the expansion phase of the business cycle because the euphoria associated with a mania leads to increases in spending that accelerate overall economic growth and further generate positive speculation on self-sustaining growth rates. The increase in the rate of economic growth induces investors and lenders to become more optimistic about the future and as a consequence asset prices increase more rapidly (at least for a while). During these euphoric periods, an increasing number of investors seek short-term capital gains from the increases in the prices of real estate and stocks rather than from investment income based on the productive use of these assets.

Kindleberger's analysis of manias emphasises their irrational character which implicitly contradicts the foundations of monetary theory. Often, in times of manias, an increase in prices is strangely accompanied by an increase in trading volumes, as individuals are eager to buy before prices increase further. However, the upward changes in prices might not necessarily depict the increased productive capacities of an asset but rather the result of market speculation and short-selling. Bubbles are described by Kindleberger as price changes that cannot be explained in terms of the assets' or commodities' fundamentals and consequently comprise an additional case of irrationality in the markets. Manias reflect irrationality while bubbles foreshadow the bursting of certain prices such that a 'rational market agent' could in an Efficient Market Hypothesis way perfectly foresee the unsustainability and inevitable implosion of the system. It is precisely at this point that Keynes' rejection of the ergodic axiom comes to complicate the ability of a 'rational market agent' to understand the mania and foresee the bubble.

The process

Similarly to Minsky, Kindleberger recognises the inherent fragility of the financial system and agrees with the proposition that the capitalist economy endogenously generates a structure susceptible to financial crises. Kindleberger also agrees with Minsky's argument regarding the functioning of financial markets in years of economic boom and how this will eventually trigger a crisis through the unsustainable debt structures developed in years of prosperity.

Financial crises are, according to Kindleberger, distinct from unemployment crises or wartime devastations for the precise reason that the rapid change in the supply of credit cannot be explained by sociopolitical or macroeconomic indicators. It can rather be explained by the change of the wealth owner's expectations that will quickly shift from one to another type of asset, leading to price decreases and most often bankruptcy.

The causes of the 'exuberant' expectations leading up to crises are separated by Kindleberger in two categories, the *causa remota* and the *causa proxima*. *Causa remota* assigns the onset of any crisis to the expansion of credit leading to speculation, while *causa proxima* refers to some incident that weakens confidence in the system and induces investors to sell commodities, stock, real estate, bills of exchange *inter alia* and increase their money holdings (Kindleberger and Aliber, 2005). This sudden change in the direction of credit's supply (commonly addressed as displacement) can be triggered by a large set of varying objects of speculation. These could range from deregulation policies, productive and financial innovations to changes in sovereign debt, exchange rates, real estate prices, commodity prices or national trade balances. These objects of speculation could even be trivial events such as: a bankruptcy, a revelation of fraud, a refusal of credit or some change of view that leads a market participant with a large position to sell. Hence, the following procedure occurs: prices fall, expectations are reversed, downward price movements accelerate, and borrowers find themselves in financial distress and need cash so they liquidate. As prices fall further, bank loan losses increase, one or more large banks fail, the credit system appears shaky and a surge in demand for liquidity arises.

The original credit displacement occurs as an autonomous shock which completely alters the nature of business and investment opportunities. In situations where new profit opportunities change market expectations and spending behaviour, investors rush to take advantage of this and, in the course of doing so, may overshoot the equilibrium price level. Investment may cumulatively increase under agents who price correctly, invest in the right amounts and have rational expectations. However, an excessive response to the displacement is likely given the increased price euphoria being transformed into a financial boom where more than one market is set at unsustainably high levels (Kindleberger and Laffargue, 1982). This exact procedure is examined and traced in all three economies studied. It is investigated and found that in Mexico, Brazil and Korea new profit opportunities were created. These changed and positively re-shaped market expectations, spending and investment behaviours and, given independent displacements for each case, all led to a financial meltdown.

Keynes' central book on the conception of uncertainty is that the future is unknowable in principle, or fundamentally uncertain, and that human decision-making takes place in a non-ergodic, ever-changing economic and structural environment (Crotty, 1994). Kindleberger builds on this Keynesian critique and frequently identifies a 'follow the leader' pattern of investment, often caused by the market participants' lack of information, which eventually produces overshooting and overtrading. Overtrading may involve profit overestimation, pure speculation for price increases (meaning buying not for use but for release) or excessive gearing (resulting from cash requirements which are low, relative to prevailing price or near-future price changes of the goods in question). In a situation of persistent overtrading, financial distress may follow as the result of the collapse in expectations on which the original euphoria was based. Distress may also be the result of a downward shift in demand resulting from an attempt by a large group to curtail its economic activities. Kindleberger explicitly states that 'a company, and by extension a financial market is in distress when it considers the probability of an acute cash squeeze to be high, and how high and how to measure high in this instance, I would not want to be precise about' (Kindleberger and Laffargue, 1982, p. 111). Distress is therefore perceived by Kindleberger as a general precipitator of crises, not a disaster in itself but, instead, the realisation that a disaster is perfectly possible. Part of this collective irrationality lies in the individual's delusion that each agent can sense the arrival of the impending disaster and will exit the market securely.

When followed by the reversal of expectations and further revulsion – as described above – distress may result in crashes and panics.

> A crash is a collapse of the prices of assets or perhaps the failure of an important firm or bank. A panic is a sudden fright and may occur in asset markets or involve a rush from less liquid securities to money or government securities – in the belief that governments do not go bankrupt because they can always print more money. A financial crisis may involve one or both and in either order.
>
> (Kindleberger and Aliber, 2005, p. 94)

Kindleberger describes the process leading to the outbreak of a financial crisis as the consequence of the following events. An autonomous shock/displacement changes and increases profit opportunities, thereby causing euphoria and excessive investment. As positive expectations continue to increase markets are set at unsustainably high levels. Financial distress occurs, investment profits diminish and, in a case where expectations are fully reversed (if not contained by a lender of last resort), further depression takes place and a crash is likely to follow.

The challenge to mainstream theory of finance

As mentioned above, a theme emphasised by Kindleberger is the incompatibility between the monetarist assumption of rational economic agents and the frequency with which speculative manias take place. Kindleberger recognises the existence of a complex relationship between the rational individual and the irrational market exists. The 'rational expectations' assumption commonly used in classical economic models is based on the notion that investors react to changes in economic variables as if they are always fully aware of the long-term implications of these changes. This is reflected in the economists' commonplace assumption described above that 'all the information is in the price' reflects the view that prices in each market react immediately and fully to all newly acquired information. The description of perfectly rational markets is, for Kindleberger, an *a priori* assumption about the way the world should work rather than an accurate description of the way in which the world actually works.

Manias are often associated with mob psychology or general 'irrationality'. Kindleberger attempts to explain this complex relationship, whereby mob psychology is an inevitable deviation from rational behaviour, through the development of the following propositions (Kindleberger, 2000):

- Mob psychology (group thinking) exists when all market participants change their views at the same time and act in concert.
- Different individuals change their views about market developments at different stages as part of a continuing process; most start rationally but increasingly move towards irrationality.
- Adherence to rationality differs among different groups of traders, investors and speculators, and an increasing number of individuals in these groups succumb to the hysteria as asset prices increase.
- All the market participants succumb to the fallacy of composition, meaning that it is often the case that the behaviour of a group as a whole differs from the sum of the behaviours of each of the individuals within.
- Irrationality may exist because investors and individuals choose the wrong model, fail to consider crucial information or make invalid assumptions – such as the aforementioned delusion that they will be able to timely and securely exit the market.

The critical transformation from euphoria to financial distress is related to the prolongation of overtrading based on the expectation of further price increases. Neoclassical monetary theory assumes that it is the fundamentals of an economy that, through changes in profit opportunities and investment patterns, initiate price changes. It suggests that asset prices in financial markets accurately reflect fundamentals, and consequently, only markets can provide an optimal allocation of resources as government intervention only produces distortions and Moral Hazard. This argument is contested and elaborated in the Efficient Markets Hypothesis (EMH). There are numerous different ways of interpreting EMH and, as a result, a lot of confusion has been created. The distinction between 'fundamental valuation efficiency' and 'information arbitrage efficiency' (Tobin, 1984) differentiates asset prices accurately reflecting the future payments of the underlying assets from asset prices reflecting the speed of relevant information. 'Fundamental valuation efficiency' is implicitly assumed in most mainstream finance literature.

'Information arbitrage efficiency' is embodied in the majority of modern EMH theory through the inclusion of rational expectation agents. Fama (1970 and, slightly adjusted in, 1991) distinguishes 'information arbitrage efficiency' in three forms. The 'strong form', according to which both private and public information are fully reflected in securities prices, the 'semi-strong form', where prices reflect all available information that is publicly available, and the 'weak form', in which prices reflect the information implicit in the sequence of past prices (Fama, 1970).

Fama, following Grossman and Stiglitz (1980),[5] later readjusted his understanding of 'information arbitrage efficiency', introducing the proposition that prices reflect information to the point where the marginal benefits of acting on information do not exceed marginal costs (Fama, 1991). Since the 1970s EMH has come under sustained attack mainly from within the neoclassical school. The attack has been based on informational asymmetry and behavioural finance perspectives. However, while the key question on the fundamental difference between risk and uncertainty in EMH remains unanswered, EMH still implicitly remains the dominant perspective in mainstream economics.

The EMH provided much of the theoretical justification for the 'New Financial Architecture' (NFA). NFA was characteristic of the radically deregulated, globally integrated financial system that began in the 1980s and continues to the day. This will be described in the next chapter.

International dimension and contagion

Kindleberger, unlike most authors, emphasises the international aspects of financial crises. Intense economic interactions across borders, he argues, can greatly contribute to both the boom and the collapse of financial markets. Acknowledging Minsky's work, Kindleberger develops the single-country financial instability model into an international one. In his cross-country contagion model, a bubble can easily spread internationally. He argues that whenever a bubble explodes in an area, money is transferred to another and the latter's currency appreciates. The external inflow of money, in the logic described above, is argued to frequently result in the continuous increase of domestic security prices in the liquidity-receiving economy. Analytically, Kindlebergers' argument can be described by the sequence of the following events: liquidity is internationally circulated and unavoidably leads to the appreciations of the recipient countries' currencies; these currency appreciations together with capital account liberalisation policies create an ever-growing but unsustainable cycle of domestic price increases, which – given the event of an exogenous displacement – could result in a rapid exodus of funds, increasing debts and bankruptcies in the liquidity-receiving countries.

Aliber, Kindleberger's collaborator, asserts that since the 1990s the world has experienced this continuous generation and circulation of credit and consequently bubble shifts. In detail, early in the 1990s, a climate of economic euphoria was prevalent in Japan where the liberalisation of financial regulation and rapid growth in its monetary base produced a rapid increase in financial asset and real estate prices. When the Japanese bubble imploded a surge of funds to Thailand, Indonesia and Malaysia followed and produced equivalent price increases in assets and real estate. As the bubble similarly burst in these countries – with contagious effects to countries with a more sound fundamentals' position like Korea – capital flew to the US. The US economy experienced an enormous appreciation in its currency, suffered a large deterioration of its trade deficit and saw its stock prices surging in an asset bubble larger than the one of 1920s (Kindleberger and Aliber, 2005, pp. 160–62). The factors to which Kindleberger attributes this cross-border contagion involve international capital flow links, arbitrage-entailing asset price increases in one market given increases in another, income changes via import changes and the foreign trade multiplier, exchange rate fluctuations and even purely psychological speculative reasons.

Concluding remarks

After this theoretical summary we proceed with an investigation of the internal and external factors behind the liquidity jumps in the economies studied, the specifics of economic and financial developments in each one of them, and we conclude on the importance of the liquidity surges and liberalisation schemes on the crises' occurrence despite the different routes undertaken. The theoretical background and argumentation of Keynes, Minsky and Kindleberger is used throughout this book and is found, at times, imperative for the understanding of the *modus operandi* of investment decisions,[6] liquidity moves and the general operation of financial markets.

3
Post-1980 Global Liquidity Data: Exponential Flows

This chapter delivers an analysis of the indicators related to the growth of financial capital in international markets since the beginning of the 1980s. It sets out the evolution of international financial markets in order to then investigate the reasons behind the remarkable increase of capital flows and the causes behind the redirection of some to the financial markets of middle-income countries. The chapter briefly describes the historic dynamics of the markets and concludes that the best way of investigating the causes behind the rapid increase of financial capital in international markets and its direction to emerging economies is by structuring the factors involved into a supply-push and demand-pull framework. The question of why developed economies generated a considerably increased level of financial flows since the 1980s can be answered through the identification of the supply-push factors (Chapter 4), whereas answering the question of why middle-income developing countries suddenly became an attractive outlet for this liquidity is central to the determination of the demand-pull indicators (Chapter 5).[1]

From the introduction of the 1933 Glass-Steagall Act of the F.D. Roosevelt administration, up until the 1970s, there existed a tight regulatory system, which found reflection in Keynesian counter-cyclical fiscal and welfare policies. Following the paradigm and policy regime shift from this regime, a transition to a radically deregulated, globally integrated financial system occurred during the 1980s and 1990s, justified by efficient financial market theory. This financial regime, referred to as the 'New Financial Architecture' (NFA), was based on self-regulation and market discipline – a combination that was considered crucial for the function of financial markets. This combination relied on the central claim of neoclassical financial economics that markets priced securities correctly with respect to expected return and risk – as long as governments did not distort incentives through intervention and regulation (Crotty, 2009).

Data on global liquidity for the post-1980 period, proxied by the value of financial assets in the USA, are illustrated here to demonstrate the actual historical evolution of financial flows. The growth of financial capital *vis a vis* the growth of real output circa 1980 summarised in Figure 3.1 is used as a starting point when investigating the sudden divergence of the two. The figure clearly illustrates the remarkable – in both size and speed – growth of financial assets against real output. In fact, the multiple of the stock of global financial assets to world output increased to 4.2 from 1.1 in the 1980–2007 period. This could be broadly considered as the result of the twin trend of financial liberalisation and financial innovation which resulted in the aforementioned quadrupling of global financial assets from 109% of global GDP in 1980 to 421% in 2007 (Palma, 2013).

In order to determine the reasons behind the change in the relationship between global financial assets and global output, the resulting asymmetry is first illustrated and then decomposed in the aforementioned supply-push demand-pull dynamic through the analysis of a series of key variables.

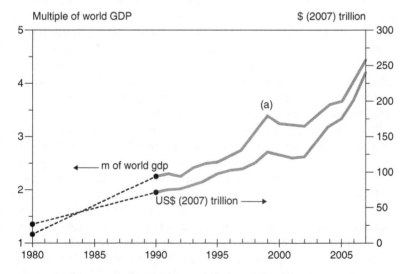

Figure 3.1 The stock of global financial assets, 1980–2007
Note: (a) collapse of the 'dotcom' bubble
Source: McKinsey (2008) and IMF (2009); from Palma (2009).

When considering the post-1980 increase in the supply of global liquidity, the major influences discussed are: the rapid market deregulation policies implemented in the US and the UK; the rise of institutional investors; the remarkable developments in financial innovations; the steep fall in the US dollar interest rate; and the rapid advances in information and communication technology. These factors created vast opportunities for the redirection of liquidity into new geographic and product markets. An environment was created where the majority of liquidity was not translated into actual investment in the real economy, but instead into financial savings. This vast direction of liquidity supply to the financial markets together with the development and increasing sophistication of financial markets – which was mostly reflected in the evolution of complicated derivative markets – resulted in financial markets creating their own liquidity and thereby greatly contributing to the post-1980 global liquidity boom. Emphasis is given to the dimensions, development, and implications of the economic deregulation policies adopted by most developed countries during this period, as they gave rise to portfolio diversification and, as a consequence, increasing investment in emerging markets. In addition to the growing deregulation framework established, the creation and expansion of complex structured financial instruments is also critical to this study. As a result of the above changes it will be demonstrated how the direction of liquidity shifted from productive investment – resulting in a capital formation[2] – to the vast trading of financial instruments. The relatively lower profits in the traditional markets of Organisation for Economic Co-operation and Development (OECD) countries *vis-a-vis* the financial profits of emerging market outlets and the role of technology and innovation will be discussed in this part, and it will be proposed that the innovation of new financial products produced, by itself, its own liquidity.

The increasingly important presence of credit and the deepening of international financial markets will be also studied through their supply-push and demand-pull implications on household income, expenditure, and consumption. The increasing household dissaving patterns in both developed and developing markets quickly generated additional monetary flows which via the new tools shaped by the New Financial Architecture resulted in an exponential increase of the capital circulated. Since the 1980s household expenditure started to strongly exceed household income. As Palma explains, this divergence resulted from the constant – if not increasing – trend of consumption, the higher access to consumer bank lending, and the real fall in personal income (Palma, 2009a). In the developed and gradually in the emerging economies, household expenditure increased – clearly not independently from the increased access to and supply of new credit – as a proportion of household income. This post-1980s increase in consumption as a share of national income has been strongly correlated with a net increase in household borrowing.

When examining the demand-pull variables related to the direction of financial flows in emerging economies, the reasons behind developing countries appearing to be highly attractive to global liquidity flows and capital investment after the 1980s are discussed. In this section, Palma's proposition that developing countries provided a 'market of last resort' for international liquidity flows will be investigated (Palma, 1998; 2003b). This proposition suggests that the perceived drainage of highly profitable activities in the developed world in relation to developing economies directed a vast amount of capital in the latter in the pursuit of higher and quicker returns. In the face of competitive alternatives, Western financial institutions started to intensely invest and lend to emerging economies in search of more profitable investments. This collective market move, being a combination of higher liquidity and a chase for higher yield, was followed by a fall in the risk spreads of the emerging markets, allegedly reflecting the lowering of the receiving economies' actual risks.[3] Incentives for international financial agents to invest in emerging economies such as Brazil were further strengthened by local attempts to reduce and stabilise the exchange rate risk.[4] The timing and direction of liquidity shifts to the developing world will be examined together with the overall economic and political background of the recipient economies to examine the formation of the overall context that enabled and strengthened the direction of flows to the economies in question. The reshaping and restructuring of the economies' financial market regulation is analysed in order to understand the reasons underpinning the purported attractiveness of developing economies. Thus, the major influences discussed in this section are summarised by the changes in the economies' domestic markets with regard to trade and capital liberalisation policies, deregulation of financial markets, and privatisations of state-owned enterprises.[5]

Data on global liquidity flows and stocks

The composition of financial flows has historically varied within the 20th century according to historic socio-economic developments and the resulting risk and liquidity preferences of financial investors. The pre-World War II structure of financial flows dominated by bond portfolio investment was reshaped into a market structure where equity investment dominated. The gradual privatisation of state-owned companies (most notably transportation and telecommunication networks) after the 1970s provided additional sources of equity opportunities for an ever-increasing pool of investors, including banking institutions, insurance companies, pension, and mutual funds. The region of Latin America, which extensively incorporated these changes, comprises a clear example of these jumps in investment (Figure 3.2).

The increasing presence of international investors was compounded by an additional significant development – the volatile nature of financial flows was now not only found in its absolute volume but further in the great variance of its dominant type. The dominant types of financial stock and flows have varied from bank assets in the 1960s and 1970s to stock market investment in the 1980s; private bonds making a strong presence from the late 1980s onwards, and a dominance of FDI, bonds and equity investment in the 1990s. Bank lending peaked in the end of the 1970s when it accounted for two-thirds of total funds raised in international capital markets. However, from the beginning of the 1970s until 1986, alternative forms of liquidity started to flood capital markets. Between 1972 and 1986 private bonds increased by a factor of over 20 (from US$11.2 to US$228 bn), syndicated loans by a factor of 6 (from US$8.7 to US$52.8 bn), while total securities by a factor of 16 (from US$20 to US$322 bn) (OECD Financial Markets Trends, various issues).

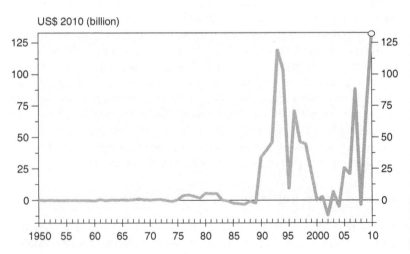

Figure 3.2   Gross Portfolio inflows in Latin America, 1950–2010
Source: IMF WOE (World Economic Outlook) database; from Palma (2009a).

The introduction of new financial instruments in the 1980s served as a market response to the greater price volatility of the period. The Latin American debt crisis of the early 1980s and the higher interest rates in the US – introduced by P. Volcker to fight domestic inflation – resulted in lower returns in traditional markets and higher overall return-uncertainty. As a consequence, market agents started distributing and hedging against the risks involved. New instruments hedging against the risk of interest and exchange rate fluctuations such as interest options, futures, and floating rate notes started to be traded in much higher levels. By 1986 around 85% of global market activity was associated with security-related funding. The increasing presence of securitisation was associated with the establishment of new instruments which encompassed the flexibility and security of securitised instruments and further provided a back-up line of credit (Cosh, Hughes and Singh, 1989).[6]

The composition of flows has varied throughout the century, and the dominant themes of investment have been changing according to the conditions of the countries concerned and ensuing preferences of the time. For example, bank lending to Latin American countries was not growing at radically high rates within the 1980s, while the same could not be said for their East Asian counterparts. East Asian economies operated as a magnet for bank lending, given that domestic borrowers were particularly attracted to syndicated lending – being flexible in structuring drawdown and hence useful in the financing of infrastructural investment (IMF, 1997, p. 30). Overall, at times where interest and exchange rate volatility were really high, the bond markets were severely hit and bank lending revived as a result.

Given this historically changing nature of dominant financial flows what has been exceptionally striking, in addition to the aforementioned changes in volume and type, is the sudden and unprecedented change in the direction of the flows (see 'euphoric' direction of flows as described by Rodrik, 1994, and Krugman, 1995). In 1980 just 5% of American institutional investors held foreign securities while only a decade after the share had increased to 20%[7] (Ocampo et al., 2007). This change of direction for institutional investors' market positions developed into a complicated 'double causality' relation[8] with the evolution of financial products but also integration throughout international markets. The development of new underwriting facilities and products like swaps was critical to the tying of domestic to international markets. Hence, markets enjoyed an overall climate of much higher cross-border linkages caused by, but also further reinforcing, institutional investors' return-seeking behaviour across borders.[9] Western governments made no significant attempts to minimise or even control the size of increasing cross-border financial transactions. The resulting market environment was such that deficit economies borrowed heavily, the creditor ones constructed and equipped themselves with an overabundance of guarantees against solvency, while concurrently the entire institutional framework was encouraging excessive risk-taking behaviour.

Financial deregulation: the post-1970s path

After the end of the 1970s international currency flows were moving at a much higher speed as a result of the gradual dismantling of the 1950s' Bretton Woods system that culminated with the 1979 British abolition of all remaining exchange controls. The deregulation of the New York Stock Exchange in 1975 together with the UK Big Bang, which followed a decade after, permitted the internationalisation of trading and the consequent external re-orientation of businesses which, searching for a higher yield internationally, diversified their investments.

As outlined above, the changing conditions in financial markets starting in 1980s are reflected predominantly in the changes in the volume, type, and direction of the flows. Another critical factor, albeit commonly ignored, is the change in the size and character of financial agents themselves. Within the two decades between 1983 and 2003, financial markets consolidated in an unprecedented way. In the OECD economies the number of active banks halved from 15,084 to 7,842, while at the same time the concentration of banking assets in fewer and fewer financial institutions was further strengthened. From the beginning to the end of the 1990s, the business share held by the 50 largest banking institutions increased from 55% to 68% in terms of banking assets (FDIC data). Together with this horizontal consolidation and as a result of deregulation, international capital markets further merged in a vertical fashion. Banking, fund management, insurance, and securities' businesses were all equally conglomerated. The most common trend was for large commercial banks to purchase fund managers or investment banks. Dutch businesses were some of the first to enter this tendency of vertical mergers and acquisitions: in 1991 ING was formed as an independent company resulting from the merging of National Nederlanden and the NMB Postbank group. Throughout the 1990s the business of mergers and acquisitions had grown so much that huge international business conglomerates such as the Allianz group purchased Dresdner Bank and the asset manager PIMCO, Citigroup was formed through the merging of Citibank with the insurance company Travellers Group, while huge banking institutions like Deutsche Bank and UBS rapidly absorbed much smaller banks, funds and trusts (Sheng, 2009).

The changes in the political economy scene of the 1980s, shaped and developed by the liberalisation policies of Reagan and Thatcher, resulted in a huge jump of international liquidity through financial innovation and a change in its direction through series of trade and capital deregulation policies. The deregulation of financial markets was seen at the time by policy-makers as a necessary move towards achieving greater efficiency, transparency, and productivity in international markets. Deregulation was expected to increase competition, which would spur these gains through the adoption of best practice and highest efficacy operations. The introduction of financial intermediaries and international accounting was viewed as a stepping stone towards higher transparency, while the move towards a greater financial globalisation was seen as being critical for the improvement of corporate governance. The liberalisation of markets and the consequent increase in the freedom of their agents were expected to improve the markets' monitoring systems and enhance the spillover effects of technological capabilities, which would contribute to more efficient investment placements.

Within the 1980s, financial assets circulated in international markets experienced a nine-fold jump. The collapse of the Bretton Woods system in the early 1970s created a new system of market incentives where sovereigns' consensus rested upon the premise that their economies could do better outside a fixed exchange rate system. Instead, economies trusted their ability to borrow offshore without altering their domestic fiscal policies while simultaneously hedging for any speculation against their home currencies – through using the credit lines and liabilities held in their own currencies (Pringle, 1989). The Western shift of the 1980s towards increasingly floating exchange rates created market conditions facilitating and pushing towards the direction of higher financial exposure as floating rates were automatically associated with increasing demand for new financial services and financial intermediation. The need to increase securitisation in capital markets was intertangled with the collapse of fixed exchange rate policies. The latter resulted in higher risk-taking and speculation on exchange rate developments, inflationary pressures and a consequent need for risk hedging.

Final remarks

In order to understand the actual volume of the financial flows, especially *vis-a-vis* the size of the real economy of the time, we continue by investigating in further detail the historic origins of this development and the political economy framework that initiated and supported this surge. The causes of the increased inflows are the result of first changing economic policies, predominately in the US, as well as market liberalisation policies in the capital-receiving economies. The first policy changes are examined through investigating developments resulting in the lowering of speculative and overall-financial domestic saving opportunities together with the creation and development of financial products with intrinsic properties benefiting from risk diversification. The policy changes in capital-receiving countries are then analysed through investigating the financial market deregulation changes and new inflow-enhancing policies introduced in three middle-income economies that are the focus of this study – Mexico, Brazil and South Korea. Through outlining the policy background prior to each economy's individual and differentiated handling of global financial inflows, the following chapters' emphasis on major international and domestic economic policy changes is key to the understanding of the crises' evolution. Mexico, Korea and Brazil are chosen as economies with striking differences regarding the handling of their own crises but whose routes to crisis all evolved against very similar international market conditions. The countries' 'three routes' to financial crises were all underlined by the framework of rapid financialisation and lower profit opportunities in the West together with market deregulation and liberalisation policies domestically.

4
Supply-Push: The Western-Induced Endogenous Generation and Proliferation of Liquidity

In the international context, the changing conditions of financial markets from 1980 onwards can be characterised by the increasingly dominant role of institutional investors, the spread of innovative financial instruments and techniques, a remarkable growth of securitised forms of lending and a much faster paced network of information, technology and communications. All these factors became increasingly present against a policy background of liberalisation and growing integration of different economies, institutions and market segments.

Overall, the changes applied not only enhanced considerably the flexibility of Western capital markets but also enabled the participation of emerging market firms into US stock markets and allowed emerging economies investors to gain access to additional financing. Through the trading of domestic shares, predominantly in the form of depositary receipts in the major stock exchange markets of the world, emerging market firms obtained finance capital in international equity markets via initially international financial intermediaries and local investors and subsequently directly.

The rise and development of institutional investors occurred following the exit of the US from the gold standard in 1971, the US acceptance and development of the Eurodollar market in the early 1970s and the overall market liberalisation policies of the late 1970s. Within the 1970s in the US and a decade later in the UK, the market share of institutional investors increased considerably. In the US, pension funds' share of total corporate equities increased from 0.9% in 1952 to 6.4% in 1968 and 9.9% in 1974. Equivalently, but with a shorter time lag, British pension funds' share of domestic stock market increased from a fifth to a third between 1978 and 1986 (Cosh, Hughes, Lee and Singh, 1989). The abolition or lowering of exchange rate controls in numerous countries together with the changing markets regulations, allowing international financial institutions to take part in domestic stock exchanges, initiated the release of additional international capital, gave rise to international equity markets and consequently resulted in the further rise of institutional investors. Given the deregulation of capital markets and the consequent remarkable enlargement of the spectrum of possible investment choices, the scope behind the institutionalisation of investors became larger than ever before. The expected ability of life insurance or mutual funds to make more profitable and insightful market placements than individual investors was directly related to the enlargement of both products and markets of the time. At the same time, the sheer volume of financial assets held by institutional investors determined their role as not just market agents but several times as market makers – see Figure 4.1 for the evolution of US financial assets within the 1990s. From 1980 to 2000 the stock of all financial assets increased by a factor of 23 (from $USbn 339 to $UStr 8.07), while just for the specific period 1990–1998 studied in this book, the sum of US financial assets increased by a factor of 4 (from $UStr 1.77 to $UStr 6.61).

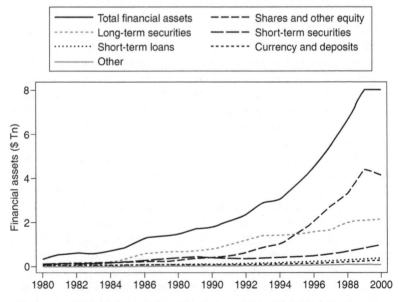

Figure 4.1   Evolution of financial assets, USA – deflated to 2010 US$
Source: OECD Statistics.

Institutional investors quickly acquired the capacity to take influential short positions (e.g., in currency from the 1980s) through spot and forward markets and the rapidly growing structured product markets. Thanks to the great bulk of their asset holdings and the augmented profit opportunities at the time, institutional investors started to diversify their investments in both new markets in emerging economies and non-traditional products which, as will be discussed later, contributed to the creation of additional capital circulated in the markets in self-generating ways.

Financial innovation and engineering

Since the 1990s the notional value of global derivatives has developed into being a large multiple of the world GDP. The level of imbedded leverage in derivative products resulted in an unprecedented contribution of additional liquidity into international capital markets. Given other financial developments, such as the expanding role of institutional investors discussed above, the establishment and increasing trading of derivatives and securities greatly contributed to endogenous creation of liquidity by financial markets.

Financial innovation and deregulation resulted in the creation of several new instruments instigating and further developing high-risk or even toxic products in financial markets. Often, the securitisation of loans and mortgages implied that assets moved off balance sheets into some special investment vehicles that often required no capital supply. Within the decade, the collateral offered by Collateralised Default Obligations (CDOs) was most often corporate and emerging market bonds and bank loans (US Government Printing Office, 2011). This was often embodied in the securitisation and engineered collaterisation of firstly corporate debt markets and then mortgages, a large share of which were subprime. CDOs functioned via the bundling of high-yield bonds and loans by investment banks and following this – along with the 'contribution' of Credit Rating Agencies (CRAs) – their slicing into different layers of risk that would ultimately prove more profitable than the individual sale of included assets. Specifically, in the case of the US, instruments such as 'vanilla' residential mortgages[2] were securitised as mortgages or asset-backed securities by government-sponsored mortgage institutions. In addition, other mortgages and corporate debt were broken down into shares of different risk qualities, which were then collaterised with assets or guarantees to form CDOs with triple A ratings. On the last point the fee-contingent provision of triple A ratings on structured products by CRAs was a key contributor to the escalation of toxic products' generation. The operation of CRAs, together with the function and milieu of the market overall, developed in a way that the riskiest and lowest investment grade CDOs would be traded in the markets and offer highly competitive rates of return – several points above the London interbank offered rate (Tomlinson and Evans, 2007).

Through deregulation and financial innovations, liquidity was giving birth to additional liquidity, while the overall technological developments of the time were facilitating its circulation. As accounting and regulatory changes permitted certain liabilities to be moved off companies' balance sheets, banks and other financing institutions were allowed to increase leverage with no change in the capital held. This was expressed through the rise of special purpose vehicles (SPVs) or separate legal entities functioning via operating leases, which were used to circumvent financial covenants – such as debt-to-equity ratios – and allowed firms to increase their lines of credit without changes in the liabilities' side of their balance sheets.

The gradual decline of the traditional commercial banking system and the rise of highly leveraged investment banks completely reshaped financial markets. Investors would position their money into the newly developing shadow banking system[3] in the pursuit of higher returns despite the absence of the Federal Insurance Deposit Corporation's protection. Through the development of the shadow banking system, the market for 'repos', or repurchase agreements – essentially a spot market transaction accompanied by a forward contract on the repurchase of the same asset – also grew significantly. Wall Street securities firms would sell Treasury bonds – a traditionally low-risk low-return asset – to banks and other investors and would very soon repurchase them at a small price premium. This transaction would offer easy and immediate liquidity to investors via the investment of the cash proceeds in the meantime in high-risk high-return assets. Repos were frequently rolled-over or renewed, allowing lenders to rapidly move in and out of their positions and transforming their assets into 'hot money'. Operating essentially like collateralised loans, the initial investors were able to borrow nearly the full value of the Treasury-collateral and invest it in high-yield assets, often found in emerging markets like the ones studied.

In the late 1980s, and more specifically in 1987, the overall deregulation climate in the US was further strengthened. Commercial banks exerted intense pressure upon the Federal Reserve to permit the undertaking of several activities forbidden by the Glass-Steagall Act and its modifications. The newly established regulations allowed 'bank-ineligible' activities, such as the holding or selling of securities not permissible for national banks to underwrite or invest in and to be undertaken by non-bank subsidiaries of bank-holding companies. The initial framework was such that the Fed had the authority to limit such bank-ineligible securities activities to 5% of the revenue of any bank subsidiary. Overtime, however, these restrictions were relaxed and ultimately abolished. From the middle of the 1980s to the middle of the 1990s, the Office of the Comptroller of the Currency (OCC)[4] was enlarging the overall framework of permissible activities for national banks. This enlarged spectrum of newly permitted activities included underwriting as well as trading bets and hedges (derivatives) on the prices of certain assets. 'Between 1983 and 1994 the OCC broadened the derivatives in which banks might deal to include those related to debt securities (1983), interest and currency exchange rates (1988), stock indices (1988), precious metals such as gold and silver (1991), and equity stocks (1994)' (US Government Printing Office, 2011, p. 35).

The newly advanced Credit Default Swap (CDS) markets and insurance companies' products were used to heighten the credit quality of debt obligations underlying papers. Thus, if the underlying assets traded were weak, the purchase of CDSs was used to enhance the perceived quality of the assets. Rapidly growing institutional investors, which had benefited from the liberalisation of the exchange rates, heavily purchased leveraged debt and equity products tied to exchange rate fluctuations. Structured foreign exchange products were among the first securities which institutional investors started trading heavily.

In the US the approval of two bills in 1990 – 'Regulation S' and 'Rule 144A' – was key to the lowering of transaction costs but also the speeding up of transactions in capital markets. Regulation S exempted securities from registration and disclosure requirements, while Rule 144A increased the flexibility and speed of trading of private placements. Rule 144A withdrew the need of investors to hold private placements for a minimum of two years after the initial offering (so that post-1990 'qualified institutional buyers'[1] had the two-year holding condition withdrawn) (Watson et al., 2012).

Financial markets' speed of transactions and circulation of capital changed considerably, and the dominant principle of 'lend, buy and hold' was replaced by the norm of 'originate and redistribute' (Gross, 2008). This institutionalisation of liquidity supply, opening of new markets and increasing participation in them (predominately generated by the rise of institutional investors) shaped a new source of demand for products and securities from emerging markets. At the same time, however, it also contributed to the sudden growth of highly leveraged funds and proprietary trading institutions, equipped with high risk and an ever-increasing demand to identify weaknesses and risk in international markets. The latter could not but automatically create a positive feedback mechanism that involuntarily generated higher risk in the sought-after markets.

The development of new financial products and institutional investors' search for higher yields in new markets – previously perceived as too risky – was enhanced by the relative decline of yields in traditional domestic investments. Emerging market opportunities seemed even more attractive for capital investors, given the 1980s' economic recession in several industrial economies of the OECD. External factors, taking place in the financial centres of the world, such as general events in their business cycles, liberalisation and deregulation policies affecting the diversification of investment portfolios, and the fluctuations in the economies' terms of trade were critical to the direction of capital flows in emerging economies.[5] Equivalently, and especially for small open economies, fluctuations in world interest rates were key in inducing capital flows in the same direction (Calvo and Reinhart, 1995). Since 1980 both long-term and short-term interest rates in the US were experiencing a downward trend. By 1993 real interest rates were at the lowest level since 1980, while in 1992 short-term interest rates were at a historic low since the 1960s (US Treasury data) (see Figures 4.2a and 4.2b). Lower interest rates, apart from releasing liquidity to alternative financial savings, further improved the creditworthiness of debtor countries through their effect on the stock of emerging countries' nominal debt. The risk of default of these recipient economies was significantly reduced, prompting a striking increase in the price of secondary market bank claims in numerous heavily indebted countries.

The speed and dynamism of this post-1980s jump in capital flows was conclusively facilitated by the fall in transaction costs resulting from the rapid developments in information and technology of the time. The combination of innovations in technology and dissemination of information together with the deregulation changes in the legal background of markets facilitated both the rise of new products and, as a consequence, the soaring of the overall stock of international capital. Institutional and regulatory changes such as the brokerage fee deregulation contributed to this capital increasing as early as 1975. The 1975 brokerage deregulation, or else the much-celebrated May Day of the financial world, entailed the US Securities and Exchange Commission abolishing fixed fees in the trading of stocks and deregulating commissions such that they would be 'competitively' priced on the trading floor. IT advancements and the rapid sophistication of the market

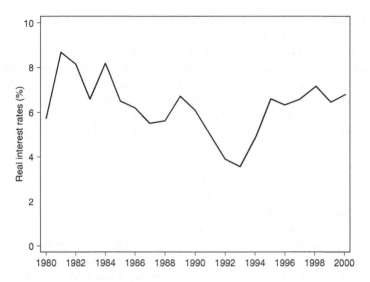

Figure 4.2a Real interest rates, USA
Source: orld Development Indicators, World Bank.

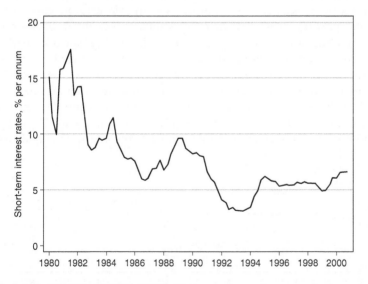

Figure 4.2b Short-term interest rates, USA
Note: Short-term rates are usually 'either the three month interbank offer rate attaching to loans given and taken amongst banks for any excess or shortage of liquidity over several months or the rate associated with Treasury bills, Certificates of Deposit or comparable instruments, each of three month maturity' (OECD).
Source: OECD Statistics.

culminated in 1996 in the establishment of online trading in the discount trading industry.[6]

Additional reductions of transaction costs and developments in information availability came with the introduction of market credit ratings for many emerging economies certified by Western institutions from the beginning of 1990. Within the decade certified credit ratings got hardwired into the system. Accordingly, CRA ratings were used in the issuance of securities, such as Eurobonds, in determining net or regulatory capital requirements for banks, securities firms and insurance companies under the Basel Treaty (Basel Committee of Banking Supervision, 1997 and BIS 2013).

Ratings were often hardwired into the investment mandates of institutional investors such as insurance companies, pension and mutual funds, which might have not been allowed to hold securities below a certain credit grade. CRA ratings also developed in a fashion so as to be indispensible when determining the criteria on the eligibility of companies' inclusion in bond indices, and were also frequently used in financial contracts like collateral agreements and loan contracts (Deb et al., 2011). The dominant theory behind the benefits of this elimination in transaction costs and increase in information symmetry is built upon the belief that investors would reduce inefficiencies such as moral hazard and adverse selection and, as a consequence, markets would operate more efficiently and the availability of credit would be further enhanced. As a result, the costs faced by investors were reduced, enabling them in this way to decrease their risk and enter new markets.

Overall, between 1989 and 1996 the number of countries rated by international credit rating agencies increased from 11 to 49 (Cantor and Packer, 1995) while from 1996 to 2010 from 49 to 124 (Standard &

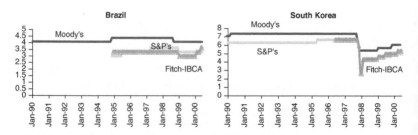

Figure 4.3   Ratings of foreign currency sovereign debt
Note: See Appendix 1 for a Scale of Ratings for Sovereign Debt.
Source: Kaminsky and Schmukler, 2001.

Poor's, 2011). Within the 1990s sovereign ratings, by all 3 major CRAs, in Mexico changed nine times (with five upgrades), ten times in Brazil (with seven upgrades) and 18 times in Korea (with as many upgrades as downgrades). Mexico received its first sovereign credit rating by Moody's in 1990, just below investment grade, and via the pressure of markets and the large inflowing investment, the score was upgraded shortly thereafter. Korea and Brazil also became hard-wired into the CRA system and were generously given investment grade ratings for their sovereign debt – Brazil to a to a lesser extent though (see Figure 4.3).

5
Demand-Pull: The Internally Induced Attractiveness of Emerging Markets

Record capital inflows in new directions outside traditional markets resulted in and also resulted from the decrease in the interest rate spreads of emerging economies. This fall in spreads was stimulated by a combination of several newly established dynamics. Among these dynamics, three were of particular importance. Firstly, investors in the 1990s identified an overall improvement in the emerging economies' fundamentals *vis a vis* the 1970s.[1] Secondly, the rise of institutional investors, together with the very high stock of the assets accompanying them, induced a growing tendency to diversify their portfolios – and hence increase their exposure to new markets. Thirdly, the overall risk effect of the growth of international liquidity supply was that, in order to maintain high yields and profits, investors moved down the credit spectrum via investments in emerging markets state and corporate bond investments.

From the start of the 1990s, a movement of international actions to stimulate the soundness and stability of emerging economies' financial markets was developed. As a result of investors' growing preferences for these new markets, institutional coverage and analysis was initiated. Early on in the decade two influential reports were produced guiding and encouraging investments in these markets. The first was from the Basel Committee on banking supervision (BIS, 1995), while the second was published from the G10 working party on financial stability in emerging market economies (BIS, 1997).

Emerging economies were subject to several monetary, fiscal, trade and financial changes that enabled these liquidity inflows to take place and enhanced the motivations of institutional investors to continue supplying their capital in that direction. Starting in Latin America, the political establishments recognised the evolution and development of capital markets and proceeded to liberalisation and deregulation, tailored to suit the inflows of funds from the world financial centres. The vast privatisation schemes in the majority of Latin American economies comprised a very significant contributing factor to the increased attractiveness of these markets and the direction of capital inflows. The causality of the direction of the flows is not uncomplicated. The identification of a direct causality between the increased attractiveness and eventual direction of liquidity inflows in the emerging economies and the deregulation of their markets remains problematic and unclear. What is clear, however, from the historical record, is that the deregulation policies in the emerging markets followed the ones of the West. Overall, it can be argued that the legal background against which the development of all securitised products took place was established before the great influx of funds into alternative markets, while the sudden jump in derivatives and securities did take place almost in tandem with the enlargement of the emerging economies' financial markets.

The overall positive economic environment favouring emerging economies allowed the sovereigns to restructure their existing liabilities in improved terms and reduce their refinancing risk through practices such as extending their debt maturity, diversifying investors' bases and setting benchmarks for corporate borrowers (IMF, 1997). For example, Brady Bonds[2] in Mexico (between 1994 and 1996) comprised the single most traded instrument in Latin America (IMF, 1997). Their liquidity was considerably increasing, and thus, despite a moderate increase in their issuance, there was a very large increase in their turnover.

From the beginning of the 1990s most of the Latin American economies operated as liquidity magnets after the introduction of significant reforms which contributed to the liberalisation of international trade, external capital controls, and the domestic financial sector. The growing trend in bond issuance was matched by, if not initiated by, increased demand for emerging markets debt. Significant financial sector policies introduced included: the abolition of the majority of exchange controls; the granting of independence to central banks; the elimination of most restrictions on foreign investment; the removal of regulations on interest rates and credit allocation; the reduction of reserve requirements on domestic deposits and the privatisation of numerous state banks (O'Campo, 2004). Fiscal changes related to the markets liberalisation included reforms on reducing income tax rates, increasing VAT and strengthening the overall tax administration.

Starting in the 1990s, when most emerging economies liberalised their capital accounts, the circulation of international capital was at its high historical levels. Private equity was relatively cheap *vis a vis* the equivalent stock prices in the Western financial centres, while external liabilities were low. Equity prices in the majority of Latin American countries were depressed in the early 1990s. Between 1990 and 1994, average capital gains in the Latin American stock markets were in the region of 230% (Table 5.1). The Mexican Tequila crisis of 1994 shook international confidence in the markets and resulted in an abrupt 40% fall in equity prices. However, the trend of increasing returns resumed between 1995 and 1997, attracting even more portfolio inflows. In both Latin American and East Asian markets, bond issuers increased their issuance. The average maturity of sovereign bonds also increased starkly, while yields on them experienced a remarkable decline – for example, there was an average fall of 62 basis points for both regions from 1995 to 1996 (IMF, 1997).

As a result of booming inflows, a vicious cycle was generated in most emerging economies whereby inflows were prompting currency appreciation, which was in turn prompting the attraction of additional inflows. The augmented supply of external financing in both the Latin American and, more moderately, East Asian regions initiated a process of currency appreciation. As long as positive expectations on currency appreciation were held, additional inflows flowed from investors with maturity horizons that incorporated the rise of domestic currency. This currency appreciation effect of liquidity inflows should also be considered when thinking about the repercussions of an abrupt discontinuation in the supply of such flows. In the case where capital inflows

Table 5.1   Latin America stock exchange prices, 1990–1998

	Indexes July 1997=100					
	Dec. '90	Sep. '92	Sep. '94	Mar. '95	Jul. '97	Aug. '98
Latin America	21.7	44.6	92.5	52.3	100	47.2
Argentina	13.4	46.9	78.2	53.5	100	53.4
Brazil	8	22.1	71.8	42.8	100	44.4
Chile	24.5	51.4	93.1	89.4	100	48
Colombia	16.6	65	113.1	96.3	100	49.9
Mexico	38.6	72.7	132.1	45.9	100	49.7
Peru	n.a.	n.a.	72.9	56.4	100	57.3
Venezuela	84.9	82.2	50.8	37.9	100	26.2

Note: Data in US dollar, 1998 prices
Source: Based on Standard & Poor's stock market review, several issues.

are suspended, additional pressure would incur testing an emerging economy's strength to defend its currency against speculative attacks. In this logic what needs to be considered is that the same structural and regulatory changes that allowed emerging economies to augment their access to international financial markets also created networks and mechanisms through which the same economies can be subjected more intensely to speculative attacks. The deregulation of these economies, especially when combined with the development of financial products such as securities and derivatives, surely increased financing access. But it also contributed to the growth of highly leveraged funds and pro-prietary traders in search of high yields, high risks and weaknesses in foreign exchange rate arrangements. Accordingly, on several occasions, institutional investors pursued strategies of taking significant short positions in currency, through the purchase of equivalent structured products and options, contributing to the volatility of the economies' currencies.

In the aftermath of trade liberalisation in Latin America, the region experienced its highest share of exports in world markets since the export promotion era. From 1990 to 2000, the continent's export growth was substantially high and coupled with historically high levels of FDI. The collapse of several trade agreements in the 1980s was fol-lowed by their revival, strengthening and the introduction of numer-ous new agreements – primarily the establishment of Mercosur (the Southern Common Market) in 1991. Within the decade, and until the Asian crisis of 1997 that disrupted the regional integration of the econo-mies, intra-regional trade exploded particularly in the Mercosur and the Andean regions – with an average annual growth rate of 26% and 23%, respectively (Ocampo, 2009). The introduction of the North Atlantic Free Trade Agreement (NAFTA) in 1994 comprised the most notable institutional change towards trade liberalisation and contrib-uted towards discussion on developing additional free trade areas such as the Free Trade Area of the Americas (FTAA). As a result of policy changes and deregulation of the American markets for goods and ser-vices, a clear North–South pattern of trade was observed within the Latin America region. Accordingly, the North, predominantly Mexico, operated as the manufacturer of industrial exports, whose construction greatly depended on US manufacturing imports. The industrial basis of Mexico, the maquila industry, could be briefly described as a simple assembling manufacturing unit putting imported goods together – what Palma calls screwdriver manufacturing (Palma, 2005). The South was characterised by a pattern of extra-regional commodity exports and intra-regional natural resource-concentrated manufacturing. Brazil predominantly followed the later trend, as its exports were comprised of primarily commodity-rich and some technology-intensive goods to the rest of the Americas. This division in the production of tradable goods was accompanied by different patterns of dominant financial inflows. Mexico, with its maquila industry, attracted high levels of equity investments, whereas in the case of Brazil private acquisitions were mostly prevalent.

Trade liberalisation and investment patterns especially for the Latin American region were closely linked. Multinational companies, and specifically financial savings firms, participated in the emerging markets tradable sector via privatisations, private buyouts and equity investment. This, however, did not imply that the growth of exports in the capital-receiving economies was translated into higher GDP growth rates. In fact, when comparing the 1990s' decade with the period of Import Substitution Industrialisation (ISI), Latin American countries grew at half the speed (Palma, 2003b). The 1990s' weakening of the link between GDP growth and the export balance and hence the low multiplier effect of high exports and FDI on economic growth (negligible in the case of Mexico and its maquila industry) can be explained by the interplay of two factors. First, the absence of a manufacturing revival investment policy after the termination of the ISI policy. Second, the structure of the 1990s' industrial production that required a great share of imported capital and intermediate goods. Thus, the opening of the region's economic borders, the increase of goods traded as well as the consequent influx of finance for these industries did not yield the expected growth effect. In order to understand better the implications of this, a broad picture of the region's capital markets' liberalisation schemes should be portrayed.

Financial liberalisation started to be implemented from the late 1980s[3] in most Latin American economies and from the early 1990s in the majority of the East Asian ones. Capital account liberalisation induced an increase in equity investment, which was seen by markets as a more secure and lower risk investment opportunity than public debt, given its weaker linkages to interest rate fluctuations. Overall, in both regions, the influx of capital and the easy access to consumer credit were broadly translated into a portfolio substitution from bank deposits to tradable securities, and national savings were largely diminished as a percentage of GDP. The performance of emerging economies' equity markets however diverged greatly among regions. In 1996, while Latin America was still recovering from the Mexican crisis, equity issuance in the region's stock markets grew by 17.2% while in East Asian by 10.5%.[4]

This sudden increase in investment in private equity and the consequent volatility of equity prices was especially worrying for emerging markets (see how price volatility in the Mexican stock market was 15 times larger than its US equivalent from 1983–1993 (McKinsey, 2008). The financial markets of the economies in question were so suddenly and abruptly deregulated that premature and volatile capital inflows could directly undermine the financial system as a whole. Financial markets in Latin America were remarkably thin and, as a consequence, any internal or external disturbance could directly affect capital flows inducing uncontrolled volatility. High volatility levels can suggest the absence of coherent information flows, the prevalence of herd behaviour from market agents, a misplaced euphoria on financial developments and, consequently, price fluctuations not acting as effective criteria on resource allocation. Further to that, and as a result of higher price volatility, risk-averse investors developed diminished interests in the region, triggering adverse selection problems and with higher finance prices.

The combination of trade and capital liberalisation had yet more ambiguous effects on the economic performance of most counties in the two regions. Large capital inflows essentially led most of the economies (especially the Latin American ones) to an enduring deficiency in effective demand for non-commodity tradables – weakening any remaining incentives to develop their manufacturing base and ultimately strengthening their dependence on manufactured imports. This resulted from the escalation of the economies' real exchange rates and the very low levels of expected demand stemming from the very high level of input leakages. The growth of manufacturing in horizontal and mostly vertical supply ways was constrained by the capital influx.[5] Incoming capital concentrated in a small number of, mostly post-privatised, companies. The absence of investment spillovers was enhanced by the absence of domestic public investment, the over-valued currencies of the regions and the high domestic interest rates.[6]

The rapid influx of capital into emerging markets as a result of a combination of domestic markets' liberalisation and the international rise in the generation and circulation of finance prompted large international institutions to engage in further research on the impacts of such changes. Towards the end of the 1990s wider concerns regarding the volatility of finance in emerging markets became institutionalised in the form of a joint programme of the IMF and the WB for Financial

Sector Assessments (FSAP) and the development of IMF Reports on Standards and Codes (ROSCs). The latter attempted to evaluate sovereigns' compliance with IMF codes on monetary policy and fiscal transparency and much wider issues extending to accounting principles and corporate governance (Peretz, 2010). Following the Mexican crisis concern on the sustainability of financial flows and their discontinuity effects grew further. IMF consultations structurally got extended to financial regulators, financial institutions and to capital markets. The 1995 Whittome Report on financial surveillance recommended tighter surveillance and contacts between the Fund and capital markets, while the Fund commissioned in both the 1980s' and 1990s' country missions for global capital markets under the title 'International Capital Markets: Recent Developments and Near-Term Prospects' in the 1980s and as 'International Capital Markets: Recent Developments and Key Policy Issues' in the 1990s (Whittome, 1995).

By the 1990s several additional international institutions started compiling similar analyses of economies' capital developments with regard to the sustainability of the financial sector and risks involved: the WB in country's economic memoranda and country-strategy papers, the OECD, the BIS, private research bodies such as the Brookings Institute, the Institute for International Finance and the Economist Intelligence Unit as well as many others. The volume and the quality of the research, unavoidably influenced by overall market enthusiasm and pessimism, did not seem adequate to shield emerging economies from a multiple of additional crises following the Mexican one of 1994 for the rest of the decade. In the rest of this book the crises of Brazil and Korea and their economic evolution after the Mexican and prior to their own crises are examined with the precise target of understanding the implications of hot, volatile and unstable capital movements.

Concluding remarks

Two important questions were addressed in these last three chapters. Why has the world economy experienced such an increase in international liquidity since the 1980s? And why did middle-income developing countries suddenly become attractive as an outlet for this liquidity in the late 1980s and early 1990s? These questions are addressed through an analysis and evaluation of the enlargement of international financial markets since 1980 and the reasons why additional liquidity was generated in developed countries (mostly in the US) and why it was directed to emerging economies.

The enlargement of the financial sector is examined together with its rapid consolidation. The marked increase of financial assets managed by banking and non-banking institutions is analysed along with the horizontal and vertical consolidation of the sector. This ultimately portrayed an image whereby the liberalisation of finance did not automatically result in its enhanced competition, as predicted by the Efficient Market Hypothesis, but in fact contributed towards an increasingly oligopolistic structure. These chapters (3, 4 and 5) further investigated the reasons behind the influx of financial liquidity in emerging economies. This was primarily achieved through their categorisation into supply-push and demand-pull factors. The first encompassed all policy, legislative and technological changes within the financial centres of the world, directing liquidity externally, and the latter embodied the changes in the external environment that pulled financial capital. It was found that a combination of different-natured changes, endogenous and exogenous to the economic advancements of the liquidity-receiving economies, were responsible for the direction of vast amounts of finance into emerging economies.

6
Mexico: The Laissez Faire Paragon Gone Wrong

Introduction to country analysis

The following chapters (Chapters 6, 7 and 8) explore how three different middle-income emerging economies, Mexico, Brazil and South Korea, headed towards financial crises in the 1990s. These economies are chosen as the best representatives of different economic policy designs devised to deal with the problem of the absorption of foreign inflow surges following Palma's 'three route approach'.

Economic and financial developments in Mexico, Brazil and South Korea

The most significant economic trends characterising the period from the late 1980s to 2000 can be summarised by decreasing interest rates in the financial centres of the world (Figures 6.1.a and 6.1.b are indicative of the US real interest rate,[1] US dollar LIBOR[2] and 'immediate' interest rate[3] developments), recovering rates of profitability in emerging markets, and a decreasing share of labour in GDP pushed by a spirit of markets' liberalisation. The economic trends most frequently observed in developing countries in particular in the same period were: the opening up to trade, the liberalisation of their financial sectors and the privatisation of state-owned enterprises.

In the 1990s growth rates in the advanced economies were fairly stagnant, real interest rates in the financial centres of the world were very low and asset prices were rising rapidly. These factors have historically comprised systematic determinants of capital flow surges (Calvo, Leiderman and Reinhart, 1996). Harcourt similarly suggests that recently the system has been made conducive to financial crises – especially

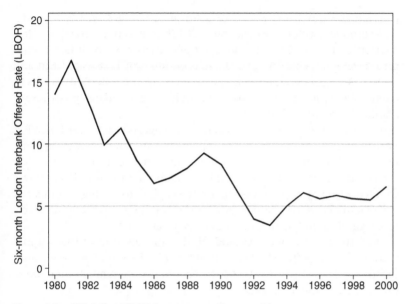

Figure 6.1a   US dollar LIBOR interest rate (six-month)
Source: WB, World Development Indicators.

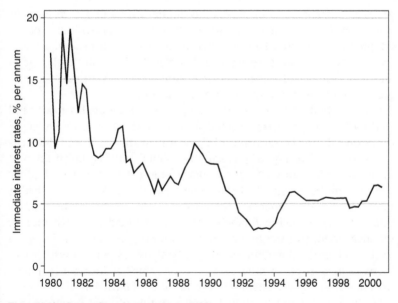

Figure 6.1b   Immediate interest rates, USA
Source: OECD Statistics.

through the unsettling effects of asset price bubbles on the financial and corporate sectors (see Harcourt, 2013b and 2001). After the introduction of the Brady Bonds in 1989 and the return of inflow surges into developing countries, the large economies of East Asia, Latin and Central America became the major receivers of these liquidity waves as alternative outlets or, as Palma would call them, 'markets of last resort' (Palma, 1998, 2000, 2003a).[4]

In the 1990s most emerging economies engaged in deeper liberalisation policies and attempted to deepen their integration with international markets via opening up to trade and finance. In the first half of the decade, there was a considerable reduction in import tariffs that was coupled with a strong increase in foreign capital, following a number of agreements between the domestic authorities and international creditors regarding middle-income countries' foreign debt.

In all the three economies studied, the liberalisation of their capital accounts was rapidly achieved within broadly the same timeframe and, subsequently, in the early 1990s the economies were much more open to the international markets.

The three cases

Mexico is used as an example of an economy with a mostly *laissez faire* policy *vis-à-vis* the surge of inflows. The non-interventionist policy adopted by its central bank resulted in such a search of liquidity and credit that ended up creating asset bubbles (both in the stock market and real estate) and a consumption boom. These eventually led to a gigantic increase in non-performing household debt.

Brazil is studied as an economy that instead adopted a nearly full sterilisation policy. It is selected as a characteristic example of an economy whose central bank sold government bonds to withdraw the excessive levels of liquidity created by capital inflows. In an attempt to avoid a Mexican-type bubble, Brazil engaged in a policy of costly sterilisation that eventually led to what Minsky would have described as public sector Ponzi finance. The full sterilisation policy of the country unavoidably resulted in financial instability through the high interest rate needed for this sterilisation and paid for by the state. The latter led to the collapse of the domestic private banking system as a result of an increase in non-performing debt, and of a further increase in public debt due to the government rescue plan of the failing banks.

Lastly, South Korea is studied as an example of an economy where even though the additional finance created by inflows was used productively by the corporate sector (and, as a result, no sizable asset bubble or consumer boom was generated), the economy still experienced a severe crisis, this time via an excessive increase in corporate debt. In South Korea, the collapse of profitability in the corporate sector (which was mainly due to falling micro-electronic prices) meant that corporations required the additional finance for investment needed to continue at the cutting edge of technology. An additional significant problem of the economy was that its central bank was caught with low levels of reserves at the apex of the crisis (Palma, 2000).

The rationale behind choosing such contrasting economies, in terms of the ways in which they formulated policy to deal with inflow surges, is to emphasise the difficulties of dealing with such surges once capital accounts have been liberalised. This study of existing literature understands and portrays the reasons why the chosen domestic policies were adopted and the economic and social implications that arose as a consequence.

Chapters 6, 7 and 8 set the background for understanding how three middle-income economies followed independent and differentiated routes to financial crises.

MEXICO: THE LAISSEZ FAIRE PARAGON

Liberalisation

Prior to 1982, the Mexican economy generated a twin public and current account deficits – mostly as a result of servicing its public debt. The 1979 increase in US interest rates – that led to a surge in the Libor-rates – and the 1981 collapse in the global price of oil induced catastrophic effects on the Mexican economy and contributed to the 1982 currency crisis. In 1982 falling oil prices and high Libor rates rapidly deteriorated the economy's tax revenues and trade balance. This, together with the Mexico's falling reserves, historically overvalued exchange rate,[5] and rising domestic inflation spurred capital flight and deteriorated the economy's current account balance. The inability of the authorities to continue to service their foreign debts, finance the country's current account deficit and defend the overvalued currency, together with the increase in capital flight, resulted in the depletion of Mexico's foreign exchange reserves and the consequent need for the government to devalue the domestic currency. The Peso was devalued three times in 1982 and between August and December 1982 lost nearly 50% of its value against the Dollar (Public Finance Statements, BoM).

In the period following the 1982 crisis up until the introduction of Brady bonds in 1989, the major objectives of the Mexican authorities were to control the very high levels of inflation (averaging over 100%

between 1982–1986, Public Finance Statements, BoM) and promote growth while maintaining the country's exchange rate (Calvo and Mendoza, 1995). Mexican authorities tried to use all means available to maintain the fixed currency peg and internal and external balances – especially given the constant reality of capital flight and the uncertainty that this produced. This left the economy increasingly vulnerable to external economic conditions. Accordingly, it was foreseeable, at least to some domestic agents in Mexico, that given negative changes in external economic conditions financial fragility could be rapidly induced in the economy.

In the years following 1982 the Mexican economy was faced with an external transfer problem induced by the high levels of external debt and the deteriorating terms of trade. Its large magnitude was due to the high level of indebtedness, the severe contraction of international financing within the 1980s, the implications of the terms of trade losses, the low-value-added composition of exports and the increasing consumption of imported goods (Moreno and Ros, 2009). The external and domestic policy constraints resulting from the debt crisis and the persistent need of the economy to refinance its debt meant that the generation of a fiscal surplus was needed to pay for this debt.[6]

In 1988 a new economic stabilisation programme *Pacto de Solidaridad Económica* (Economic Solidary Pact) was introduced by the newly elected Salinas government. The program was targeted at reducing inflation and servicing foreign debt while maintaining exchange rate stability. The main instruments that were used included neoliberal reforms of trade liberalisation, a wide-ranging privatisation and deregulation scheme, and a call for a renegotiation of externally held sovereign debt. From the beginning of 1989 the government used the exchange rate as a nominal anchor to stabilise the economy and reduce inflation. This exchange rate stabilisation policy was additionally complemented by several income policies. These included wage freezes, job cuts and reduced benefits. The resulting dynamic, typically observed in similar nominal exchange rate stabilisation schemes, was an appreciation of the real exchange rates – which was effectively a consequence of the inflation differentials between the domestic economy and the US. Between 1988 and 1994 the Mexican real exchange rate is calculated to have appreciated by 40% despite the numerous changes in the country's exchange rate policy (World Bank Development Indicators).[7] As a result, the country increased its exposure to and reliance on short-term capital flows, which are knowingly determined by indicators more investors'-appetite specific than overall macroeconomic fundamentals.

In this manner, the capacity of markets and policy-makers to identify signals of changes in the economic fundamentals of the country further increased in complexity. The deterioration of Mexico's current account together with the growing exposure of domestic banks to foreign debts increased the vulnerability of the economy and was closely tied to the credit boom it experienced.[8] The authorities effectively pursued policies to enhance the credit boom taking place in the country's markets, by allowing the domestic commercial banking system to increase its leverage, enabling the significant growth of the mortgage market, permitting very high interest rates on credit card loans and, at the same time, maintaining a very relaxed mechanism for the monitoring of the commercial credit expansion.

Despite the relatively low contribution of Mexico towards the combined GDP of emerging economies in the early 1990s, the economy was attracting a disproportionately large amount of capital (see Figure 6.2). In 1991 the Central Bank introduced a band establishing the limits within which the nominal exchange rate was allowed to fluctuate. Accordingly, to limit nominal depreciation and enhance investors' confidence in a strong Peso, the Central Bank (CB) would intervene each time a 1.5% change[9] in the currency's value took place within a day. This contributed to a level of interest that was considerably lower than before – reflecting, among others, the lower risks perceived by investors. Overall, the band system enhanced security of a strong Peso and encouraged additional optimism on holding a currency with a strong potential to further appreciate – given the fact that the Peso was

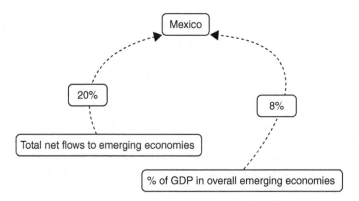

Figure 6.2 Mexico's contribution to emerging economies' GDP and asymmetrical share of capital flows
Source: IMF data.

allowed to appreciate but not depreciate more than the value that the band dictated. Overall, access to vast amounts of international capital, resulting from the variables analysed above together with the timely introduction of Brady bonds in 1989, enabled the Mexican government to manipulate exchange rates so as to ensure price stability and – at least in the short term – resolve or tame domestic social problems.

Finance intensification

After the 1988 election of President Salinas the entire economic and financial regulation framework of Mexican markets changed remarkably. The banking system was re-privatised, reserve requirements for banks were decreased, quantitative credit controls were reduced and the overall conduct of monetary policy changed radically. The M2 money multiplier nearly doubled between 1988 and 1994 (from 4.2 to 8) – a change which was attributed by many to the extensive liberalisation that took place (Calvo and Mendoza, 1995).

Under the Salinas government and given the immediate effects brought about by the Brady bonds, the provision of credit ballooned in Mexico. A large boom in consumption credit took place in the economy, and the commonly anticipated overvaluation of the currency followed soon thereafter. Between 1987 and 1994 bank credit experienced a remarkable expansion – in real terms overall commercial bank credit grew by more than 100%, mortgages grew by 966%, consumer credit increased by 548% and credit to retailers by 513% (IMF, 1995b). An implication of this expansion of bank credit was its allocation to high risk and sub-prime borrowers and the consequent increase in the volume and value of non-performing loans. This can be seen as a combined result of domestic banks' structural inability to effectively assess risk and the improvements in public finances. Mexican banks were generally inexperienced, having little knowledge and organisational networks to facilitate the assessment of credit, investors and other market risks. On the other hand, the improvement of state finances, which was expressed via a lower demand for bank credit, directed the banks to shift away from their traditional state client to more risky borrowers.

By 1994 the Mexican economy was characterised by heavy speculative portfolio inflows and high private foreign indebtedness. These were the combined result of security placements and high banking and private sector indebtedness attached to the security provided by the overvalued exchange rate. As a result, portfolio inflows in Mexico were highly sensitive to a possible exchange rated evaluation.

Capital inflows were not only large in absolute volume but they came to comprise a large part of the economy's GDP. A significant characteristic of the flows was that a very large proportion of them were directed towards portfolio investment (67% in 1993, BoM data). Much of this portfolio investment was directed into very short-term government paper, which made incoming capital more unstable and prone to reversals. Figure 6.3 shows that between 1990 and 1993 the deregulation and internationalisation of Mexican financial markets further allowed a substantial increase in the direction of foreign inflows to the Mexican private sector. The immediate effects of Mexico's liberalisation policy and its perceived lower investment risk can be clearly seen in the rapid growth in the accumulation of private debt from 1991 until the 1994 crisis.

Economic liberalisation was swift and very extensive – from 1989 to 1993 most markets of finance were opened, deregulated and liberalised.[10] Starting in 1989, deregulation of foreign portfolio investment in domestic stock and money markets was applied. In order to stimulate the participation of foreign investors the 1986 stock markets 'neutral investment regime' was eliminated in 1989, while in 1990 restrictions on foreign purchasing of fixed-interest government bonds were also removed. The elimination of the 'neutral investment regime' effectively

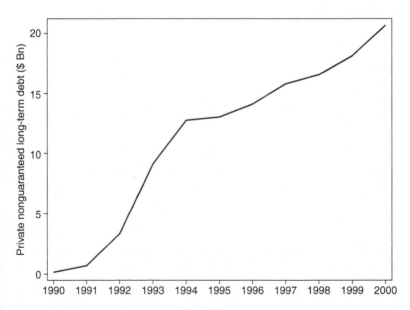

Figure 6.3   Mexico's private debt, US$ (2012)
Source: World Bank.

meant that foreign investors were eventually allowed to buy voting shares in companies (Cuevas et al, 2002). Overall, reforms in the domestic regulatory framework had two major targets: enhancing market participation and reducing the prevalent administrative, distribution and communication costs. This was achieved through changes in the domestic competition regulation, with an emphasis on the service sector where the previous framework of permits and legal constrains limiting market participation, entry and exit was eradicated (Ros, 1991b).

Private equity and bonds

Investment in private equity and private bonds increased remarkably. Until the late 1980s foreign ownership and equity enlistment in the Mexican stock market were highly constrained. It was only at the end of 1989 that the revised Stock Market Law enabled the access of foreign investors. As a result, foreign investment acquisitions of Mexican net equity holdings increased from US$1bn in 1983 to US$29bn in 1993 and international participation in domestic stock markets reached a total of 27% in 1993 – whereas in 1989 it accounted for 6% (BoM).

Public bonds

Mexico returned to international bond markets in 1990. American Credit Rating Agencies gradually improved the rating of the country's sovereign bonds – to just below investment grade – and within three years the government raised US$24 bn (IMF).[11] After the introduction of Brady bonds, Mexican government securities became more attractive to international investors, especially given the deregulation of Mexican capital markets.

During the 1980s, access to Peso-denominated government bonds was practically restricted to domestic investors as foreign investors' access to such instruments was very limited and could only operate via secondary purchases from Mexican banks (BOM, 1992). In 1990 the public bond market was liberalised, and direct sales of Mexican securities to foreign residents were allowed (IMF, 1995b). In 1991 foreign investment in government securities was US$3.4 bn, but two years later such purchases totalled US$18bn. Overall, holdings of government paper were increasingly dominated by foreign investors. Between 1990 and 1993 the share of foreign investors in total government securities increased from 8% to 57%. At this point, it is interesting to point out the different composition of domestic and foreign holdings' maturities.

In the purchases of Peso-denominated government bonds, domestic investors would acquire government paper with longer maturity while their international counterparts would mostly purchase bonds with shorter maturity, typically between 1 and 12 months (see Table 6.1). Accordingly, the average maturity of residents' holdings was calculated to be an average of 350 days, while the equivalent figure for non-residents' holdings was 280 days. The fact that the majority of government securities were held by international investors and had shorter maturities contributed additional volatility in the economy.

Mexican authorities briefly but unsuccessfully attempted to alter the international investment trend of short-term capital flows. In 1992 the monetary authorities imposed a cap of 10% on the share of foreign liabilities in the total liabilities of Mexican banks. Additionally, a floor of 15% of low risk or risk-free assets was placed in foreign currency liabilities (Gurria, 1995). These regulations originally resulted in the fall of financial flows channelled through the banking system. Soon thereafter, however (in 1992), banks managed to circumvent the regulations through adjusting their portfolio and capital inflows and benefiting, in this way, from their growing balance sheets.

The heavy bias of capital inflows towards short-term portfolio investments had important consequences for the economy as a whole. These consequences operated through three major channels: real exchange appreciation, increasing consumption and higher overall financial fragility (see Moreno and Ros, 2009, for a detailed analysis). First, the rapid real exchange appreciation had adverse effects on the level of private

Table 6.1 Government bond investments

	1991	1992	1993	1994
NRPGB*	3,406	8,147	7,013	−1,942
TB	253	−62	1,063	14,338
Other	3,153	8,209	5,950	−16,280

Note: *NRPGB – Non-Resident Purchases of Mexican Government Bonds; TB – Tesobonos; Other – Primarily CETES.

The Fed's definition of Cetes and Tesobonos is the following: 'Cetes are government securities and are the equivalent of Mexican T-bills. They are denominated in Pesos and are sold at a discount. Cetes have maturities of 28, 91, 182, 364, and 728 days (though this maturity is presently discontinued). Cetes are highly liquid instruments and have an active repo market . . . Tesobonos are Dollar-indexed government securities with a face value of U.S.$1,000. At the investors' option, they are payable in Dollars, and they are issued at a discount. Maturities include 28, 91, 182, and 364 days... they comprised the majority of debt offerings in the time leading up to the 1994 Peso crisis' (US Federal Reserve, p. 6, 1998).
Source: MCB, US$mn.

investment. The Peso appreciation, taking place in tandem with the intensification of trade liberalisation, reduced the profits of the tradable sector and adversely affected the levels of private investment (Ros, 1995). Second, an allocation of resources towards consumption – at the expense of mostly private savings and investment – resulted from the difficulties in dealing with the unprecedented volume of capital inflows. Lastly, the concentration of inflows in highly liquid assets, together with the rapid expansion of consumption credit, resulted in the imminent deterioration of the banking sector's balance sheets and the consequent increase in the financial fragility of the sector as a whole.

At this point, the increase in the financial fragility in the banking sector needs to be understood through an additional perspective that is related to the currency appreciation and finance liberalisation policies that were implemented. Other than the banking mistakes conducted as a result of excessive liquidity inflows, the lower returns of the banking sector – reflecting the lack of experience of the new bankers – were highly related. The average annual rate of return from private and commercial loans in the banking sector decreased from 50% in 1987 to 12% in 1994, while the share of non-performing loans steadily increased throughout the period. The combined effect of the above, together with the increased borrowing of Mexican banks from international capital markets in order to lend domestically, increased the susceptibility of the domestic banking sector to exchange rate movements and contributed to the sector's general vulnerability (Moreno and Ros, 2009).

Crisis and post crisis: the developments

Following the Chiapas uprising in early 1994, the assassination of the presidential candidate Colosio on 23rd March and several other events, panic spread in the markets. Speculation against the economy as a whole resulted in a large exodus of capital, a collapse of foreign exchange reserves, a significant devaluation of the Mexican Peso (by 15% in December 1994) and a sharp deterioration of the economy's current account. On the 20th of December 1994 the Mexican monetary authorities agreed to widen the band limit for the currency by 15%.[12] At the same time, however, the authorities did not announce a broad adjustment or monetary tightening program to reassure investors of their determination to take control of economic developments. This led to a gigantic increase in the exodus of capital from the economy, a large fall in foreign exchange reserves and a consequent decision to allow the currency to float and subsequently devalue.

The economy's stock of foreign exchange reserves fell remarkably within a month (a US$10bn decline after the assassination of the Presidential candidate and an additional fall of almost $3bn resulting from other political developments prior to the elections[13] – see points 1 and 2 in Figure 6.4). The Mexican monetary authorities assumed that the fall of inflows was only a temporary phenomenon and decided to sterilise the monetary effect of the foreign currency. This was delivered through a large expansion of domestic credit and thus an increase in the monetary base at a time of falling international currency reserves (Griffith-Jones, 1997). The expansion of domestic credit led to a fall in domestic interest rates starting in July 1994 and an increase in the spread with the US dollar – as the US dollar followed the reverse trend. Ultimately, the authorities' assumption that the fall in capital inflows was solely a short-term result of the temporary political uncertainty proved to be unsubstantiated and excessively risky.

The political economy of the time and the developments in the domestic political sphere were signalling high instability in the near future, a prediction greatly reflected in the position of the country's foreign reserves (see Figures 6.4 and 6.5). The introduction of a swap line with the US and Canada of US$7 billion was announced after the Peso devaluation by the Mexican authorities, but this was not perceived

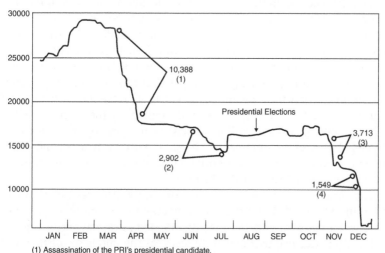

(1) Assassination of the PRI's presidential candidate,
(2) Resignation of the Secretary of the interior.

Figure 6.4 Stock of net Foreign exchange reserves in 1994 ($US mn)
Source: Griffith Jones, 1997.

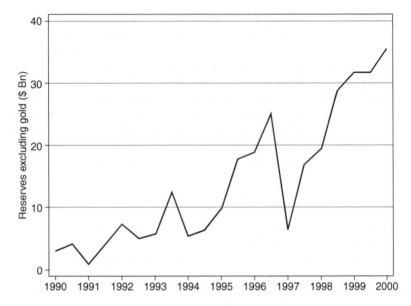

Figure 6.5   Mexico's reserves position, US$ (2010)
Source: OECD Statistics.

as an adequate commitment to prevent the additional escalation of the capital exodus (Lustig, 1995). The Mexican authorities discussed possible options for a viable and effective macroeconomic policy through an atypical meeting with the Pacto – a forum formed by the government, business and workers to discuss macroeconomic policy prospects and policies concerning exchange rates, inflation targeting and wage determination. At that meeting an agreement to increase the exchange rate band was reached, and this was implemented on the 20th December 1994. However, several objections have subsequently been raised on the legitimacy of the discussions, the clash with macroeconomic policy targeting on the part of the Central Bank and the ulterior motivations of different participants of the Pacto.[14]

The current account deficit of the economy, which was around 8% of GDP in 1994 (OECD Statistics), was mainly due to the economy's private sector net savings deficit. Starting in 1990, external borrowing was primarily performed by the private sector as the public sector financed its liabilities through the increasing stock of foreign exchange reserves (see Figure 6.5) – mainly as a result of the aforementioned capital inflow sterilisation schemes of the Central Bank. In February 1994 the level of foreign exchange reserves peaked at US$29bn (BOM, 1995), and a discussion on revaluing the Peso was introduced by the local authorities. As mentioned above, within the first few months of 1994 social and political uncertainties were high. This was primarily a result of the Chiapas uprising but this was, at least in the short term, offset by the domestic and international optimism resulting from the approval of NAFTA by the US Congress.

The NAFTA negotiations between the US, Canada and Mexico started in 1990, the countries that signed the treaty in 1992, and it came into effect in 1994. The US and Canada together with Mexico – already one of the world's developing economies most open to trade (OECD, 2002) – agreed to the elimination of tariff and non-tariff barriers to intra-regional trade and to the gradual elimination of foreign investment restrictions within by the end of the decade.[15] Mexico committed to further liberalising its trade sector but retained restrictions in certain sectors – primarily oil refinery, agriculture (particularly corn production) and the transportation equipment industry[16] – which would only be gradually liberalised. Optimism regarding the overall performance of the economy resumed as exports to the US and Canada were expected to rise and FDI flows from the two economies to Mexico were anticipated to grow rapidly. The Agreement was predicted to increase domestic and foreign firms' investment in the production of tradable goods in Mexico, which would in turn place the economy into a phase of export-led growth and guarantee Mexico's economic reform process.

In 1994 the Peso had already started to depreciate against the US dollar (10% in March 1994, see Figure 6.6) at a period when the Dollar itself was depreciating in real terms against the Yen and most European currencies. Prior to the crisis the Mexican Peso was strongly overvalued, and this was further compounded by the government's strict inflation-targeting regime. At the same time the current account deficit was rapidly deteriorating, reaching 5.2% of GDP in 1993 and 6.3% in 1994[17] (see Figure 6.7). It needs to be emphasised here that the current account deficit of the Mexican economy was partly financed by short-term capital inflows contributing to its volatility. The level of public debt at the time, however, was lower than the OECD average (67% in 1993, WDI WB). In 1993 Mexico's public debt accounted for 30% of the GDP (WB, see Figure 6.8) – a level that encouraged international investors to count on the continuation of Mexico's international borrowing given the expectation that NAFTA's approval by the US Congress would consolidate additional international capital inflows in the domestic economy. However, the fact that both a large stock and a high share of government debt paper were both short term but also held largely

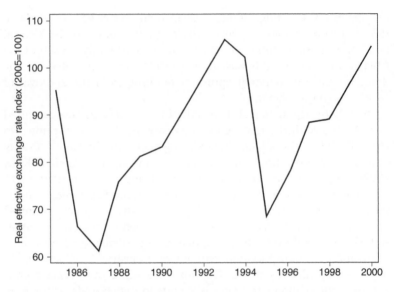

Figure 6.6 Mexico's real effective exchange rate
Note: The IMF defines the Real effective exchange rate as 'the nominal effective exchange rate (a measure of the value of a currency against a weighted average of several foreign currencies) divided by a price deflator or index of costs'.
Source: International financial statistics, IMF.

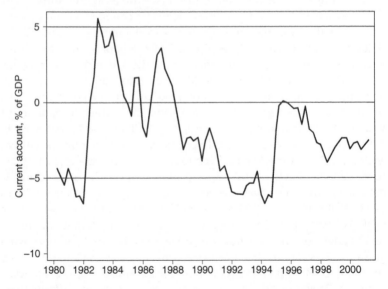

Figure 6.7 Mexico's current account balance, percentage of GDP
Source: OECD Statistics.

by non-Mexicans contributed to an increase in the volatility of public debt subject to changes in international markets and shifts in investors' expectations (Figure 6.8).

The composition of domestic public debt changed very rapidly. Most domestic investors quickly switched from Mexican Peso-denominated public bonds (CETES) to their US dollar-indexed counterpart (Tesobonos). Virtually the entire stock of short-term government debt shifted from CETES to Tesobonos as fears regarding the government's inability to exchange the Peso-denominated debt for US dollars at the official exchange rate started growing. The level of foreign currency reserves unavoidably exacerbated this dynamic. The stock of Tesobonos increased from $1bn in January 1994 to US$3.1 in March, US$12.6bn in June and $14 billion in July of the same year (BoM). By December 1994 the composition of government paper held by non-residents had changed remarkably, so that 10% of the total government paper held was in CETES and 87% in Tesobonos, while exactly a year earlier the equivalent shares were 70% and 6% (BoM Statistics). From the middle of 1994 the stock of Tesobonos exceeded that of the foreign exchange reserves held in Mexico. By the end of 1994 the level of foreign

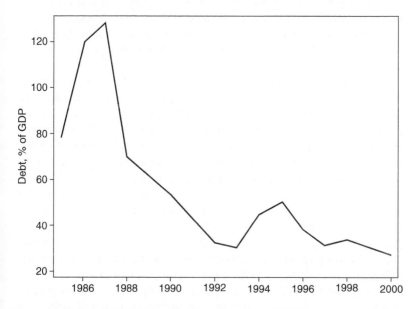

Figure 6.8 Mexico's public debt, PPG*, percentage of GDP
Note: PPG* – Public and Publically Guaranteed Debt
Source: Global Development Finance, World Bank.

exchange reserves had fallen to US$6.3bn – a level considerably lower than the stock of Tesobonos expected to mature in the first quarter of 1995 (a total of US$9.9bn, BoM). This imbalance was highly volatile and proved problematic for the economy. Tesobonos' very short maturities negatively affected the economy's ability to service its debt and, being US dollar indexed, would further inflate the stock of public debt in the case of a Peso devaluation. The increasing speculation against the ability of the Mexican government to pay its debt spread panic to international financial markets, and the resulting necessity for a lender of last resort to halt this panic became increasingly apparent. Up until 1995, when the IMF credit package was granted (see IMF, 1995c), a self-fulfilling prophecy with foreign investors unwilling to purchase Tesobonos and falling levels of foreign exchange reserves was aggravating the crisis.

The interest spread between CETES and Tesobonos can be considered as a good indicator of expected exchange rate fluctuations, while the spread between Tesobonos and US Treasury bill can be viewed as the risk premium of international investors holding Dollar-indexed domestic securities (see Figure 6.9). After the assassination of Colosio in March 1994, both spreads increased and then decreased as a result of the electoral success of President Zedillo in August 1994 and the expectation of stability following the election (IMF, 1995c). These optimistic expectations were held constant until November of the same year. After the official devaluation of the currency in December, both spreads rose steeply again.

Following the crisis an immediate redemption of all Tesobono holdings took place, while the Mexican government, heavily constrained by its existing foreign debt maturities, was forced to seek assistance externally and ultimately receive in early 1995 a 'rescue package' from the US, IMF and several international commercial banks. In addition to this credit 'rescue package', Mexico introduced a series of sharp fiscal adjustments to deal with the resulting extra deficit. The IMF's credit package was the largest ever financing package approved by the Fund – both in terms of the absolute amount of money provided and in relative terms given Mexico's quota in the institution.[18] The package was designed to provide an adequate international response to the economy's financial crisis and was primarily intended to revive the confidence of the international financial system (IMF, 1995c). The program aimed to address Mexico's liquidity problem through the supply of external financing, which would help in converting short-term government debt into medium- and long-term debt while assisting domestic commercial banks to meet their short-term external obligations. In this manner,

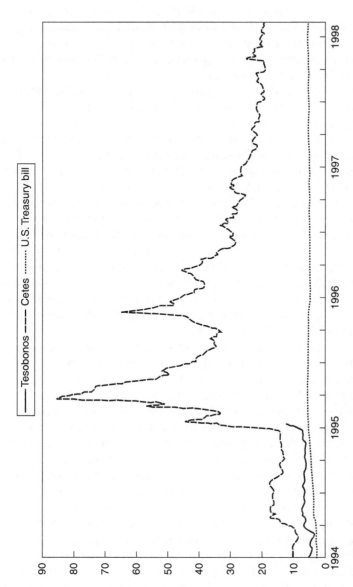

Figure 6.9 Yields on Mexican and US Government securities, January 1994–January 1997 (in percent)
Source: Bloomberg Financial Markets, from Flood and Marion (1998).

investors' interest in the Mexican economy would be renewed, confidence would be restored and the over-shooting of the depreciation of the Peso could be reversed. The IMF package, together with additional bilateral loans, was designed to operate alongside a fiscal tightening policy by the Mexican state. The latter was considered necessary for achieving the stabilisation of financial markets and the reduction of the trade and current account deficits.

The economy's debt crisis generated ample economic problems on two fronts. First, the repayment difficulties due to the high-level and short maturity structure of external debt and, second, the consequent inability of the government to design and implement a sound macroeconomic policy given its resulting constraints in issuing debt, borrowing from international capital markets and retaining savings domestically. Accordingly, on the fiscal front, the government proceeded in a series of tightening policies such as taxation changes and wage and price restraints. To contribute towards the formation of a primary surplus VAT rates were increased from 10% to 15%, while wages in the public sector were allowed to increase by a maximum of two-thirds of the expected rate of inflation (IMF, 1995c). On the financial front, the recapitalisation commitments to the government deposit guarantee fund resulted in a sharp increase in the ratio of equity of the banking sector to non-performing loans from 137% to 149% within a year (from the end of 1995 until end of 1996).

Other than the deterioration and escalation of both the current account deficit and the economy's public debt (with regard to its volume and structure), several additional influences, mostly resulting from the swift liberalisation of the economy, are of great significance. It has been argued that the absence of transparent and timely information on several economic indicators and their appropriate dissemination was critical to the escalation of the Peso devaluation.[19] Indicators such as the economy's position on international currency reserves and exposure to foreign banks and financial institutions were not widely and comprehensively available – especially to international investors. Information on the level of reserves was only released every three months, except that Mexican insiders knew what was going on, which gave them an advantage against foreign investors. On this point questions unavoidably arise regarding what detailed and comprehensive data are, and the difference in their definitions prior to a crisis, when they tended to be a fluid and flexible notions, and after a crisis, when they are presented as objectively defined concepts.

Concluding remarks

When examining the consequences of the rapid liberalisation of the Mexican economy, it is evident that both the authorities and the economy as a whole were unable to cope with the speed of the changes and the simultaneous adjustments in several parts of the financial sector. As a result of the rapid financialisation asset prices in the Mexican economy were inflated to a level that could not be sustained. The market euphoria brought along increases in the prices of financial assets that were not fully supported by changes in the economic fundamentals of the country. In fact, it was exaggerated market optimism rather than signs of equally increasing productivity or output that stimulated this asset price inflation. The Mexican asset price inflation needs to be viewed concurrently with the overall limitations of international capital markets, which, in the case of Mexico, acted in a way so as to accumulate an investment mania in times of euphoria and exacerbate speculation against the domestic currency in times of panic. This resulted in manic reactions, which manifested themselves suddenly when compared to the sedate rate of change of the economy's official fundamentals' indicators.

7
Brazil: The Anti-Mexican Public Debt Failure

The pre-1998 economic experience

In the 1990s Brazil engaged in deep liberalisation policies and attempted to enlarge its integration with international markets by intensifying its opening up to trade and subjecting its domestic industries to foreign competition. The economy gained access to international capital markets by a combination of a wide spectrum of macroeconomic policies, the liberalisation of its capital account and debt restructuring through the Brady Plan. In the first half of the decade – following agreements between the domestic authorities and international creditors regarding the country's foreign debt in the late 1980s – there was a considerable reduction in import tariffs that was coupled with a significant increase in foreign capital inflows.[1] The latter enabled the economy to reduce a large part of its current account deficit. The current and capital account liberalisation were achieved rapidly, and by the second half of the 1990s the economy was much more open to the international product and financial markets. The main challenge faced by the authorities, dating to the 1980s, was soaring inflation, and the opening up of the economy (and especially finance) was, as a consequence, geared towards the state's anti-inflationary policy.

Economic developments and the role of inflation: an historical view

Between 1980 and 1985 the Consumer Price Index (CPI) of Brazil had escalated from 86.3% per annum to 248.5% (BCB, 2012a). In 1986 the first major attempt to stabilise inflation was made. The new Cruzado currency replaced the existing Cruzeiro: all the prices – including the exchange rate – were fixed to the 27th of February 1986 level; all wages, contracts and payments in the old currency were converted into the new currency based on the average value of the previous six months; and all indexation of prices, wages and contracts was eliminated (Fonseca, 1998b). The Plan appeared to be an immediate success as inflation was remarkably reduced – falling to almost zero percent within the same year. After 1986, however, the adjustments proved too large to prevent a gigantic increase in aggregate demand and the resulting inflationary pressures (Baer, 2008). The limited, or rather non-existent, access to external funds (predominately prior to the introduction of Brady bonds) implied that the programme ultimately fell on the economy's current account deficit and lack of reserves.

During the 1990 Presidential election, and after the failure of the Cruzado Plan, the country was still suffering from severe hyperinflation, large primary deficit and very high rates of public debt[2] (see Figure 7.1 for annual inflation rates). The newly elected President Collor de Mello introduced a set of policies primarily targeting the opening of the economy, via several privatisation schemes, and the taming of inflation. The plan included: the introduction of another new currency – the Cruzeiro; the freeze of 80% of all deposits, transactions and saving accounts larger

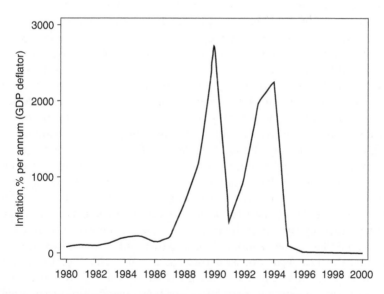

Figure 7.1 Brazil's inflation, GDP deflator (annual percentage)
Source: WDI, World Bank.

than Cr\$50,000 (for a period of 18 months); the increase of taxation on foreign investment in fixed income instruments (from 5% to 7%); the introduction of taxation on bond placements (5% tax); the prohibition of new foreign investment in stock options and futures' markets; the introduction of directly indexed taxation; and the initial freeze of prices and their gradual replacement with new ones based on inflation expectations (Cardoso and Helwege, 2001). The very limited success of the programme to stabilise inflation together with high political distress and corruption accusations prompted the termination of the plan and its eventual replacement with the future President Franco's Real Plan.[3]

Despite the failure of the Collor plan to contain inflation, foreign capital was already flowing into the Brazilian financial markets – between 1992 and 1993 foreign exchange reserves more than doubled (from \$8bn to \$22bn, WDI World Bank). The influx of financial flows at the time should be seen in conjunction with the success of the Brady Plan for Latin America analysed above. Accordingly, the implicit agreement that the economies of the region would be unable to repay their debts through trade proceeds and would instead be able to borrow from international capital markets restored confidence in the markets (Kregel, 2000). The effects of the Brady Plan, the resulting dynamic of restored capital flows and investors' manic behaviour to diversify their portfolios in emerging markets set the backdrop to the 1994 Real Plan.

The Brazilian Real was introduced as a new currency in 1994. Initially, in February 1994, while the Cruzeiro continued to be used as legal tender, the authorities introduced the Unit of Real Value (URV) as a standard of monetary value. The introduction of URV (essentially an average index of the most representative Brazilian inflation indexes) intended to equilibrate the economy towards a sustainable price set where the indexation processes of all nominal contracts would eventually be removed. Later in the year (July 1994) the URV completely replaced the Cruzeiro as a legal tender and thus acted as the medium of exchange, unit of account, standard of deferred payment and store of value for the Brazilian economy. At the same time, the Central Bank of Brazil established an exchange rate anchor to reduce and control the inflation rate. Thus, the Central Bank controlled the maximum price of the currency such that the one Real could not be worth more than one US dollar (Ferrari-Filho, 2001). Together with the currency adjustments, the Real Plan operated through a combination of fiscal and monetary reforms. A policy of fiscal tightening was followed whereby government spending was cut and a social emergency fund (to be used in welfare crisis situations) was established and financed by the federal government – as a result states' and municipalities' access to credit was largely constrained. On the monetary sphere, between February and July 1994, the Brazilian Central Bank intervened in the markets on a daily basis to determine the parity between the Cruzeiro Real and the Unidade Real de Valor in accordance with inflation rates as reflected by the three most followed price indexes. Thus, every day all prices and wages were linked to a single unit of account. The exchange rate was used as a nominal anchor, and all previous contracts were converted into the new currency.

The Real Plan managed to be remarkably effective at lowering inflation and induced higher growth rates for some years. Inflation fell from 50.7% in June 1994 to 0.96% in September in the same year. In the aftermath of the introduction of the Real Plan the highest base interest rate, reached in June of the following year (BCB), was relatively low – at 5.14%. However, the task of maintaining low inflation rates continued to be very demanding as the authorities' tools to contain inflation – interest and exchange rate policies – manifested complicated dynamics. The Real's overvaluation contributed to large trade deficits, the deterioration of the economy's current account balance, the resulting contraction of the country's foreign reserves and, most importantly, the marked surplus in its capital account. Given the large emphasis attributed to inflation-targeting, the economy became even more vulnerable to excessive capital flows as the traditional macroeconomic tools became unavailable as instruments to secure capital stability. The 1994 Mexican crisis and the resulting capital flight from the entire Latin America region comprised important additional constraining factors, encouraging the exodus of capital flows, decreasing confidence over the robustness of the Real and further contributing to the necessity of the Dollar peg.

The inflation elimination success was certainly associated with the appreciation of the Brazilian currency: between 1994 and 1998 the average real exchange rate was 31% higher than the average of its 1980–1994 value (Baig and Goldfajn, 2000). However, one of the results of the overvalued currency was the deterioration of the economy's terms of trade. Overall, the accumulation of this great volume of capital inflows greatly eroded Brazil's current account. Figure 7.2 demonstrates that in every year following the Mexican crisis and the implementation of the Real Plan, the current account of the economy was in deficit and in some years (see prior to the 1998 crisis) very high deficit – the deficit increased from 2.5% in 1995 to 4% in 1998. Between 1994 and 1997 imports nearly doubled from US$33 to US$61bn, the net exporting

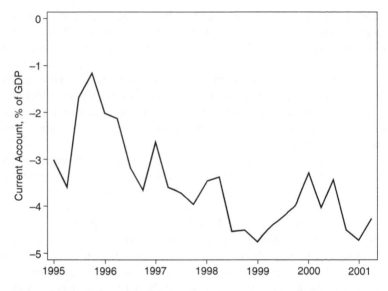

Figure 7.2   Brazil's current account balance, percentage of GDP
Source: OECD Statistics.

balance turned from a surplus of US$10bn to a deficit of $US8bn, while gross national savings fell from 19.7% of GDP to 16.8% (BCB, 2012a). The authorities unsuccessfully attempted to introduce a series of measures to promote export competiveness. These were mostly channelled through the Brazilian Development Bank (BNDES) and took the form of either direct credit subsidies to exporters or legislation that exempted the manufacturing,[4] semi-manufacturing and primary exports sectors from taxation.

The developments in the financial sector

The types of financial flows dominant in the capital markets of Brazil diverged a great deal between 1980 and 2000. In the 1970s, the dominant kind of finance was commercial bank loans. In the 1980s it was sovereign bonds, while in the 1990s they were all almost entirely replaced by private equity investment (see Figure 7.3 for the higher scale of stock market investment illustrated in the right axis of the graph). Portfolio capital flows, mainly in the form of bonds and equity investments, and often related to new credit products such as derivatives and securities, dominated the Brazilian capital markets since the 1990s. The domestic deregulation of finance in the early 1990s, together with the increasing

Brazil
GDP and liquidity flows

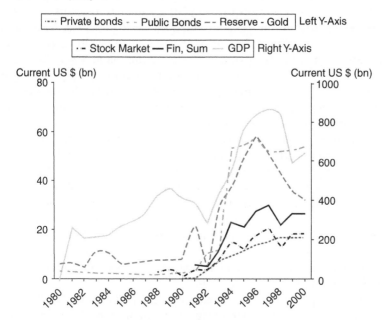

Figure 7.3 Composition of capital flows, US$ (2012)
Source: World Bank and Datastream.

levels of trading in currency markets and the access of Brazilian firms to foreign stock markets that enabled them to raise equity finance, facilitated portfolio inflows. The domestic banking sector was liberalised and, as a result, domestic banks were, by the beginning of the decade, allowed to take loans from foreign financial and non-financial institutions and use them to issue domestic market loans.[5]

In addition to the usual arguments underpinning the liberalisation of financial markets, there were two Brazilian economy-specific causes of the 1990s' liberalisation. First, there was a need for non-inflationary-growth capital to finance the high and increasing private and public debt. Second, the high inflation rates of the previous years had made domestic investors and even households able to deal with more sophisticated financial instruments, and thus, there was increased demand for product diversification (Morvan, 2000). Prior to the 1998 crisis, loans represented less than half of all bank assets in Brazil. Specifically, an increasing share of lending was dedicated towards households to finance increased consumption expenditures.

The spectrum of possible investments for foreign investors increased remarkably within the decade. Financial regulation was eased and numerous legislations were introduced or amended to cater for the demands of the newly flexible markets. Central Bank Resolution 1289 (BCB, 1987) was created to regulate the formation and supervision of equity portfolios kept domestically by foreign investors. It also allowed the formation of mutual country investment funds, which mainly comprised investment portfolios including a wide spectrum of financial products ranging from bonds, stocks and commodities' tradables to investment and mutual privatisation funds. This resolution also amended the regulation of foreign borrowing through the listing of domestic firms in foreign stock and bond markets. Brazilian firms in search of credit in foreign markets started growing in numbers and in type. Private sector issuers such as export-oriented industrial companies and, most importantly, banking institutions accounted for an increasing share of bond issues. Overall, returns on these bonds were higher than the return of the US dollar LIBOR and, consequently, international credit was amply allocated to them.

A sharp expansion of credit took place in the beginning of the decade. This was further compounded by the high domestic interest rate, stemming from the inflation stabilisation project and resulting in the increase of high-risk borrowers in search for credit. Foreign investors' appetite for credit provision in the economy resulted in a self-sustaining circle of credit expansion, which generated a state of high liquidity for debtors, further disorienting banks' ability to engage into effective risk assessment. The latter resulted in the problematic dynamic of adverse selection with regard to credit allocation. The traditional norms under which Brazilian banks used to operate further aggravated the problem of adverse selection: 'Historically Brazilian banks tend to base their lending decisions on the quality and size of the collateral, rather than on projections of borrower's repayment capacity' (Morvan, 2000, p. 14).

Starting in 1994, a major restructuring of the banking sector took place in the economy. An important contributing factor behind this vast restructuring was the loss of an important source of revenue for the banking sector as a result of the stabilisation process. The pre-Real Plan inflationary revenue of the banks ('the float') was a result of the daily decreases in the real value of the deposits and their attached interest rates that were typically lower than the value of the ensuing inflation rates. In the early 1990s (see Table 7.1) 'the float' was accountable

Table 7.1 Inflationary revenue contributions in the early 1990s

Year	As % of Bank Value Added	As % of GDP
1990	35.7	4.0
1991	41.3	3.9
1992	41.9	4.0
1993	35.3	4.2
1994	20.4	2.0
1995	0.6	0.0

Source: BNDES

for practically 40% of the Bank Value Added – meaning the difference between interest receipts and payments in the banking sector – which had grown to represent as much as 4% of the economy's GDP (BNDES). The equivalent rates for the period just after the implementation of the Real Plan suggest that by 1995 the contribution of this inflationary revenue was negligible to both GDP and banking value added. It is clear that banks lost a substantial stream of revenue from the success of the inflation stabilisation policy. The domestic banking sector was thus forced to retrench, redirect its activities and develop alternative sources of financing.

The changes and evolution of the financial system reforms brought about by the Real Stabilisation Plan could be described as the succession of three phases: first, Central Bank's intervention and direct liquidation reduced the number of commercial banks; second the inception and application of PROER and PROES[6] to rescue the banking sector; and third the allowance of foreign banking institutions to enter the domestic market (BIS, 1999b).

The first phase included a gigantic state scheme to intervene and reduce the number of banks in the system. Given the bankruptcies of commercial banks, within a bit more than three years (July 1994–December 1997), the Central Bank had intervened in 43 banks (32 of which were private) and liquidated all but one of them (Kregel, 2000).

The second phase was marked by the inception and implementation of the Programme of Incentives for the Restructuring and Strengthening of the National Financial System (PROER) in November 1995 and PROES[7] in August of the following year. This phase was characterised by the restructuring of private and state-owned banks via the implementation of the two programmes which targeted the protection of depositors' interests by preserving overall confidence in the banking sector, containing the exposure of banks and acquiring the ownership of the troubled ones (BCB, 1995). The main principles of the two schedules can be summarised as safeguarding deposits and penalising banks that followed high-risk strategies. Safeguarding deposits implied that deposits were protected and could be claimed at any time, while penalising bad banking policies entailed the transfer of shareholding control to new owners.

PROER operated via two major streams: one for large and one for small and medium banks. The first split the large troubled banks into 'good' and 'bad' banks according to the quality of their assets and deposits.[8] Thus, the 'good bank' was rebranded and acquired by another bank, while the 'bad bank' became a liability in the Central Bank's balance sheets as it was liquidated. The second stream, that of small and medium banks, entailed their direct purchase by another bank – PROER would directly grant a line of credit to the acquiring bank as 'a liquidity cushion against potential deposit withdrawals or as a lever to help to replace the troubled bank's impaired assets' (BIS, 1999, p. 114).

PROES was introduced to restructure, privatise or convert state banks into non-financial institutions with the aim of ultimately reducing the intervention of the state into the financial system. Under PROES the federal government was allowed to acquire shareholding control for the sole purpose of privatisation or liquidation. Additionally, the government could finance the liquidation of the state bank and the adjustments required to privatise it or transform it into an NBFI.

Both PROER and PROES were introduced to prevent the total collapse of the banking sector and to protect depositors' money (Goldfajn et al., 1997). The scheme facilitated mergers and acquisitions through offering a direct line of credit where all bad debts were transferred to the Central Bank. By the end of the decade, it was evident that the introduction and operation of PROER and PROES were responsible for the eventual consolidation of the banking sector.[9]

The third phase of the reforms in the financial system included the entrance of new foreign institutions into the domestic banking system. This, together with the bank foreclosure and restructuring policies, brought about great changes in the structure of the banking industry. The entrance of new foreign institutions took place under two channels: the direct entrance of new banks and the increase in equity held by foreign banks that were previously minority shareholders. The increase in equity participation of foreign banks was subject to a toll – established according to the entry-capital required for the setting up of all foreign banking institutions. As a result of the developments in this last phase of financial markets' restructuring, the share of foreign banks' assets in the total banking system within the period December 1994–December 1998 doubled from 7% to 14% (Maia, 1999).

The effects of this restructuring in the domestic financial sector could be divided into two major streams: the additional increase in the availability of liquidity via the augmentation of bank credit and the increasing accumulation of government debt. Despite the immediate increase of reserve requirements on sight deposits after the introduction of the Real Plan (see Fonseca, 1998b), financial sector loans to the private sector increased by an astonishing 60% as early as the first year after the implementation. This large increase initially compensated the loss of revenues in the banking sector given the lower inflation rates and the consequent absence of the float. However, the overall slump in economic activity and the rise of interest rates caused by the Mexican 1994 crisis resulted in a significant increase in non-performing loans.

Overall, the restructuring of the financial system following the implementation and relative success of the Real Plan was a significant change in the *modus operandum* and balance of the system itself. The combination of an environment with low inflation rates and a surge in loan-provision served to destabilise the financial system, which was for decades operating under high and volatile inflation and a generally underdeveloped credit culture. To understand more clearly the impact of the above dynamic, the increase in public debt needs to be emphasised. The increased levels of public debt that developed both independently and as a consequence of the government policy changes in the banking sector need to be analysed.

The above-described restructuring and liquidation process of the banking sector were responsible for a massive increase in domestic public debt – it is estimated that 20% of government outstanding debt by 1997 was attributable to this (IMF, 1995a).[10] In 1997 the federal government issued nearly 100 billion Reais in treasury securities to finance PROES and general state debt restructuring. A total of 20 billion Reais was spent between November 1995 and mid-1997 (around 2.5% of the 1996 GDP) on disbursements under PROER (IMF, 1998). The implementation of both PROES and PROER substantially changed the dynamics of public finances and contributed to the escalation of public debt. In addition to the financial stabilisation-related build-up of federal public debt, the economy's indebtedness was exacerbated at the state level too. The fiscal position of the majority of the state governments started to deteriorate significantly from 1995 as a result of numerous factors analysed later on in this part of the book.[11]

The authorities' choice to control and maintain low levels of inflation resulted in very high short-term interest rates. The policy to sterilise capital inflows and the allocation of foreign savings to domestic money markets resulted in high short-term interest rates, which further encouraged capital inflows in the form of portfolio investment. The inflation history of the economy had shaped the revenues of the banking sector to be mostly based on overnight investments in the government-bonds market or else from foreign exchange revenues. At the time, the size of revenues from the floating exchange rate were so high that banks did not even engage in credit operations that were almost risk-free. However, as soon as the economy was stabilised under the Real Plan, inflation revenue[12] and the interest from float virtually vanished as a source of banking income. Banks therefore switched into credit operations in private sector as their main source of income (Morvan, 2000).[13]

The clients of domestic banks were transformed as well. The increase of competition in credit allocation and the ability of domestic investors to bypass domestic banks – as a result of international capital markets developments – induced a rise in credit allocation towards middle market borrowers[14] and consumers. Thus, a consumer credit boom was initiated together with a rise in sub-prime borrowers with access to credit from second-tier banks.[15]

The financial liberalisation and consequent deepening of the Brazilian economy must be investigated in conjunction with the overall developments in the international financial markets. Two main elements of financial developments need to be recalled at this point. Firstly, the rapid increase in the securitisation of financial markets and, secondly, the concurrent rise of new sources of demand for financial products – namely the significant rise of institutional investors such as hedge, pension and insurance funds. The rise of private investment, especially through portfolio capital flows, was predominantly geared towards new types of credit lines such as securities and derivatives. This trade was definitely facilitated by the integration of exchange markets and the increasing flexibility among international financial markets to list bonds and equity without major regulations.[16] It is under this specific historical background that the foreign capital inflows into Brazil are studied in the rest of this book.

Capital flows, the private sector and privatisations

The vast inflow of foreign capital to the economy was almost uninterrupted after the implementation of the Real Plan. It was only temporarily reversed in early 1995 given the spillover effects of the Mexican crisis. The Tequila crisis of 1994 induced a large but short-lived contagion effect in the Latin American markets. Capital flows in 1994 dried up throughout the region, investment in bonds and equity fell remarkably, while the price of Brady bonds, primarily the Brazilian ones, plummeted. The authorities responded with a series of measures easing controls on capital inflows and reversing some tightening measures imposed only months prior to the Mexican crisis. Government intervention was large, but the Brazilian currency nevertheless continued to depreciate until the first quarter of 1995 (see Figure 7.4 for a picture of the Real Effective Exchange Rate and the currency's depreciation resulting from the Mexican crisis spillover effects). The Brazilian authorities decided to proceed towards the implementation of an adjustable band on the exchange rate against the US dollar to allow for small currency depreciations. This measure was implemented in March 1995, but soon thereafter speculators attacked the currency, forcing the central bank to devalue by adjusting the band. International institutional consultation at the time, predominantly the IMF, advised the authorities to allow for further currency depreciation in case the speculation attack continued. The authorities, however, persisted with their inflation targeting

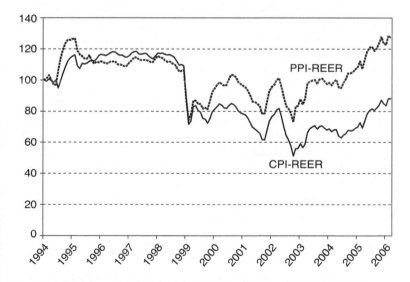

Figure 7.4   Brazil's real effective exchange rate (REER), (1994=100)
Note: CPI = Consumer Price Index; PPI = Producer Price Index.
Source: Brazilian Institute of Applied Economic Research (IPEA) database. From Paiva, 2006.

policies, high short-term interest rates, partial liberalisation of the exchange market and structural reform programme.

Brazilian public companies' privatisation schemes and the institutional changes accompanying them provided the government with an additional source of finance. Resolution 1810 on Mutual Privatisation Funds was created to stimulate investment and foreign participation in the Brazilian privatisation programme through the formation of highly variant investment portfolios. Prior to 1995 no equivalent participation of foreign investors in privatisation funds existed, while in 1994 and 1995 annual investment of close to US$2bn was made in portfolios composed of new external investment sources, government external debt and voluntary hedge deposits (BNDES, 2002).

The expansion of credit in the private sector was very high. In the period following the implementation of the Real Plan and preceding the 1998 crisis, the credit directed to the private sector averaged at around 60% of the country's GDP at the time (BNDES). Credit allocated to bonds and stocks increased remarkably. In 1992 the Brazilian stock market opened to foreign investors and portfolio investments, predominately in the form of stocks, flourished. Large volumes of foreign capital were attracted until 1998 – with a temporary intermission in 1995 when the economy experienced an exodus of funds as a result of the Mexican crisis. Additionally, direct purchases in the domestic stock exchange market through mutual investment funds increased from US$171 million in 1990 to US$28 billion in 1995 (Morvan, 2000, p. 9). Banking liberalisation and the consequent increase in the influx of capital induced the abrupt regulatory changes in the banking sector described above, which were not implemented in tandem with a well-developed monitoring and assessment system. As a consequence, depositors had a constrained ability to assess and value the risk encompassed in banks' asset and liability sheets. In a Kindlebergian logic, this absence of information can – and has historically on several occasions – lead to simultaneous panic behaviour. An adverse shock indicating the higher risk of loan portfolio investments could prompt depositors to collectively withdraw deposits without precise knowledge of the specifics of the institutions and products involved.

Sterilisation

Brazil is studied as an economy adopting a nearly full sterilisation policy in the face of large capital inflows, which through high interest rates and other events, such as the rescue of the banking system, produced large public debt problems. The experience of Brazil is selected as a characteristic example of an economy whose Central Bank sold government bonds to withdraw the increased liquidity created by inflows. The government, trying to avoid a Mexican-type bubble, of an asset price inflating *laissez faire* policy *vis-à-vis* the surge of inflows, engaged in the costly policy of sterilisation that eventually led to what Palma would describe as public sector Ponzi finance (Palma, 2003a).[17]

The full sterilisation policy of the country led to financial instability through several channels. These primarily included: the high interest rates necessitated for its implementation, the consequent high level of public debt it produced and the additional – though sterilisation-independent – cost incurred from Brazil's need to defend its fixed exchange rate. The latter, as explained above, predominately took place as a result of the Brazilian anti-inflationary policies combined with the appreciation pressures brought about by capital inflows. This sterilisation practice necessitated the introduction and selling of new government bonds serving as a mechanism to eliminate the monetary expansion induced by the capital inflows. Accordingly, to avoid a monetary expansion accompanying the financial inflows, the incoming capital was sterilised and the resulting high interest domestic bonds[18] produced large problems for fiscal policy implementation. The high cost of sterilisation was evident in the large divergence between what was paid for the paper sold (as the instrument of sterilisation) and what was retrieved from the returns of foreign exchange reserves holdings. Even the IMF in a 1997 pre-Brazilian crisis report emphasised the financing problems produced by sterilisation schemes in emerging countries:

> Half of the total capital flows undertaken in search of higher returns have ended up as foreign exchange reserves, which are typically composed of highly liquid and risk-free but relatively low-yielding assets such as US treasury bills. This sterilization of capital flows into emerging markets and their recycling through investment into mature market securities implies a significant cost for emerging market countries. In essence, residents of emerging markets countries have to pay the difference between the cost of these external funds and the return on reserve assets multiplied by the stock of foreign exchange reserves.
>
> (IMF, 1997)

The Brazilian paradigm illustrates well the excessive burden of the sterilisation commitment and demonstrates how the problems created around debt servicing further led to the collapse of the domestic private banking system. The latter resulted from a dynamic combination of the increasing non-performing debt and the additional increase in public debt resulting in the government rescue plan for the failing domestic banks. In 1994 net public debt was 20% of the economy's GDP, in 1996 it was 35%, while just four years after the implementation of the Real Plan it had more than doubled – reaching 44% in 1998 (IFS, IMF). The state policy of keeping the domestic currency to the US dollar interest rate differential high enough to attract foreign capital to finance the current account deficit and ensure economic stability necessitated a high real interest rate, which caused a very large debt burden to the economy.[19] Given the size of public debt (Figure 7.5) at the time high interest rates resulted in large fiscal imbalances through the impact of the increasing debt service on government deficit. The eradication of inflation in Brazil through the Real Plan produced a very large fiscal deficit. The Plan was hugely successful in eliminating inflation, but at the same time its persistent reliance on high interest rates reinforced the economy's imbalances. High real interest rates not only increased the difficulty of the country servicing its debt, but further increased banks' needs for subsidies to be used for recapitalisation (Cardoso and

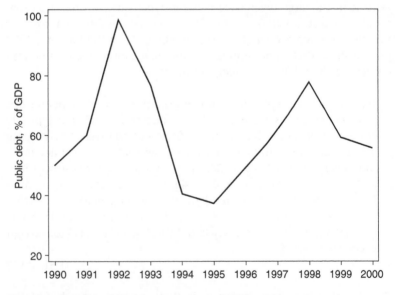

Figure 7.5 Brazil's public debt, percentage of GDP
Source: World Bank.

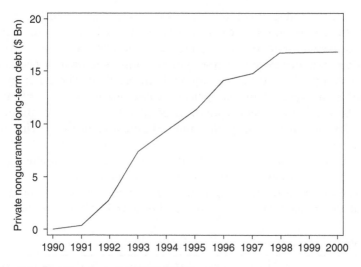

Figure 7.6   Brazil's private debt, US$ (2012)
Source: World Bank.

Helwege, 2001). The Plan was able to control inflation but in the long run produced an internal public debt structure such that – as a result of the high interest rates and inflow sterilisation policy – long-term growth with price stability would eventually be in danger and the prospect of an expansionary monetary policy would be highly improbable.

The sudden and volatile injections of capital in Brazil (Figure 7.3) together with the persistent expectations for them to be prolonged, given the policy of the Dollar peg, were constantly pushing towards an increasingly overvalued currency. This brought the economy into the oxymoronic predicament of needing to maintain both high and low interest rates. The overvalued currency was needed to attract inflows and fight inflation; thus, high interest rates were maintained to keep the reserves of the Central Bank in line with the incoming capital, while at the same time low interest rates were needed to support the lending of domestic banks, which was denominated in US dollars (Figure 7.6).

The role of interest rates

The ensuing use and significance of maintaining an extremely high interest rate[20] did not only serve Brazil's need to defend its overvalued exchange rate and overall stabilisation programme but also to avoid being trapped in a Mexico-type crisis. Accordingly, the Brazilian authorities endeavoured to avoid a Mexican-type evolution where the effects of unrestrained liberalisation inflated the economy in a Kindlebergian-style mania. According to Kindleberger the external inflow of money frequently results in the continuous increase of domestic security prices in the liquidity-receiving economy. These give rise to exuberant expectations and generate consumption booms, real estate bubbles and investment manias. As positive expectations continue to increase and investment profits diminish, financial distress occurs and, in a case where expectations are fully reversed, further depression takes place and a crash is likely to follow (unless they are contained by a lender of last resort) (Kindleberger and Laffargue, 1982).

The policy of maintaining high interest rates (Table 7.2) and accumulating foreign reserves (Figure 7.7), however, had two main negative

Table 7.2 Real interest rates (average annual rates)

	1989	1990	1991	1992	1993	1994	1995
S-R private bonds	44.3	23.9	26.8	29.7	16.9	25.3	29.8
Consumer loans	193	138	231	165	104	175	207

Source: BCB 2012b, several issues of Boletim Mensal.

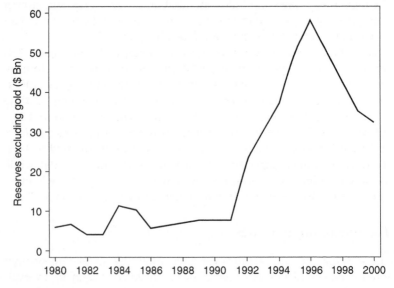

Figure 7.7 Brazil's reserves position, US$ (2010)
Source: OECD Statistics.

Table 7.3   Outstanding government debt, bn of Reais

	March	June	September	December
1994	50.5	61.3	62.5	61.8
1995	65.3	69.5	98.5	108.5
1996	133.6	154.3	162.5	176.2

Source: BCB 2012b, several issues of Boletim Mensal.

Table 7.4   Total and non-performing* loans to the private sector, mn of Reais

	Dec. 93	June 94	Dec. 94	June 95	Dec.95
Bank Loans (a)	94,162	74,299	103,964	126,784	126,784
In arrears and non performing (b)	6,716	7,964	10,708,	19,205	26,189
(b)/(a)	7.13%	10.71%	10.30%	15.93%	20.66%

Note: Non-performing loans refer to those that are more than 180 days overdue, with insufficient guaranties, and to operations of more than 360 days overdue, with sufficient guaranties.
Source: BCB 2012b, several issues of Boletim Mensal.

consequences. First, and as already analysed, the Brazilian level of public debt increased sharply, as a result of the combined sterilisation policy pursued and high levels of interest rates (see Table 7.3). Second, several additional difficulties were subsequently produced in the economy's banking sector with regard to its exposure and risk adopted.

The banking sector in the first half of the decade faced large problems as the percentage of non-performing loans to individuals increased to unprecedented levels. Between 1993 and 1995 non-performing loans increased from 7% to 21% (Table 7.4). This produced an additional destabilisation in the entire banking system and even more in the state-owned banks. The latter became over-equipped with non-performing assets and entrapped themselves in rolling over the state's non-performing loans – when their traditional role was to bridge the credit shortfalls of state treasuries.

Maturity mismatch in the banking sector's assets and liabilities

A significant variable that aggravated the problems faced by the banking sector was the long-built maturity mismatch of the banks' assets and liabilities. The liabilities of most of the country's banks were usually very short-run, while the earnings from their assets had much longer maturities. The high likelihood of contagion resulting from multiple banking failures – associated with the increased risk in the banks' portfolios and the large-scale maturity mismatch of banks' assets and liabilities – further aggravated the situation. The latter was exacerbated by the fixed exchange rate of the time being used as an inflation anchor and consequently limiting the abilities of the Central Bank to act as the lender of last resort. This asset and liability maturity mismatch aggravated developments in the banking and contributed to an eventual crisis of confidence in the banking sector which forced several small banks to go out of business and coerced the state to bail out numerous others (Sheng, 2009).

Given all of this, the difficulty of maintaining high interest rates needs to be studied together with the aggravated state of Brazil's deficit and debt positions. From 1996 to 1998 the budget deficit of the country increased from 5.9% to 8%, while in the same period its net public debt[21] almost doubled to 50% of GDP (BCB).

Ponzi finance and the crisis

The country's public sector's primary accounts deteriorated throughout the decade. At the time, a common misconception was established regarding the impact of the state bailouts on the public accounts. The establishment of this misconception was encouraged by local media – as a result of the government's historic influence in them (Palma, 2002b). The liberalisation policies and all the privatisation and state bank bailouts that they entailed were subject to severe time lags. Specifically, the government only acknowledged the bad debts produced by the bank bailouts when they actually matured –so debts that would never be paid were accounted as assets until they were actually in default (Palma, 2006).

This flawed representation of public accounts directed attention away from the real cost of the bailouts and enabled the government to incur additional deficits while ignoring the deleterious implications that the high interest rates would bring about. Brazil engaged into a 'Minskyan' scheme of Ponzi finance as it entered into a dynamic where the interest portion of its cash payment commitments – or else the returns given to domestic public bond holders – exceeded its net cash receipts – or else the interest paid by the US Treasury for the bills that the Brazilian authorities were sterilising.[22] Effectively, the Brazilian government capitalised its current interest payments by borrowing more.

The economy became vulnerable on two fronts as a result of engaging in Ponzi finance. Firstly, as with any agent engaging in credit operations, Brazil was vulnerable to product market developments such as cost escalations or revenue decreases mostly resulting from changes in the markets for goods and tradables. Secondly, and most precariously, Brazil became vulnerable to developments in financial markets. Interest rate escalations effectively increased the economy's financial commitments and contributed to widespread private and public default. The developments in international financial markets, and specifically, the drop in US interest rates, and also the domestic deficit-deepening activities of the government, forced the Brazilian authorities to engage in continuous debt generating activities in order to service the increasing amounts of public debt resulting from the adopted inflow sterilisation policy, the rescuing of the private sector banks and the recapitalisation of some public sector banks, under PROER and PROES, respectively.

This part of the story needs to be emphasised when dealing with Brazil's eventual Ponzi finance scheme, which is often considered a clear result of its sterilisation policy. The state banks' rescue operations did have a vast impact on the country's gross debt and their incorrect and underestimated accounting in the public deficit balance sheets aggravated the financing schemes that were adopted.

Concluding remarks

The financial crisis and the consequent 1999 Real devaluation hit Brazil after a series of repeated endogenous and exogenous shocks, which had adverse effects for the growth rate of the economy. Following several desperate efforts to prevent the exodus of capital through further increases in the interest rate, it became evident that capital outflows could not be reversed.[23] The exchange rate was subsequently allowed to float freely, and within two months it was devalued by 40%.

Brazil went through a financial crisis by initially trying to avoid a Mexican-style credit expansion and asset bubble. The Brazilian authorities managed to engage in Ponzi finance and produce a crisis when following a route designed to avoid it (Palma, 2013). The authorities attempted to prevent a private sector credit explosion equivalent to the one experienced by Mexico earlier in the 1990s. By imposing very high interest rates and consequently accruing a large public debt, the authorities managed instead to destabilise both the financial sector and general public finances in a completely indefensible way. Instability in the financial sector was created by the high interest rates that needed to be paid as a result of Brazil's sterilisation policy, its underperforming banking assets and the bailout of several of them. More general problems in public finances were a result of the growing and unsustainable deficits in the state's finances compounded by the costly rescue operations of the domestic banking system.

8
South Korea:
The Private Debt Story

East Asian market developments

The economic and financial developments of Japan in the 1980s, and the rise of the telecommunications and electronics industries, were critically linked to the performance and competitiveness of the East Asian economies. The large volumes of cross-border trade and investment inflows shaped a high financial multiplier for the entire East Asia region. However, as the Japanese Yen appreciated in the 1980s, non-Japanese East Asian goods became even more competitive in international markets (see the continuous appreciation of the Yen for the entire 1982–1988 period, Figure 8.1). The loss of competitiveness of Japanese firms induced many of them to move out of Japan, searching for lower costs and higher profit opportunities. This resulted in technological spillovers, which further contributed to the rise of East Asian productivity. East Asian firms were thus building up their export capacity, among other means, through Japanese and US FDI and its consequent technology transfers.[1]

Sources of overall Asian vulnerability

In the 1990s the majority of East Asian markets faced similar economic problems and imbalances. The combination of three elements – modest macroeconomic imbalances, significant banking problems and the mismanagement of the maturity structure of private debt – created highly problematic dynamics in the majority of East Asian economies (Eichengreen, 2004). The region's high growth rates were partly sustained by the high level of foreign capital inflows, and the large current account deficits of the region were coupled with overvalued exchange rates. The economies were all subjected to financial investors' moves

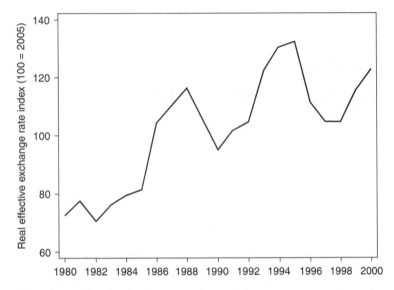

Figure 8.1   Japan's real effective exchange rate (2005=100)
Source: International Financial Statistics, IMF.

and transfers, so in the case of investors' panic the financing of their current account deficits could be disrupted, creating large-scale problems for the economies.

The weaknesses in the economies' financial sector were the combined result of the high interest rates of their banking sector and the short-term nature of the Asian banks' and corporations' foreign financing. The high levels of interest designed to attract foreign flows that was prevalent in most economies destabilised most Asian economies' banking systems. In particular, higher interest rates raised funding costs relative to the sector's incomes, resulting in higher exposure to non-performing loans and consequently damaging the banks' balance sheets. Regarding the maturity structure of private debt, short-term lending (indexed mostly in foreign currency) increased remarkably as a share of total debt in the early 1990s (Chang R. and Velasco, 1998). As illustrated in Table 8.1, in 1994 73% of total debt consisted of short-term borrowing in South Korea and 74% in Thailand compared to 66% and 60%, respectively, four years earlier. The high interest rates in the banking sector and short-term maturity structure of private debt contributed to 'stock and flow' problems in the entire region. High interest rates created a 'flow problem' whereby there was a continuous need for foreign

Table 8.1   Short-term and total debt in East Asia

Total Debt (US $mn)

	Indonesia	Korea	Malaysia	Philippines	Thailand	Total
Jun-90	20,076	23,369	6,864	9,055	11,675	71,039
Jun-94	30,902	48,132	13,874	5,990	36,545	135,443
Jun-97	58,726	103,432	28,820	14,115	69,382	274,475

Short-Term Debt (US $mn)

	Indonesia	Korea	Malaysia	Philippines	Thailand	Total
Jun-90	10,360	15,528	1,761	3,019	7,026	37,694
Jun-94	18,882	34,908	8,203	2,646	27,151	91,790
Jun-97	34,661	70,182	16,268	8,293	45,567	174,971

Short-Term/Total Debt (%)

	Indonesia	Korea	Malaysia	Philippines	Thailand	Total
Jun-90	51.6	66.5	25.7	33.3	60.2	53
Jun-94	61.1	72.5	59.1	44.1	74.3	67.8
Jun-97	59	67.9	56.5	58.8	65.7	63.8

Source: Bank of International Settlements Statistics.

capital flows to finance the current account deficit, while the short-term nature of private debt created a 'stock problem' whereby the large stock of foreign debt needed to be rolled over frequently (Eichengreen, 2004).

An historical perspective: Korea from the 1960s

The financial monitoring and regulatory framework of South Korea that was established in the 1970s, following the little known (outside Korea) crisis of the early 1970s, was based on rigorous state involvement, close supervision to ensure the efficiency of policy loans and the establishment of regulatory and allocative state policies surrounding the formation of the 'main-bank' system in 1974.[2] The role of the state in credit allocation was significant. Finance was channelled by the state into specific sectors through numerous policies and institutions aiming at the enhancement of overall economic performance. Ownership of banks was either public, or if private, was subject to an ownership ceiling, dictating the maximum ownership share by private agents.[3] With regard to state banks, the government owned several 'special purpose banks', including the Korea

Development Bank, the Bank for Small and Medium-Sized Firms, the Korea Exchange Bank and the Korea Housing Bank (Kim, 1988).

The political urge to maintain economic stability, especially given the geopolitical volatility rising from the North Korea tensions, combined with the chronic foreign exchange shortage of the economy, necessitated a very tight control over capital outflows.[4] Severe restrictions were in place that dealt with the use of the incoming foreign exchange, under acts such as the Foreign Exchange Management Act in 1961 and the operation of Foreign Exchange Concentration System, whereby all incoming exchange was directly channelled to the Central Bank. Via the Foreign Exchange Management Act and the 1962 Law for Payment Guarantee of Foreign Borrowing, the government was in control of the channelling and the use of capital from institutional borrowing. This was translated into both the engineering of the use of capital inflows at the macroeconomic level and the vigilant direction of investment at the microeconomic level. To secure the attraction of foreign exchange, the government introduced a series of measures to attract foreign capital through developing incentives for foreign lending along with establishing an overall security mechanism discouraging the exit of capital inflows. As early as 1966, The Foreign Capital Inducement Law was merged with the Special Law to facilitate Capital Equipment Imports and the Law for Payment Guarantee of Foreign Borrowing Law to form the Foreign Capital Inducement Law, which gave government guarantees on the capital of foreign lenders (Kim K., 2006).

Korean economy characteristics

The evolution and development of Korean industry was achieved through a series of long-term state-engineered policies generating and directing capital to specific industrial functions. The government introduction of the Heavy and Chemical Industrialisation (HCI) programme in 1973 established an emphasis in the allocation of credit to six strategic industries: electronics, machinery, steel, non-ferrous metals, chemicals and shipbuilding (Galbraith, 1998). Accordingly, through HCI, the government heightened overall economic activity through the empowerment of big industrial companies – the *chaebols*. Specifically, the government engineered its industrial policy via the direction of capital to the six key industries and indirect support practices. Key to this programme was the establishment of state-funded industrial estates, the granting of state investment provisions, preferential bank loans, reductions in import tariffs for intermediate goods, and a series of tax exemptions and benefits.

To promote industrialisation, the state disciplined, penalised and rewarded the *chaebols* according to their performance. In underperforming, badly managed or bankrupt cases, the state refused to bail out firms and allowed better managed ones to acquire them very cheaply. The state awarded good performance with licenses in other industries while rewarding entrance into more risky sectors by providing licenses in more secure sectors – cushioning in this way the high-risk infant industries (Amsden, 1992). The above practice resulted in the rapid growth and diversification but also concentration of the Korean industry. By the end of the 1970s 93% of all commodities and 62% of all shipments were produced in monopolistic, duopolistic or oligopolistic market conditions (Kim, 1993). The Korean industry was largely segregated (see also the work of Sheng, 2009). In fact, 30 large industrial conglomerates dominated the entire manufacturing sector. Specifically, 40% of the manufacturing value added was attributed to these 30 largest conglomerates. In the early 1980s, similarly, the revenues of the ten largest *chaebols* accounted for almost 50% of the economy's GDP – a concentration higher than the equivalent of Japan or Taiwan (Chenery et al., 1986). Taiwan, the main industrial competitor of the economy, was mostly dominated by private small- and medium-sized enterprises (which had very limited and overall unsophisticated access to credit) and large state-owned enterprises.

Throughout the 1980s the Korean government introduced additional industrialisation policies enhancing the policy framework of the economy's industrial pillars and channelling further resources to this cause. The government established the Industrial Policy Deliberation Council as a medium with which to identify the industries with high efficiency and profit opportunities that should be given additional state support. This council acted as the state instrument to identify and target the future industrial opportunities and consequently approve any merging and financing suggestions proposed by lending institutions. Between 1985 and 1988 the government, through the operation of the Industrial Policy Deliberation Council, channelled additional capital to previously low-performing industries. Shipbuilding and construction were among the chief credit recipients (Chang, 1994).

Financial markets

Traditionally, financial markets in Korea had a supporting rather than protagonistic role in the overall economic activity and development of the country. Their operation was central to the function and expansion of the industrial sector, which remained the central pillar of economic activity (Kim, 1993). Only in the late 1980s did the growth of the financial markets start accelerating significantly and this can be mainly attributed to the sudden growth of non-bank financial institutions (NBFIs). By the end of the decade their significance in economic developments and channelling of industrial capital started to overshadow the equivalent role of banking institutions. The regulatory framework around NBFIs was largely underdeveloped at the time, making them much more flexible and hence attractive as an untamed source of finance for the *chaebols*. Through a long but rapid series of mergers and acquisitions, the NBFIs quickly became integral parts of the *chaebols* as, unlike banks, they were able to retain the ownership of NBFIs and facilitate their financing needs (Park, 1990).

Prior to 1993 the role of financial markets was seen as an integral part of the economy, essential in providing credit and enabling investments in the industrial sector. The government through 'Policy Loans' established a series of credit programmes linking the banking system to industry, serving and targeting the growth of specific industries. Peaking in the mid-1970s the system of Policy Loans and the engineering and financing of industrial policy were strengthened through several government tools. These included severe monitoring schemes to ensure the efficiency of credit allocation in maximising long-term profit opportunities but also in minimising the cost incurred in the form of foreign debt that commonly accompanied credit provision (Chang, 1994).

Financial liberalisation

Within the 1980s the government's attempts to liberalise the capital account were little and very gradual (Amsden and Euh, 1990). It was only in 1993 with the newly elected government of Kim Young Sam that a large plan on deregulation and liberalisation of financial markets was introduced. Starting in 1993 the five-year market liberalisation plan of the Kim government attempted to open capital markets through deregulating interest rates, enabling higher managerial autonomy to banks, reducing entry barriers and transaction costs in financial markets, and eliminating previous policy loans targeting the growth of specific industries. Specifically, in 1993 an announcement was made on the termination of all policy loans (including loans to SMEs and export targeting industries) and by 1996 all remaining credit controls were dissolved.

The economic success of the country following the 1980s, together with the rise of financial institutions in international markets, contributed to the decision of the government to liberalise domestic credit markets (Chang, 1998b). The success of Korea's industrial policy, combined with the authorities' decision in the 1980s to impose strict exchange controls, resulted in the inflows of very high levels of liquidity in the early 1990s. In 1986 the Korean government, in an attempt to deal with persistent current account deficits, intensified its exchange controls under the Foreign Exchange Concentration System and the Foreign Exchange Management Act. The first ensured that all foreign exchange entering the economy would be channelled through the Central Bank, while the latter established severe regulation on the use of foreign currency. These regulation policies ranged from limits on remittances and overseas real estate acquisition to foreign tourism receipts (Chang et al., 2001).

The results of the economy's successful industrial policy and foreign exchange regulation were reflected in the economy's current account performance. Starting in 1986 the economy experienced a huge reversal in its balances: from 1986 to 1990 the constant deficits of the early 1980s turned into large surpluses (higher than 7% of GDP in both 1987 and 1988; see Figure 8.2 for quarterly data). These surpluses generated additional liquidity in the system, compelling the government to relax

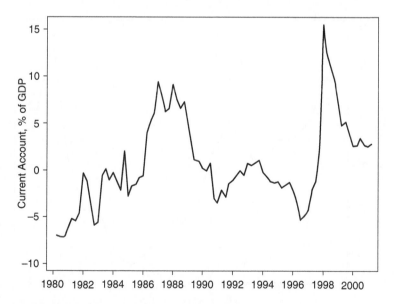

Figure 8.2 Korea's current account balance, percentage of GDP
Source: OECD Statistics.

its exchange control programme. Increasing incoming liquidity forced the authorities to continuously increase the regulatory ceiling on foreign exchange reserves, which culminated in the eventual decision to almost eliminate the entire programme in 1995. This reduction in government monetary intervention was coupled with the increasing importance of CRAs, which by continuously upgrading the rating given to Korean private enterprises and banks made the role and impact of government intervention of even lower importance (Chang, 1998b).

At the end of the 1980s and beginning of 1990s both domestic and international developments contributed towards the deregulation of Korean financial markets that were discussed above. Internally, additional pressure for financial deregulation came as a result of the large trade surpluses in the economy. The large surplus during the 1985–1988 period prompted the inflow of increasing amounts of foreign exchange (see Figure 8.3). This clashed with the highly regulated government mechanism of the Foreign Exchange Concentration System described above. The policy of all foreign exchange being directed to the country's Central Bank became increasingly hard to maintain, and foreign exchange ceilings, which were continuously updated, were gradually

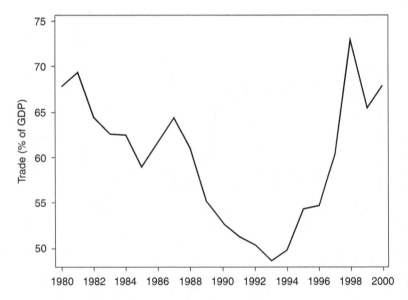

Figure 8.3   Korea's trade balance, percentage of GDP
Source: WB, Global Development Finance.

reduced until they were practically unimportant by 1995. This attraction of foreign exchange and consequent central capital stock building continued despite the disappearance of the trade surpluses in the 1990s.

A combination of international developments, such as the increasingly important role of international financial institutions – predominately the CRAs – in the ratification of domestic economic and investment opportunities, further led to the relaxation of the government's monitoring of financial markets. Korean industries, corporations and banks continuously received high and improving ratings by international CRAs which implied the increased difficulty of the state to direct all the inflowing capital. Within a short period of time the state was transformed from a guaranteeing institution essential to attract capital to an additional administrative step in the international financing process.

The internal and external pressures that contributed to the liberalisation of Korea's financial markets rapidly transformed the image of the economy. The 'much desired' diminished role of the state in the direction, administration and regulation of finance was achieved. What unavoidably followed though was the remarkable development of the Korean financial markets, which were historically viewed as underdeveloped, underperforming and inefficient – a dynamic often argued to have resulted from the erstwhile involvement of the state itself (see Krueger, 1997, and Krueger et al., 2002). The Korean banking system was historically seen as highly fragile, and it was envisaged that it would be problematic if competing in international credit markets (see Eichengreen and Hausmann, 1999, and Arestis and Demetriadis, 1997). This was a result of the norms it was traditionally operating under, characterised by strong government intervention in the allocation of credit. Thus, the traditional function of the Korean banking industry based upon explicit government-directed lending to specific industries was regarded as incapable of competing with international competitors. A perceived consequence of the government's prominent role in credit allocation was the evolution of loan collateral practices rather than credit evaluation (IMF, 1997). Accordingly, the Korean banking system was lagging in the development of a sophisticated internal credit evaluation system and ultimately placed emphasis on the loan collateral rather than an analysis of the project to be financed. The absence of an emphasis on credit evaluation was combined with the targeted, preferential and regularly criticised selection of banking clients by the government. This combination of factors was considered to be partly responsible for the system's exposure to high-risk borrowers (see again IMF, 1997).

The entrance of the country into the OECD in 1996 signalled the economy's commitment to open goods and financial markets and exerted additional pressure towards the liberalisation of markets. After long negotiations and bilateral talks with the US government, the country applied for OECD membership in 1993 and consequently went through a period of intense liberalisation changes. In 1996 the country formally joined the OECD. The domestic and international pressures on the government to liberalise Korean financial markets were further propelled by the international relations and political stance of the government. The political relation of the country with the US included long bilateral talks and negotiations towards an open financial system.

The economic policy characteristics dominant in Korea until the 1993 liberalisation reform can be described as an overall expansionary macroeconomic policy based on very cautious undertakings of public debt (Figure 8.4). The deregulation policies encompassed changes in exchange rate, interest rate, capital, banking, shadow-banking and industrial sectors.[5] In detail these deregulation and liberalisation changes, which took place in the first half of the 1990s, can be summarised below.

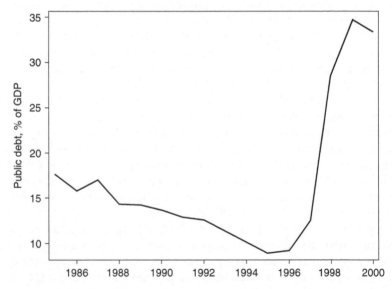

Figure 8.4   Korea's public debt, percentage of GDP
Source: World Bank.

Interest rate deregulation took place in four different stages within the decade. This started in 1991 and ended in 1997 when all lending and borrowing rates were completely liberalised – with the exception of demand deposit rates. In the banking sector a relaxation of market entrance requirements took place in tandem with the increased flexibility granted to the banks' management on issues dealing with dividend determination and capital holding ceilings. In 1996 all ceilings on maximum maturities of loans and banks deposits were abolished. Overall, banking and non-banking financial institutions were allowed to expand and multiply. Through several government acts in 1990, 1993 and 1994, securities firms and deposit money banks were allowed to expand remarkably (see S-J Chang, 2003).

Several changes with regard to the additional opening and increased accessibility of foreign investors to financial markets were made. In 1992 domestic stock markets opened to international investors (with ownership ceilings), while two years after that international investors were allowed to hold and trade government bonds at international interest rates. Foreign investors were gradually allowed to hold equity-linked (by 1994) and non-guaranteed long-term bonds of Korean SMEs (by 1997) and were also allowed to hold non-guaranteed convertible bonds issued by large Korean firms (also by 1997). With regard to infrastructure and FDI projects, private companies operating infrastructural ventures were allowed to finance their projects via international borrowing, while all borrowing related to FDI was similarly liberalised. Equivalently, in 1993, Koreans were allowed to invest in international markets and foreign securities through the formation of beneficiary certificates. A couple of years following that, domestic investors were also allowed to engage in international portfolio investments without any ceiling upon their outflowing capital.

In banking and other financial industries, the government monitoring over the financial industry became more relaxed. A series of guarantees and proofs previously necessitated by the government to permit financial trading were lifted early on in the decade. The government granted several permissions on Over the Counter (OTC) trading of numerous assets to banks and non-banking firms. Specifically, in 1995 banks and insurance companies were allowed to trade OTC public bonds, whereas in the same year all securities companies were allowed to handle foreign exchange matters. Additionally, government approvals over foreign commercial loans were equally abolished in 1995 and replaced with a simple order to follow government instructions that were established in a new investment guideline.

In foreign exchange, the liberalisation came in 1990 with the adoption of the Market-Average Foreign Exchange Rate System. Under this system the basic exchange rate of the country's currency against the US dollar was market-determined within a specified range of the previous day's weighted average of interbank rates. Accordingly, all rates against other currencies were shaped following the rates of each currency against the Dollar in international foreign exchange markets (Nam and Kim, 1999). In 1994 the Foreign Exchange Reform Plan allowed additional flexibility in the market determination of the Korean Won – US dollar exchange rate, while in 1995 the foreign exchange market was further liberalised through a substantial relaxation of the Foreign Exchange Concentration System (Chang et al., 1998a).

Korean industrial sector and corporate debt

The Korean industrial sector started suffering from increasingly lower rates of profitability. It has been proposed that this is the direct result of collapsing manufacturing prices for the goods that the majority of the Korean firms were specialising in – microelectronics (see Palma, 2003a). This fall of prices, especially in microelectronics, can be understood as a technology-led phenomenon brought about by the combination of a persistent drop in prices resulting from the rapid increase in the supply of the goods and the dynamic entrance of Taiwan in the same market (that of memory chips).[6] The latter remarkably accelerated the speed of technological innovation to such a degree that Korea necessitated gigantic investment efforts to remain its technological lead.[7] Korean manufacturing exports at the time experienced a significant price decrease as a result of the production time lag specific to technological progress of the microelectronics industry.[8] This fall in some manufacturing profitability rapidly changed the finance structure of investment for the whole industry – from one characterised by retained profits to one characterised by debt financing. The effort of the microelectronics industry to retain sales was reflected in an increase in the sectoral deficit of the corporate sector from 5% to nearly 20% of GNP in the period 1987–1996. Altogether, Korea was faced with the predicament of rapidly increasing investment to stave off Taiwan's technology advancements in microelectronics or entirely exit the industry. The latter option would entail suffering a consequent depreciation of all physical, human and social capital that it had accumulated so far (Palma, 2013).

With regard to the political side of industrial developments, a fundamental transformation of the state-business relationship took place under the Kim government (Chang, 1998b). The weakening of the state's industrial policy took place concurrently with an increasing exposure of the manufacturing sector to state corruption and vested interests. The abolition of sectoral industrial policies allowed more space and scope for policy manipulation and individualised exceptions. Chang suggests that,

> this meant the end of the 'generalistic' state–business relationship that characterised the Korean model and the rapid rise of 'particularistic' (or 'cronyistic', to use the currently popular expression) relationships, and, more importantly, as we have seen, their spread into the major manufacturing industries which were previously largely insulated from corruption.
>
> (Chang, 1998b, p. 741)

It is thus proposed that it was specifically under the King Young Sam government that 'crony capitalism' was put in operation in Korea. The elimination of the domestic sectoral policies and the diminishing transparency of the state–business relationship unavoidably aggravated the position of the Korean microelectronics industry, contributing additional pressures to its 'exogenously generated' declining profitability described above.

The outbreak of the crisis

The contagion induced after the collapse of the Thai Baht in May 1997 and the markets' revelation that Korea's short-term debt figures were, in fact, higher than the official numbers induced speculative attacks against the currency (Eichengreen, 1999). In a Kindlebergian logic, panic was spread among market investors and a simultaneous exit out of the Korean markets developed in a contagious manner. The government appeared reluctant to foreclose the problematic banks, and foreign commercial banks refused to renew short-term loans that were close to maturity. This prompted large and rapid capital flight. The burden of short-term debt was highly destabilising for the economy, and the level of foreign exchange reserves was so low that it appeared that they would be exhausted by September of the same year (Figure 8.5). At the time short-term foreign debt was maturing at a rate of US$1 billion a day (Eichengreen and Hausmann, 1999), and the inability of the authorities to defend the currency and the economy as a whole became apparent. Between 1993 and the beginning of 1998 gross external debt

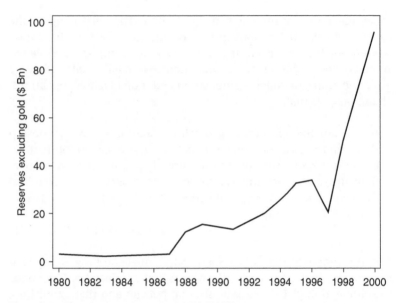

Figure 8.5 Korea's reserve position, US$ (2010)
Source: OECD Statistics.

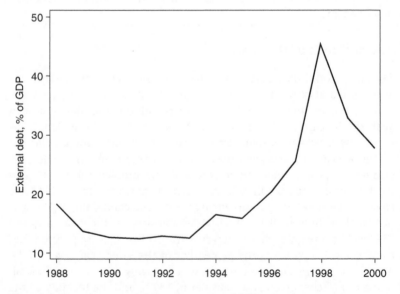

Figure 8.6 Korea's external debt, percentage of GDP
Source: World Bank.

more than trebled – it grew at an annual average rate of 33.6% – as a result of the authorities considerably relaxing all previous regulations on debt accumulation (Figure 8.6).[9]

One of the main sources of concern about the rapidly growing foreign debt was its maturity structure. Debt grew mostly as a combined result of investment financing of Korean corporations and the relaxation of banking regulations limiting the ceiling of foreign borrowing. The debt to GNP ratio of the economy was 19.9% in 1996, lower than the equivalent figures for the Indonesian, Thai or Latin American economies (such as Argentina or Brazil), or the OECD countries, for that matter. Correspondingly, the external debt service ratio of the country was at 5.8% in 1996 – much below the World Bank's warning threshold of 18%.

The maturity structure of overall foreign debt, however, was alarming. The share of short-term[10] to total debt was high and increasing within the 1990s. In 1993 short-term debt was 43.7% of total foreign debt, while in 1996 it was 58.3% (BAI, 1998). Chang (1998b) explains the increase in the accumulation of short-term debt as a result of both domestic legislative changes and international developments in financial markets. The liberalisation that the economy underwent offered higher incentives to short-term debt borrowers. Specifically, short-term foreign borrowing required a much simpler information provision procedure, whereas the undertaking of longer maturing debt needed an additional complicated and time-consuming approval from the Ministry of Finance and the Economy.[11] Chang further argues that the uncertainty following the 1993 liberalisation plan over the exact dates of the various deregulation implementation, together with the increasing creditworthiness of the domestic firms, as endorsed by international credit rating agencies, resulted in the accumulation of continuously re-rolled short-term rather than long-term debt.

The rising power and influence of merchant banks as a result of the Kim government's financial liberalisation schemes intensified the build-up of maturity mismatches between their lending and borrowing. Specifically, by the end of 1996, 64% of the merchant banks' total foreign borrowing was short term, while 86% of their lending was long term (Chang et al., 2001).

Concluding remarks

Within the 1990s the debt burden of Korea increased at historically high rates. In fact, between 1993 and 1997 the foreign debt of the

Korean economy nearly trebled and increased at rates almost double the equivalent ones of the 1976–1985 debt crisis period. The unsustainable increase of the country's private and external debt was critical for the Korean economy at the apex of the Thai currency crisis. The market dynamics of contagion and mob psychology enhanced investors' panic and, when combined with the low levels of foreign exchange reserves, contributed to the inability of the authorities to support the domestic currency and consequent financial crash. The implications of Korea's growing – and ultimately unsustainable – private corporate debt will be further analysed in the next chapter, in isolation but also in comparison with the private and public debt dynamics in the developments of Mexico and Brazil.

9
Deregulation and Volatility: Where the Three Economies Meet

Chapters 6, 7 and 8: a comprehensive review

The last three chapters analysed the ways in which three different middle-income developing economies drove themselves to financial crises in the 1990s. It examined three very different sets of domestic policy design and implementation, which all resulted in a financial crisis. Mexico followed a full liberalisation policy and allowed financial inflows without any controls within its economy. Brazil and Korea followed domestic economic policies different to those of Mexico but also different to each other. In an effort to avoid a Mexican-type asset inflation, Brazil sterilised its financial inflows. This, together with the application of a very costly bank rescue scheme and a highly disputed privatisation programme, drove the economy into unsustainable levels of public debt. Unlike Brazil, Korea's private sector considerably increased its exposure to external finance and, at a time of regional market panic, found itself with a high exposure in external debt and low levels of exchange reserves to defend its currency against speculative attacks.

The analysis of this chapter is essential for the assessment of the book' initial proposition: that open capital accounts at times of high international liquidity can lead to surges in capital inflows that tend to create unsustainable macroeconomic imbalances irrespective of domestic policies devised for their absorption. That the three very different routes taken by the economies studied all resulted in the same crisis-outcome validates this proposition. In each economy the sudden increase in capital inflows and the concurrent jumps in private and public indebtedness were followed by sharp reversals in the flow of capital. This analysis is also essential when assessing the presence and extent of an association between the Keynesian and post-Keynesian tradition and the developments in all three economies examined. The extent to which the trajectories of the three crises adhere to Keynes', Minsky's and Kindleberger's analyses will be assessed and evaluated in the next chapter. The analysis of the three economies' routes to financial crises thus sets the basis for associating both the direction of international capital flows and the Keynesian literature on the systemic character of financial crises to the three routes studied.

Literature and data convergence

All the three economies analysed in the previous chapter point to the same conclusion: in the 1990s capital flows in middle-income emerging economies were all of a volatile nature, resulting in large swings of capital movements and large changes in asset prices. This volatility was not temporary but persisted throughout the decade. In fact, it has been reported that 'during the 1990s the global financial system had been in crisis for 40 out of the 120 months, or else 33% of the time' (Griffith-Jones and Bhattacharya, 2001, p. 20). Studying three completely different economies, with regard to the policies adopted prior to their crises, it could be inferred that volatility is intrinsic to modern liberalised financial markets. Since the early 1990s volatility has been most commonly associated with an abrupt increase in all price, volume and variance in the type of financial capital traded in world markets and has arisen in all economies whose financial sector experienced a rapid intensification, independently of the way it was managed.

Deregulation and volatility: data for all three economies

In all three economies, herding behaviour, especially in the short run, spreads following the deregulation of their markets. The deregulation of domestic markets, together with the rise of institutional players such as CRAs and financial information dissemination firms,[1] contributed to this herding dynamic.[2] The EMH assumptions of long-term transparency and saving and investment decisions reflecting the performance of financial indicators were undermined by the harmful short-term effects of herding behaviour. In this context, the development of new financial products distorted the market by increasing speculation, and subsequently contagion, in markets where agents based their placement decisions upon rumours circulated by other investors or financial agencies. Newly developed products such as Daily Earnings at Risk (DEaR), which measure the valuation of a specific assets' risk for a one-day period, were regularly used in international financial markets to increase returns by reducing inefficiencies arising from the lack of transparent information in different types of investment instruments.

Developments with regard to stock price escalations and jumps in the volume of stocks traded reveal the manic financial investment patterns described by Kindleberger in his attempt to explain the route to financial crises. Figures 9.1–9.3 below reveal how, in the years preceding their crises, each of the three economies experienced a significant stock price inflation reflected in: stock market indices, individual prices of the enlisted company stocks traded and the overall stock market capitalisation over their GDP rates.

Financial placements in the stock market, especially in the economies of Mexico and Brazil, followed an erratic upward pattern prior to the economies' crises.[3] It is evident from Figures 9.1, 9.2 and 9.3 that investors in all three economies became manic about this type of portfolio investment and directed financial capital to the stock markets. Prior to their crises, this type of portfolio investment amounted to 40% of the Mexican and Korean economies' GDP and 30% of the Brazilian economy's GDP.

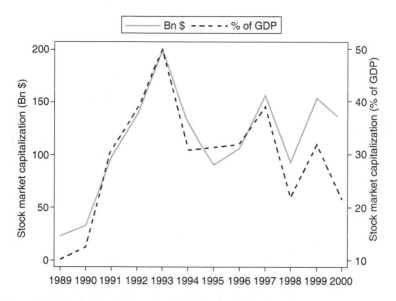

Figure 9.1   Mexico's stock market capitalisation, US$ (2012)
Source: Datastream and World Bank.

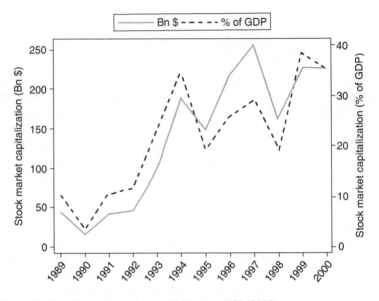

Figure 9.2   Brazil's stock market capitalisation, US$ (2012)
Source: Datastream and World Bank.

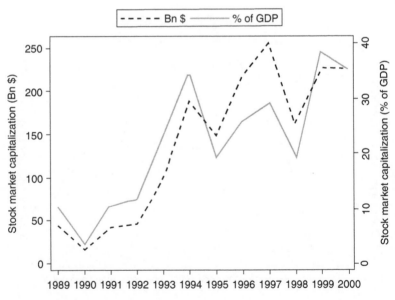

Figure 9.3   Korea's stock market capitalisation, US$ (2012)
Source: Datastream and World Bank.

In the late 1980s and 1990s investment in the Brazilian stock market followed an almost identical route to Mexico – including both its boom and bust period. Even prior to the implementation and inflation-targeted success of the Real Plan, funds entered the economy's stock market at unprecedented levels and rates. The consistency of Brazilian stock market developments with the Mexican pre-crisis euphoria, when combined with the absence of symmetrically ameliorated fundamentals in both economies, can be seen as an example of Keynes' rejection of the ergodic axiom. This rejection along with the different and much later criticism by Stiglitz and his collaborators regarding information asymmetry being responsible for the inability of agents to accurately assess the risks involved can explain part of the downward movements of financial market developments in both countries (Stiglitz and Grossman, 1980, and Stiglitz and Weiss, 1981). As a result, a major prediction of the EMH is rejected – that of prices instantly reflecting all information, available and hidden.[4] Both of these points are supported by the fact that the optimism and euphoria, that were dominant in the markets prior to each country's crisis, did not foretell the financial bust that followed. On the contrary, the agents feeding this optimism and euphoria envisaged two dynamics: the perpetuation of these super-normal returns and their own ability to rapidly and securely exit the markets in case of a sudden displacement.

Herding behaviour and its resulting enhancement of volatility were highly prevalent in the stock market and public bond trading. In all three economies and their entire regions (see Figure 9.4), bond holding trading was strongly influenced by herding patterns. In both Mexico and Brazil a manic trading behaviour by international investors was established after the deregulation of public bond markets. Figure 9.4 clearly illustrates how the jumps in liquidity resulting from public bond trading in the late 1980s in the case of Mexico and the early 1990s in that of Brazil were large enough to account for the majority of the changes in the entire Latin American region. Figure 9.4 also demonstrates how since the late 1980s public bond trading in the entire region has increased to unprecedented levels. From the slope of the curve, being substantially steeper at the periods of Mexican and Brazilian public debt expansion, it is evident that it is these two economies that are crucial to explaining sharp increases in public debt in the entire region. However, the jumps in public debt of other Latin American countries, such as Argentina and Venezuela, were far from negligible.

A comparison between the public debt routes taken by Mexico and Korea illustrates very different dynamics (see Figure 9.5). In contrast to

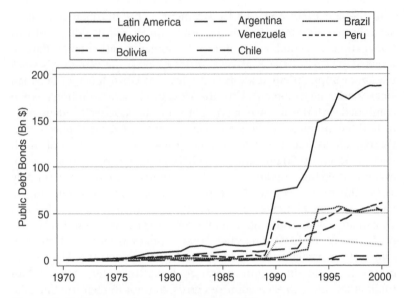

Figure 9.4   Public bonds Latin America, US$ (2012)
Source: World Bank, International Debt Statistics.

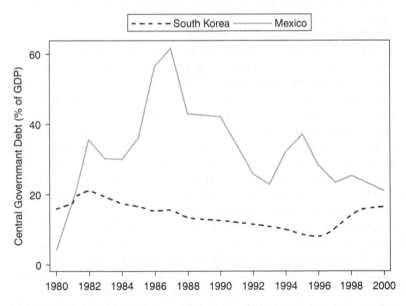

Figure 9.5   Public debt dynamics: Central Government debt, percentage of GDP
Source: World Bank, WEO.

the great stock of public debt and excessive government obligations created in the case of Mexico, Korea followed a very different path. Central government debt – in terms of absolute size, volatility and as a share of GDP – was not erratic in the case of Korea (see also Chapter 8). In contrast, Mexico had large and unsustainable levels of central government debt. This did not result from counter-cyclical fiscal provisions but instead from pro-cyclical government indebtedness that was further inflated by financial deregulation, opening and consequent increase in exposure (Dornbusch and Werner, 1994).

After the liberalisation of the public bond acquisition and ownership criteria – in 1988 for Mexico and 1993 in the case of Brazil – international acquisition of sovereign debt soared. This was accompanied by an uncontrolled frenzy on acquiring bonds by mostly international hedge funds profiting from the interest rate differentials between these bonds and US Treasury equivalents, which was even higher and more volatile than stock market investment. The work of Calvo, Leiderman and Reinhart (1996) reveals how public bond trading in Latin American countries followed a 'stop and go' pattern. Along the same lines it has been asserted that 'it would appear that bond investors are keen to get out before they are held in by a debt memorandum or orderly workout' (Griffith-Jones and Bhattacharya, 2001, p. 66). The holding of domestic public debt in emerging economies by international investors was still considered to be of risky character given the numerous concerns regarding the ability of emerging economies to service and meet their international obligations. In both cases, but also in the case of Korea, it is apparent that bond investors' decisions would be increasingly shaped by herding behaviour – even when compared to equity portfolio investors.[5]

Private debt: equity and stock markets

With regard to equity financing, much of the volatility in Mexico and Brazil could be explained by developments in newly privatised state-owned enterprises (see Figure 9.6). It is has been calculated that the cumulative privatisations carried out by Brazil and Mexico between 1989 and 1999 represented, respectively, 11% and 6% of the economies' 1999 GDP (Lora, 2001). The significant increase in international investors' purchases of developing country's private bonds should be seen in conjunction with the privatisation schemes of the economies and the consequent efforts of institutional investors to gain control of the privatised firms.[6] Private bonds trading and stock market participation

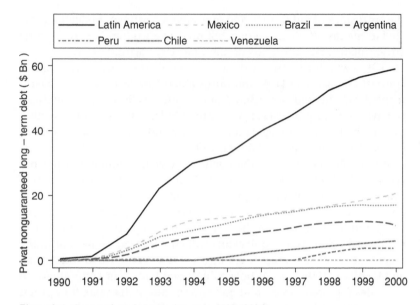

Figure 9.6   Private bonds Latin America, US$ (2012)
Source: World Bank, International Debt Statistics.

in the early 1990s were growing at high rates and reached, from the beginning of the decade, a large multiple of its earlier level.[7] The presence of large international intermediaries in the stock markets of developing countries triggered additional volatility. This increase in volatility was primarily realised through intermediate institutions being hastily developed in emerging economies and consequently unable to efficiently diversify risks in those, rapidly growing, financial markets (see Acemoglu and Zilibotti, 1997). The rapid financialisation of Mexico and Brazil enhanced the vulnerability of the economies to developments in the financial sector, which were then amplified by the increasing presence of financial intermediaries (Beck at al., 2006). The economies grew more exposed to monetary shocks, which were transmitted through the financial sector – a sector very rapidly and ultimately inadequately regulated. Given the fact that these markets did not possess or develop adequate regulatory infrastructure and that international investors were not in possession of even-handed and transparent information about them, the practice of arbitrary pricing and self-enhancing levels of even higher volatility were developed (Singh, 1997).

It has historically been the case that in most share price booms in emerging economies in the 1990s, share prices in stock markets deviated considerably from the economies' fundamentals (Singh, 2003). On this front the example of Mexico is quite striking. Within a decade (1981–1991) the stock market capitalisation of the economy grew so fast as to represent 43% of the country's GDP *vis-à-vis* an initial 25%, while in three years alone the stock market capitalisation increased from 12.5% in 1990 to almost 50% of the country's GDP in 1993. Overall, the development and expansion of international intermediaries, which traded, hedged and facilitated access to emerging world assets and debt acquisitions, contributed to this significant expansion of transactions in stocks and equities.

Banks, information and euphoric investments

Bank lending also proved less straightforward than expected in all three economies studied. The lower level of volatility that was assumed to be prevalent in bank lending, *vis-à-vis* raising debt from capital markets, was not as low as the proponents of liberalisation had predicted. The variable causing this volatility can be traced to the common short-term maturity structure of bank loans in all three economies – as explained in the previous chapter. With regard to bank lending, financial instability and volatility, Keynes' rejection of the ergodic axiom and Minsky's financial instability hypothesis are highly relevant. The vast increases in bank lending could not have reflected investors' knowledge of highly promising future returns – 'In almost every year since the 1980s, the share of trade financing commitments in total bank lending has been higher for non-investment grade or unrated developing countries than rated ones' (Ocampo, Kregel and Griffith-Jones, 2007, p. 35).

The dominance of short-term lending in pre-crisis Mexico, Brazil and Korea enabled banks to rapidly retrench in times of euphoria but, as a result of the long-term maturity of their assets, proved highly problematic. When panic was spread in the markets, capital became scarce and firms were unable to service their debts. At the same time, the consolidation of the banking sector and the increased presence of international banking conglomerates in emerging capital markets contributed to this panic and volatility in capital flow. Specifically, the banking conglomerates' *modus operandi* of wider exposure to international financial flows and highly diversified portfolio investments enabled them to have a much more flexible presence in emerging economies – which consequently increased those economies' exposure to capital outflow shocks.

Short-term cross-country banking debt

Short-term lending[8] has traditionally been the most likely type of monetary flow to be withdrawn at times of financial distress. Minsky's understanding of the change in the perception of acceptable level and structure of debt obligations is highly relevant here. Minsky's argument is ratified in all three economies. As the euphoric period of the economy lengthens, existing debts are easily serviced (though frequently in a Ponzi-manner), heavily indebted units can prosper and, most importantly, views about the acceptable structures and levels of debt change into being intrinsically elastic and considerably higher. One of the biggest concerns attached to short-term maturity of lending is the quick inflow reversal and consequent liquidity run dynamic following a 'Kindlebergian' displacement. In the 1990s several middle-income and emerging economies experienced a vast and quick reversal of financial inflows, the majority of which were of short-term nature and maturity.

In fact, the relationship between financial crises and preceding levels of very high short-term bank lending was not a phenomenon that was exclusive to the 1990s. In Figure 9.7 below the IMF effectively summarises how financial crises in the second half of the 20th century have been often correlated with an earlier significant rise in short-term maturity lending to developing countries (see also Figure 9.6).

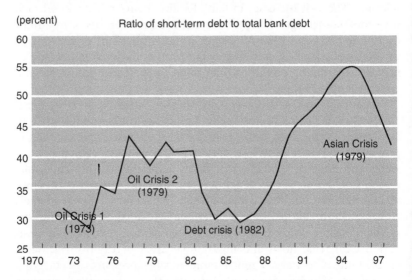

Figure 9.7   Shortening of debt maturities and crises in developing countries
Source: IMF. From Dadush et al., 2000.

Table 9.1 Growth of short-term debt to developing countries in the 1990s

	1990	1997	1998
Short-term debt WB (Original maturity) $USbn	244.6	469.3	411.9
Short-term debt BIS (Remaining-maturity) $USbn	175.6	454.1	369.1
Ratio of short-term debt BIS to foreign currency reserves (%)	119	91	68

Source: World Bank, Global Development Finance 2000 (GDF), and the Bank for International Settlements (BIS).

In the early 1990s short-term bank lending experienced another boom in emerging and middle-income economies that lasted until the East Asian crisis of 1997. By 1997 nearly 60% of all outstanding bank claims on developing countries had a remaining maturity of less than one year, while at least half of all new international bank loans to developing countries had maturities of less than a year (Dadush et al., 2000, see Table 9.1). Korea, Mexico and Brazil were all among the top 10 international receivers of short-term loans (BIS, 1999a). Throughout the period preceding their crises, each of the three economies held levels of international reserves lower than their accumulated short-term debt (See Figures 9.8 and 9.9).

Within the 1990s bank loan maturity-related concerns became increasingly prevalent in emerging markets. Following the East Asian crisis, BIS-reporting banks stated that the balance of short-term debt flows into developing countries transformed from positive $43.5 billion in 1997 to negative $85 billion in 1998 (see Figure 9.9).[9] The reversal of short-term inflows is by its own nature very straightforward in financial markets. For lenders, the cost of pulling out funds is minimal, both in absolute and in relative terms. In relative terms, especially when compared to other forms of finance, it is simple to understand the mechanics and ease of short-term loans exodus from an economy (see again Figure 9.9). Alternative forms of finance, such as investments in stocks and equity, could entail losses for the sellers if they pulled out during financial distress, whereas liquidating FDI is realistically much harder, as it could entail the sale of stocks, machinery and general capital goods, which is usually much more problematic in periods of economic downturn.

Financial instability and consequent liquidity runs are strongly associated with the increasing prevalence of short-maturity bank lending.

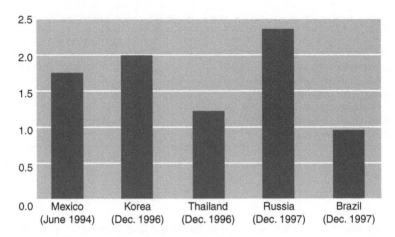

Figure 9.8 Ratio of short-term debt to reserves
Source: BIS and IMF. From Dadush et al., 2000.

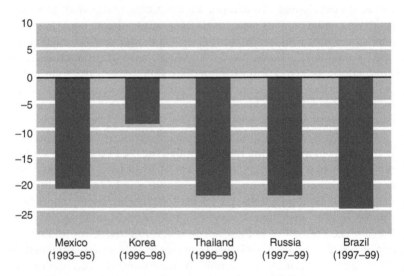

Figure 9.9 Reversal of private flows in times of crisis (US$bn)
Source: BIS and IMF. From Dadush et al., 2000.

The higher the ratio of an economy's short-term debt to foreign currency reserves, the higher is the risk of developing a liquidity run, and consequently the higher the risk of bank runs and systemic crises. Naturally, an economy with sufficient foreign exchange reserves will be able to defend its currency in the case of short-term debt exodus and avoid the consequent liquidity and bank run. Figure 9.8, combined with the previous findings of our study, demonstrates how Korea and to a lesser extent Mexico suffered strongly from the absence of an adequate pool of foreign exchange reserves.

One of the major problems of bank lending, especially short-term bank lending, is that it tends to have a pro-cyclical character. Overall, market optimism and favourable shocks attract capital inflows and consequently create equivalent investment and consumption patterns, which, according to the logic described in our literature review, are self-enhancing and unsustainable in the long term.

The reasons behind these short-term debt jumps are several and can be classified in the same way as this book has done previously with the overall liquidity surges in the three economies studied. Accordingly, demand-pull and supply-push factors can be identified. In turn, each of these factors can be subdivided into systemic, policy and cyclical factors. Demand-pull factors refer to characteristics that are endogenous to the economies of Mexico, Brazil and Korea, and that shaped their markets to be more attractive to inflows of short-term bank loans. These could be systemic causes, such as the liberalisation of trade and finance and the consequent domestic deregulation permitting lending in areas with previously higher requirements for short-term working capital and higher overall market accessibility. Additionally, cyclical demand-pull factors that were prevalent included high domestic growth rates often followed by asset price booms. Similarly, the prevalent policy demand-pull factors encompassed high interest rates often accompanied by tax incentives, and government attempts to isolate the effects of capital inflows using policies such as sterilisation. As we have seen for the case of Brazil, the sterilisation of capital inflows operated through a high interest rate differential to incentivise the purchase of newly issued domestic bonds while preventing a nominal appreciation of the Brazilian Real. The high domestic borrowing costs thus incentivised international lending – especially short-term international lending.

Supply-push variables were also significant for the attraction of short-term bank debt. These were again all of systemic, cyclical and policy-relevant nature. The high economic growth rates in the US and the majority of OECD economies comprised cyclical supply-push factors, while policy factors predominately involved changes in the US dollar interest rates. Interest rates in the US fell substantially throughout the 1990s, triggering the already described and analysed expansion in global liquidity flows. Investors, firms and financial institutions in developing economies initiated a substitution of domestic loans for foreign loans to take advantage of these lower interest rates. Supply-push policy factors pushed this further into this direction. Specifically, policy changes such as BIS' relaxation of capital adequacy criteria and international organisation rescue packages that targeted firstly short-term loans further encouraged the undertaking of short maturities in cross-border loans (Wade, 1998).

Reserves and short-term maturities

Regulation of an economy's capital account performs two roles. The first is as a vehicle for macroeconomic policy-making whereby these regulations could contribute to overall economic stability as a counter-cyclical monetary policy anchor. The second is as a 'liability policy' to smooth the profile of private and – potentially – even public sector debt (Ocampo, 2003). Liability structures together with a country's position on international reserves are two of the most significant indicators when liquidity constraints are considered. Thus, when judging the risk factor accumulated at times of mania, it is not simply the magnitude of public and private indebtedness which needs to be considered but also its maturity structure and overall level of reserve holdings. Neoliberal thinking would predict that a very short-term maturity structure in an economy's financial liabilities would be externally visible and that the markets would be hesitant in investing under such circumstances. Rodrik and Velasco (2000) argue that markets generously reward sound external debt structures. However, it seems as if the timing or ability of the markets to observe and comprehend the actual debt structure and its maturities was lagging in all of the cases studied. In times of panic, and given a Kindlebergian displacement, markets respond to gross financing requirements in a manner which makes the rollover of short-term debt far from financially neutral. In the economies studied, especially Korea, then Brazil and to a lesser extent Mexico, debt profiles that were leaning towards short-term debt obligations considerably increased the level of risk involved and unavoidably intensified the level of panic in the market.

Foreign exchange reserves: a uniform inadequacy

Throughout the 1990s a significant portion of financial flows that entered emerging markets was accumulated in the form of foreign exchange reserves. In the East Asian region 70% of all inflows were accumulated as foreign exchange reserves, while in the entire Latin

American region the equivalent share was 37% (IMF, 1997, p. 29, see also Figures 9.10 and 9.11 for the absolute increase in the volume of reserves accumulation). Starting in 1989 the entire Latin American region experienced a vast increase in the sum of foreign exchange reserves held. After a brief fall resulting from the Mexican crisis in 1994 (Point A, Figure 9.10), the region reached a dramatic peak in reserves' accumulation in 1997 (Point B, Figure 9.10). In some economies, like Brazil, this was the direct effect of the Central Bank's sterilisation policy (see Figure 9.10 Brazil's increase of reserves from 1990 until point D), while in others, such as Mexico, it resulted from Central Bank's intervention to prevent the appreciation of the national currency (see in Figure 9.10 Mexico's reserves' position rises until 1993 while suffers a sharp depletion at point A during its crisis).

The accumulation of foreign exchange reserves, especially in the case of emerging economies, where the influx of financial capital is highly volatile, is also commonly pursued as a policy buffer against abrupt capital outflows. However, in all cases studied but especially in Mexico and Korea, the accumulation – or lack of thereof – of a large stock of foreign reserves proved critical to the development of their crises. In Mexico, the outflows of capital occurred at an unprecedented rate, so

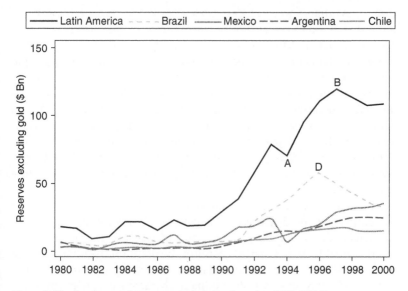

Figure 9.10   Foreign exchange reserves Latin America, US$ (2012)
Note: Points A–D are explained in the text above
Source: World Bank, World Development Indicators.

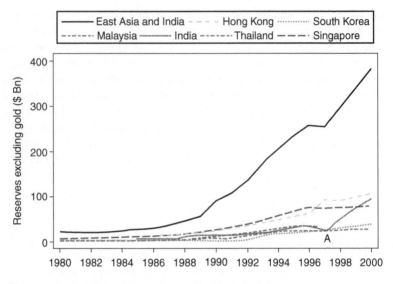

Figure 9.11　Foreign exchange reserves East Asia, US$ (2012)
Note: Point A denotes the outbreak of Korean crisis
Source: World Bank, World Development Indicators.

that in less than a week in December 1994 the Mexican economy lost more than $5bn as the authorities were forced to sell foreign exchange reserves to defend the domestic currency. Equally, in the case of South Korea, the market-panic spread in 1997 and the equally striking rapid capital exodus led to the Central Bank running out of foreign exchange reserves at such a speed that many observers believe it made a crisis inevitable (see Stiglitz and Ocampo, 2007, and *Economist*, 2007). Figures 8.5 and 9.11 are particularly illuminating on this point. The previous analysis of Korea, especially when understood in the context of the entire East Asian region, reveals the significance of its pre-crisis reserve' position but also that the contagion dynamics applied to the entire Asian region.[11]

Overall, one of the big lessons from the decade's financial turmoil for the entirety of the financially emerging world was the significance of sovereigns' accumulation of large pools of reserves. Developments in international financial markets confirm the point on the importance of foreign exchange reserve accumulation. The incorporation of a country's reserve position as a determinant characteristic of its sovereign default rating and the consequent ability to borrow from international markets are profoundly related but often ignored.

Overview of liquidity's direction in both regions

The following summary can be drawn with regard to the shape and form that incoming liquidity took in the recipient economies in both Latin American and East Asian regions:

- Most economies in both regions used the incoming funds to augment their stock of foreign currency reserves (Korea was a bright exception from his route. The lack of reserve accumulation contributed to its inability to defend its currency at the time of crisis and eventually led to a default on its debt). In the first part of the 1990s around 60% and 35% of the surge in inflows in East Asia and Latin America, respectively, were channelled towards the accumulation of international currency reserves (Calvo and Reinhart, 1996). For the first five years of the decade both regions accumulated about $209 billion in international reserves. This sharp increase in the holding of international currency could indicate how most economies dealt with the inflows by absorbing them thereby compelling their monetary authorities to intervene – in order to predominantly avert the appreciation of their domestic currencies.
- Private consumption accelerated in all Latin American economies as a combined result of higher consumer debt, higher demand for imports of durable goods, lower private savings and increased real money growth.[12]
- The effects of inflows on each country's domestic currency value were similar – even though their underlying causes were different across the three economies. The East Asian currency depreciation trend of the '80s was halted, while the majority of the Latin American currencies appreciated strongly. However, the reasons behind this movement in a similar direction were distinct. The composition of aggregate demand in the two regions diverged most significantly along its consumption, private savings and investments patterns. In the East Asian economies, investment as a share of GDP increased more rapidly than in the investment-stagnant Latin America during the '90s capital inflows decade. Brazil, following the full sterilisation policy, is different from the rest of the Latin American countries, which experienced overall currency appreciations in most of its economies. Mexico can be considered as a prime example of how an economy's currency was inflated as a result of capital inflows combined with the domestic response of declining private savings, higher consumption patterns and booming asset prices.

Volatility in stock markets

The financial developments in OECD countries in the 1990s – specifically the significant fall of US dollar interest rates, together with the volatile and debt or deficit finance needs-related interest rates in emerging economies – prompted investors to direct liquidity towards portfolio investments. This dynamic was unlashed despite the lower quality of information and lack of transparency in the emerging markets.

Portfolio investment in stocks became popular as a type of financial saving much less vulnerable to interest rate shocks than bank lending and widely available after the liberalisation of all three countries' stock markets. In all three economies higher incoming liquidity that did not enter bank deposits was converted into tradable securities rather than higher national savings. The result of this practice was generally experienced in emerging economies throughout the decade and, given among others the lack of maturity in emerging markets' financial institutions, it manifested itself in higher stock price volatility *vis-a-vis* OECD markets. The lack of increased levels of national savings is understood as a generic problem of an economy's financialisation. Discussion on diminishing national savings and their economic and social effects has a long history. From the 1970s economists started investigating the substituting effects of foreign aid. It was found that foreign aid was substituting domestic saving in most low- and middle-income aid-receiving economies (Griffin, 1970). Equivalently, and specifically in the context of post-financial reform Latin American economies, financial flows could also have a significant substituting effect on domestic private investment and savings.[13] Portfolio investments in the region resulted in a massive boom in asset prices – and in particular mobile asset prices – rather than the build-up and formation of a productive fixed capital stock.

Kindleberger and pro-cyclicality of capital inflows

In this book the problematic nature of the pro-cyclicality of finance is identified in numerous domains and instances, including the pro-cyclicality of short-term bank debt flows analysed in this book. In all forms and types of monetary flows monitored in the three economies, we can clearly infer that finance was entering the markets in a pro-cyclical fashion related to the perceived optimism and euphoria of market investors, participants and observers. Given this, Kindleberger's analysis and clear identification of the role of financial optimism and resulting mania in the formation of a crisis are key in explaining this pro-cyclical character.

Kindleberger's proposition on crisis formation entails asset price increases in times of euphoria accompanied by increases in the volume of assets traded as a result of the manic behaviour with which investors are willing to buy in anticipation of further price increases. This increase in the quantities traded and the price levels of domestic assets does not necessarily – or much, as shown in the three economies – correspond to an enhancement of productive capacities in the economies in question. In fact, the role of speculation and herding behaviour is imperative to this development. Kindleberger is deeply influenced by Keynes' analysis of the speculative motive, which has been demonstrated to be of high relevance in this analysis. Expectations were treated as having an extensive role in investment decisions, thereby determining business trading, decisions and consequent economic changes in each of the three economies. Equivalently, liquidity preference[14] was generated by market agents' expectations regarding future developments – what Keynes called 'the speculative motive'.

The pro-cyclical behaviour of monetary inflows is further verified in the reverse side of economic activity. Equivalently, given all three displacements in the economies studied – the presidential candidate assassination, the collapse of the Thai Baht, and the Asian and Russian crises contagion – the economic downswing was associated with the rapid exodus of funds and consequent financial distress in all three economies. On the bust part of the cycle expectations are reversed, financial distress creates pressure to exit the market, prices fall, additional downwards pressures on prices accelerate and the consequent need for liquidity coerces agents to liquidate their assets and flee the markets. Subsequent to the described price falls, bank loan losses increase and possible bank foreclosures disregard the credibility of the banking system as a whole and contribute to an even greater surge for liquidity.

This position on the pro-cyclical nature of international finance, and the implications that it might entail particularly for emerging economies, is very well summarised by Ocampo, Kregel and Griffith Jones (Ocampo et al., 2007). Through an analysis of the pro-cyclical character of financial flows, they reject the neoclassical assumption whereby international capital flows smooth consumption and investment gaps throughout the business cycles of capital receiving economies. The logic of capital flows moving from capital-abundant to capital-scarce markets, thereby increasing the growth and development of the latter, has been empirically rejected.

Theory and data put together

The case of Latin America

Starting from 1989, Mexico was one of the most spectacular examples of an abrupt capital flow turnaround in emerging markets. Within a decade the economy turned from being a cumulative net exporter of financial capital to a cumulative net importer. The $15 billion cumulative net outflow between 1983 and 1989 was transformed into a cumulative inflow of $120 billion just for the period between 1990 and 1994. In 1993 with a GDP representing only 8% of the world's emerging economies, it attracted 20% of the entire net flows directed in these (IMF, 1995a). The increase of liquidity directed to the whole Latin American region and Mexico in particular was initially related to and increasingly followed by a massive decline in the interest spreads of the countries' sovereign bonds *vis-a-vis* their US Treasury securities counterparts. The most pronounced decline for private sector borrowers in the entire region was in Mexico, where average spreads fell from 650 base points in 1990 to 315 in 1993, whereas specific yields on five-year Mexican government bonds fell from 800 base points in 1989 to 150 in 1993.

In the 1990s, as a result of increasing international interest rates and financial liberalisation policies designed to enhance growth in emerging economies, the relative cost of debt finance increased. Consequently, the relative cost of equity finance (in relation to debt finance) became more favourable for investors.[15] The rise of equity finance is highly prevalent in the case of Mexico as it is the most illuminating early example demonstrating the important effects that portfolio investment had on emerging economies. On a micro level, portfolio inflows contributed to the generation of vast price booms in the stock market (an increase by a factor of 10 in the Mexican case within five years from 1989) (Datastream data). This facilitated access to, and lowered substantially the cost of, capital in the Latin America region. As analysed above and supported by well-acknowledged literature (see Rodrik, 1994; Stiglitz and Ocampo, 2007; Harcourt, 2010; Ocampo and Palma, 2007), the majority, if not the totality, of these flows to Latin America, were not a market response to ameliorating fundamentals but rather the manifestations of herding behaviour initiated from a misplaced euphoria. International markets were supplying funds, which were being used for consumption purposes and the building of asset bubbles, instead of being used by domestic firms to finance investment.

Debt rollovers were widespread in the 1990s, and when combined with the dominance of short-term lending analysed previously, would often result in the additional destabilisation of the countries' financial systems. Circumstances like this would include the government absorbing the risks of interest rate hikes or a possible devaluation. In the cases of Mexico and Brazil, short-term maturities of public debt eventually manifested in instability in the markets. Mexico's move to replace the Cetes with Tesobonos in 1994, and the short-term profile of the first, was a crucial component in the build-up to the crisis. Equivalently the short-term structure of Brazil's debt could explain why since the end of 1997 fixed-interest bonds were rapidly replaced by variable rate bonds and US dollar denominated securities – a situation that cancelled out any progress made on the structure of public debt since the introduction of the Real Plan (ECLAC, 2002).

Government spending in Latin America after state-led industrialisation

In the period of market liberalisation that succeeded that of state-led industrialisation, the entire Latin American region did not undergo any major changes with regard to achieving higher growth and translating it into more progressive patterns of welfare policy. In both Mexico and Brazil two common trends with regard to fiscal policy were observed (Ocampo, 2006). The first entailed a shift in the composition of taxation away from income and property taxation and towards indirect and wage taxation. The second was that the rate of welfare spending – not to mention the absence of redistributive incomes policies – was stagnant when compared to the 1980s and substantially lower than both the 1960s and 1970s.[16]

Inflows-led appreciation: the consequences

Change of direction in obtaining competitiveness: the case of Brazil

Following the success of the Real Plan, the Brazilian economy was forced to abandon the policy of preserving an undervalued exchange rate parity aimed at maintaining competitiveness via cheaper exports. Instead, the era of high capital inflows, liberalised trade and consequent euphoria forced the economy to become internationally competitive through an internal devaluation which created downward price pressures on domestic producers (IMF, 1995a).

The jump in the size of bank deposits, private debt and public debt in Brazil was accompanied by an increased burden in the domestic

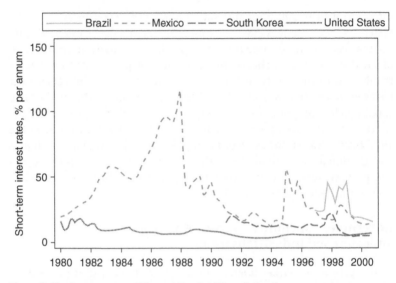

Figure 9.12   Interest rate differentials, the US and the three countries
Source: OECD Statistics.

agents' obligations to service the issued debt. The use of domestic funds and offer of high domestic returns acted not only as a prerequisite for attracting foreign capital but also as a stabiliser to secure its persistence. Figure 9.12 below clearly illustrates this point: the short-term interest rate differentials between the economies studied and the US are shown to be of substantial magnitude. Higher interest rates in emerging economies, especially in the case of Brazil and to a lesser extent Mexico and Korea, acted as a powerful source of the attraction of short-term capital inflows. An interesting aspect of the growing Brazilian public debt was its growing foreign ownership. Since the introduction of the Real Plan, more and more of Brazilian public debt came under direct or indirect ownership of international market agents. The Brazilian crisis should be seen through the prism of the increasing cost of its rising interest rate on the public sector balance sheet. The rate paid to international investors effectively became the domestic interest rate – a fact further compounded by the large amount of debt denominated in US dollars and paid in domestic overnight rate.

The case of East Asia

There are two sources that can briefly summarise the general Asian vulnerability and at the same time the post-liberalisation developments in Korea. These are the modest macroeconomic imbalances[17] and the weaknesses of the financial services, stemming from the unsustainable level of high corporate debt combined with a high short-term maturity structure. Macroeconomic imbalances included primarily overvalued exchange rates complemented by deficits in the current account and a consequent need for financial inflows in order to pay for them. These deficits implied that, once financial inflows were reversed, countries would be unable to cover them and thus would consequently give rise to deeper imbalances.[18] The problem in the region resulting from current account deficit was twofold (Eichengreen, 2004). First, capital flow problems were accumulated and high demand for them was created in order to finance the deficit. As a result, this created a problematic dynamic based on the need to regularly rollover private debts. Second, capital stock problems became further apparent. The Korean economy had accumulated a large stock of short-term debt and a great share of it was denominated in foreign currency. The majority of the debt created was private rather than public and resulted in a large destabilisation of the banking system in the country.

The overall image of the destabilised banking system in the East Asian region, and Korea in particular, would be incomplete without considering the question of loan maturity. In most of the East Asian countries the maturity of issued debt was short. From 1990 to 1996, half of all net private portfolio capital inflows to Thailand took the form of short-term borrowing, while from just 1992 to 1997 the equivalent figure for South Korea was 62%[19] (Eichengreen, 2004). In Korea, net interbank lending more than tripled within less than two years following 1994 (Eichengreen, 1999). Specifically, it increased in value from $US14 billion to $US43 billion, where 60% of the debt was denominated in US dollars and the rest in Japanese Yen. Again, in interbank lending the maturity of the liabilities was very short as an overwhelming two-thirds of them matured in less than a year.

The appreciation of the Japanese Yen (see Chapter 8) and the positive effects that it induced in the trade balance of the region eventually contributed to the growth of short-term lending. The appreciation of the Yen contributed via two major channels in the growth of the Korean economy and the entire region at the time. The first channel worked via the enhanced export competitiveness of non-Japanese East Asian exports, while the second through an overall production shift trend whereby many Japanese companies and banks moved their manufacturing and lending out of Japan and into the rest of the East Asian region. The latter initiated a self-sustaining cycle of enhanced motivation for

Japanese companies to flee domestic production, as the technological transfers were quickly established, which contributed towards the overall increase of manufacturing productivity in the region and further enhanced its export capacity, demand and production. The appreciation of the Yen, together with the low levels of international interest rates, the high financial multiplier of the Asian region[20] and the resulting high levels of portfolio investment and FDI, generated waves of optimism in the market and secured short-term stability in the exchange rate. This in turn, via the Kindlebergian mechanisms described above, contributed to the spread of euphoric short-term lending – including short-term interbank lending – in the economies of the region.

An additional development shared by most economies of the East Asian region after the liberalisation of their capital markets and the resulting financial inflow booms was the increasingly oligopolistic structure nature of the markets. The concentration of economic power in the hands of very few industrial and financial conglomerates[21] had been stark in the case of Korea but also other East Asian economies like Thailand, Indonesia and the Philippines. The shares of the total value of listed corporate assets controlled by the top 15 families in Indonesia, Thailand, Philippines and Korea in 1996 were 62%, 53%, 55% and 38%, respectively, while the equivalent shares for the top five families were 41%, 32%, 43% and 30%, respectively (Claessens et al., 2000). As analysed earlier in the book, since the 1980s the five big Korean banks successfully extended the long-established oligopolistic structure of the Korean financial markets despite the doubling of commercial banks in the 1980s (Park, Y.C., 1994). Equally, in the industrial sector, given the structure and operation of the Korean *chaebols*, 40% of all manufacturing value added in the mid-1990s was produced by the 30 largest industrial groups whose ownership was equally oligopolistic (Park W.A., 1996). Other than manufacturing and banking institutions, the structure of non-banking financial institutions (NBFIs) in the country followed similar patterns.

Korea's large industrial groups comprised the majority of the shareholders in most of the economy's security firms and NBFIs. Through this channel of direct ownership of banking institutions and NBFIs, the large industrial conglomerates were able to control and direct the management of the five largest commercial banks and bypass state regulations such as equity ownership restrictions (Chang, 1998b). Not surprisingly, large manufacturing groups comprised the larger borrowers in both commercial banks and NBFIs – complementing the argument put forward in this book, regarding market liberalisation, not only questions the benefits of a neoliberal agenda (i.e., higher competition and efficiency) but, in fact, points towards the opposite. The study of South Korea seems to contradict McKinnon's (1973 and 1993) financialisation assumptions in all degree and angles – starting from the price efficiency and volatility effects of opening up the capital account and extending to the problematic market efficiency dynamics with regard to participation to and overall development of the financial sector. The expectation that financial liberalisation will have a substantial market pay-off in terms of real and financial output is, in fact, reversed. On a different but intertwined front, the question of the social consequences of this reversed market pay-off remains to be studied.

Relevance of Kindleberger: summing up

In all three cases the growing volume of financial inflows increased the appetite for domestic credit by reducing its direct cost (see the evolution of interest rate differentials in Figure 9.12), lowering its transaction cost, decreasing its regulations, improving its accessibility and ultimately contributing towards its expansion. Cheap and easily accessible credit unvaryingly led to a surge of euphoric expectations and animal spirit behaviour equal to the one described by Kindleberger.

The pro-cyclical relation described throughout this book between capital flows and overall economic activity was characteristic in the case of Latin America in the 1990s. Figure 9.13 provides a good illustration

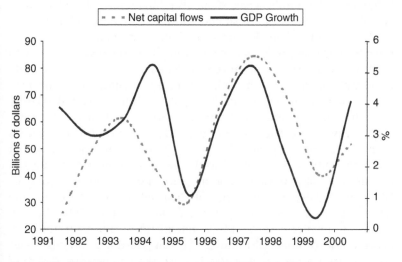

Figure 9.13 Kindleberger and data – pro-cyclical flows, Latin America
Source: ECLAC, 2002.

of this dynamic. The association between net resource transfers (capital flows) and economic activity throughout the 1990s has been really strong in the region – particularly in the second part of the decade. This could act as an indicator of the main mechanisms through which externally generated cycles of boom and bust can be transferred within the economy.

In the boom period the mania associated with investment and market placements was accompanied by a fall in all incentives to efficiently assess the actual risks. This was the main result of two mutually reinforcing sentiments: the investors' appetite for seemingly far more attractive prospective revenues and their unshakable belief in their ability to securely exit the markets prior to their collapse. While the collapse in each of the economies studied was precipitated by two sets of very different events, in both cases the economies' bust was followed by an immediate collapse of credit inflows. In Latin America, following the Brazilian crisis, net capital flows fell to negative levels – albeit only for a few months. This had immediate damaging effects on the economies' exports – mostly through weakening their ability to import intermediate goods used for exporting. While an equivalent export dynamic was avoided in East Asia, the effect of capital withdrawal on the economies' pool of foreign reserves was significant.

As Kindleberger points out, the one thing that international financial markets can do that is worse than lending excessive amounts to developing countries is to stop that lending abruptly (Kindleberger and Laffargue, 1982, Kindleberger 2000). The importance of capital flows' volatility and suspension is paramount. In the presence of highly volatile flows, the problematic character of the policy designed to counter the crisis becomes much more complicated than the policy response to problems resulting from balance of payments asymmetries. The latter could well be addressed through exchange rate adjustments and revisions of domestic monetary and fiscal policy.[22] Inflow volatility is costly in both economic and social terms. In economic terms, it increases uncertainty, reduces the efficiency of fixed capital investment and leads economic agents to prefer 'defensive' microeconomic strategies that avoid committing fixed capital to the production process and instead encourage lending towards liabilities with shorter maturities (ECLAC, 2002). In social terms, volatility of financial inflows can contribute towards social unrest and poverty (see Baldacci et al., 2002). Abrupt changes in relative prices and fiscal retrenchment can result from sudden reversals of financial inflows. This can contribute towards unrest and poverty via two main channels. First, the immediate exposure of those agents that engaged into debt at times of inflow euphoria and, second, the resulting inability of the government to provide welfare schemes that would counter the effects of inflows' reversal.

The expansion of credit during what Kindleberger describes as a euphoric period is self-reinforcing in an upward spiral manner. Great contributors to this trend are the poor regulation and monitoring of the markets where inadequately experienced authorities and investors with unsubstantiated optimism perform the risk evaluation and supervision of financial agents. These conditions were characteristic of the period of financial liberalisation in all three economies studied. Increasing private debt and to a lesser extent public debt, together with consumption sprees in mostly Mexico and then Brazil, resulted in significant asset price increases – with equity but also real estate experiencing the most significant increases in prices and demand. In a Kindlebergian logic this dynamic results in wealth effects that further accentuate consumption in euphoric times but act in the completely opposite manner when expectations are reversed. Debt, consumption and, as a result, asset prices fall substantially in such a time of reversal. This process becomes self-reinforcing when market agents become readily available to make financial decisions and buy into the markets – in this way shaping a dynamic where fixed assets are highly liquid during euphoric times and highly illiquid in times of crises. On this point it is important to recall the fundamental difference, as best described by Minsky, between a euphoric state of an economy and a steadily growing one. Minsky identifies the tendency of a capitalist economy to explode – to enter into a boom or euphoric state – as its fundamental instability and this is crucial for understanding the distinction between steady growth and mania (Minsky, 1982a, 1986).

Part of Kindleberger's 'mania, panic and crash' logic can be easily identified in the case of Mexico, where a complete Kindlebergian displacement can be identified. The case of Mexico can illustrate a perfect example of a self-fulfilling displacement in a liberalised economy with unsustainable levels of debt and a pronounced reversal of investors' expectations. The Central Mexican Bank succumbed to the attacks against the currency, and the levels of reserves held were not, as effectively they never seem to be, adequate to support the economy. As Mendoza and Calvo (1996) point out, the low ratio (below 1) of the country's Central Bank reserves to short-term liabilities contributed to the speed of the displacement. The effectiveness of the Mexican Central Bank's response to the market displacement has been long disputed. Responses to this include the widely discussed approach by

Dornbusch and Werner (1994), which argued the necessity of an earlier devaluation, to Sachs et al. (1995), who stressed the shortcomings of the monetary policy of the time. The latter emphasised the role of Mexican monetary policy in contributing towards the erosion of the country's reserves and stressed the need for tighter monetary and fiscal policies necessary to secure the long-term position of the country's reserves to shield the economy from the higher risk of devaluation and consequent debt escalation.[23]

The speed and scale of the market's response to the Peso devaluation can be also explained in a Kindlebergian logic. International financial markets responded to the December 1994 Peso devaluation in a manner that was unprecedented for the Mexican economy and the Latin American region as a whole. The response, primarily including the vast reversal of capital inflows, cannot be fully explained as the result of a sudden sharp deterioration in economic fundamentals. Such a deterioration in Mexico's fundamentals did not occur suddenly and was certainly not available as market data to international investors prior to the actual devaluation of the Peso. Similarly, indicators on the economy's increasing financial vulnerability (such as the increasing ratio of Tesobonos to foreign currency reserves) are inadequate in explaining the speed of the crisis. The crisis acted as a response that abruptly countered the previous market excesses linked to the climate of perceived euphoria. In the case of Mexico this euphoria evolved hand in hand with the neoclassical image of the economy that was perceived as a paragon of reform in the region – an image encompassing both the direct liberalisation reforms and the indirect ones such as those brought about by the membership of the country to institutions such as NAFTA.

A key distinction between East Asia and Latin America with regard to the Kindlebergian supply-generated demand argument can be identified in the very different production lines of the two regions. The key difference between the developments in both regions stem from the fact that in the first there was a collapse in confidence and a subsequent withdrawal of finance, whereas in the latter the underperforming character of the economies' fundamentals was eventually exposed to and comprehended by market agents who did not want to acknowledge it before. The fundamentals in the largest economies of Latin America were largely problematic. Their underlying problems included large public sector deficits (as predominantly seen in Brazil), mounting current account deficits (including the fastest growing imports of consumption goods),[24] weak investment and rapidly appreciating exchange rates. On the other hand, in East Asia, exports made a significant contribution to each economy's growth levels. Additionally, the growing private consumption trends of the entire region did not develop in a fashion similar to Latin America and did not distort the macroeconomic equilibrium. Lastly, the region's exchange rates did not act against the economies' exports, the current account deficits were low and the share of savings and investment in GDP was large and growing (Figure 9.14).

The Latin American dynamic of rapidly evolving consumption patterns, manias and booms, together with the much less dynamically evolving production and manufacturing, base can also be understood here through the Keynesian rejection of the loanable funds theory. The rapid and gigantic growth of credit in the region outlined above did not translate into corresponding increases in capital formation – concurring in this way with the Keynesian logic. The fruits of the credit expansion, especially in the case of Mexico, were not channelled to productive manufacturing or infrastructural investment but instead financed consumption bubbles (Baig and Goldfajn, 2000). Keynes' assertion that liquidity rather than savings can be a constraint on the accumulation of capital, together with the key role assigned to banks rather than savings in enabling capitalist accumulation, is crucial to the

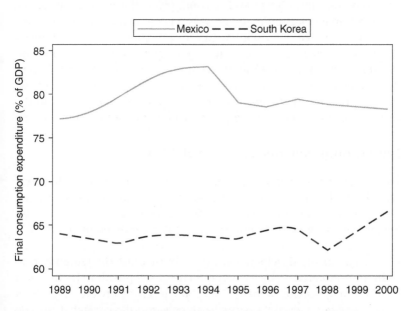

Figure 9.14 Consumption levels, Mexico and Korea, percentage of GDP
Source: OECD Statistics.

overall understanding of the relation between credit, investment and consumption studied here.

The demand-pull factors attracting liquidity in the two regions studied had a fundamental difference associated with the dynamism of their industrial sector and the resulting differences in the direction of finance to it. In Latin America, demand-pull factors directed finance outside the real economy – a dynamic partly resulting from the economies' inability to increase productivity and added value in manufacturing goods. This was closely related to the rapid and radical economic reforms of the 1980s, including deregulation and privatisation. The low manufacturing investment incentives, together with the perception of still 'undiscovered' and undervalued Latin American financial markets, the continuous expectations for currency appreciation and the higher debt returns[25] were the main determinants of liquidity attraction in the financial markets of the region. The determinants of liquidity attraction in East Asia were based on a different dynamic. This was predominately captured in the economies' need to finance the intensive capital demands of the region's growing manufacturing base and declining profits. Accordingly, it was necessary for the economies to attract external corporate investment for two main reasons. First, as their domestic funds were insufficient and, second, given the very nature of the dominant microelectronics industry. The latter, being very technology-intensive, required a constant stream of investment that was imperative to its persistence and consequent enlargement (Chang, Palma and Whittaker, 2001). However, as analysed previously, the region voluntarily switched to self-destructive forms of volatile short-term financing, misallocation of investment[26] and the accumulation – especially in the case of Korea – of very high corporate debt-equity ratios (Palma, 1998).

Implications: looking again at volatility

In the face of high circulation and volatility of 'hot money', which was sensitive to, but also related to, the generation of boom and bust cycles, domestic authorities that have abandoned the route of capital controls are left with very limited options. As Rodrik recently pointed out:

> Officials in the developing world ... must resist the temptation to binge on foreign finance when it is cheap and plentiful. In the midst of a foreign-capital bonanza, stagnant levels of private investment in tradable goods are a particularly powerful danger signal that no amount of government mythmaking should be allowed to override.

Officials face a simple choice: maintain strong prudential controls on capital flows, or be prepared to invest a large share of resources in self-insurance by accumulating large foreign reserves.

(Rodrik, 2014)

In the case of the three economies studied the accumulation of reserves by their central banks was proven to be inadequate, while the design and application of effective capital control mechanisms were completely overlooked.

The understanding of how the Kindlebergian and Minskian logics frame and explain the evolution of the events in each of the economies studied generates discussion about the possible effectiveness of capital controls. Authorities in middle-income emerging economies need to concentrate on crisis prevention rather than crisis resolution as the former clearly offers much higher degrees of freedom in policy design. Managing booms and monitoring asset prices, saving and investment placements in times of euphoria entails a much larger spectrum of possible policy prospects for both governments and monetary authorities. Minsky claims that within capitalist economies instability is inherent. Instability might be decreased by public intervention and policy (through changes in investment, wages or the government budget), but it cannot be completely eliminated. On this exact point, regarding the fact that policy design can alleviate but not eradicate financial instability, this study demonstrates the absence of such public policy interventions in the economies studied. Instead, this book exposes the existence of policy design and implementation achieving the opposite results.

10
An Endogenous Conclusion

This book investigated the relationship between the causes of financial crises and emerging markets and found two dominant dynamics: first, a high level of incoming financial flows generated in the financial centres of the world and, second, financial market liberalisation in the emerging economies. Thus, the thesis proposing that capital market liberalisation leads almost inevitably to financial crisis when a combination of sufficient push and pull factors are present is credible for the cases of Mexico, Brazil and Korea. The exact route diverged greatly between the three economies as a distinct combination of domestic policy was followed in the actual measures' design, speed of implementation and sequencing of application. However, all three routes converged in the eventual crisis through a set of commonly experienced international liquidity supply-push and domestic liberalisation-pull factors.

Each of the three cases studied provides evidence regarding the adverse effects of swift financial liberalisation in middle-income economies and demonstrates how the supposed merits of the efficient market hypothesis that endorses financial liberalisation are much more complex than commonly acknowledged. The mainstream theoretical case for free capital flows and deregulated financial markets associated with the work of E. Fama (1970 and 1985) is critically challenged and discredited.

Deregulated financial markets were subjected to investors' volatile and manic investment decisions, which drove the prices and quantities of assets traded to unsustainable levels. The heightened prices of assets produced extraordinary levels of return, contributing to a self-reinforcing system of supply-generated demand that resulted in unsustainable prices and volume levels of trading. Asset prices produced misaligned signals with regard to the assets' underlying fundamentals, initiating a cycle of high and unsustainable expectations for future performance.

This feeding of euphoric expectations regarding future returns was further exacerbated by the increasing issuance of credit by the domestic and international banking systems. Banks, via the rapid provision of credit to the private sector, fed optimistic expectations regarding the performance of the entire economy, despite their balance sheets being burdened with high levels of debt and short maturities of liabilities. In all three economies, a differently weighted combination of internal banking and external public imbalances grew and finally became unsustainable.

Each economy received high levels of short-term capital inflows. These inflows created different problems in the financial sector of each economy, but in all three they resulted in financial crises. The Mexican liberalisation experience entailed the dynamic of depressed private savings and increased private consumption with a resulting boom in the real estate market, a wild escalation in asset prices and the poor performance of private investment. The Brazilian case involved a poorly designed and badly implemented strategy to avoid a Mexican style credit and asset price bubble through a plan to avoid inflation that included policies of sterilisation and bank bailouts. This entailed the accumulation of an unsustainable level and maturity structure of public debt as a result of the interest paid on the national inflow sterilisation scheme and the costly terms of the banks' national bailout scheme (Palma, 2002b). Lastly, Korea accumulated an unsustainable amount of private debt, which, despite being correlated with high levels of private investment, was subject to sector-specific risk and a constant need for sectorial innovation to maintain not only the returns but, most importantly, the solvency of the micro-electronics industry as a whole. The theoretical framework of the book binds together the country analysis with the crisis developments and demonstrates the structural characteristics underpinning the conventions and behaviour of liberalised capital markets. Accordingly, the lessons of Keynes, Minsky and Kindleberger have proved to be integral in both the understanding of the evolution of the events and the discussion of policy alternatives.

Discussion of main findings

In Chapter 2, the literature on the inherent instability of financial markets was reviewed as an alternative to efficient market hypothesis theory and first, second or third generation models attempting to explain financial crises. The theoretical background against which the evolution of the crises was understood and explained throughout the book was presented here as the best fit to understanding how the events unfolded. Keynes' rejection of the ergodic axiom was analysed as a key factor responsible for investors' inability to accurately assess the risks involved. The rejection of loanable funds theory, which lies at the core of Keynes' analysis of financial motive, establishes how banks rather than savings have a guiding role in enabling capitalist accumulation and consequently can lead to dynamics, like in Mexico, where liquidity constrains capital formation and instead promotes a consumption mania. Minsky's work was then analysed for his key conceptualisation of a steadily growing phase of an economy *vis-à-vis* a booming one. The structural tendency of a capitalist economy with a liberalised financial sector to enter into a boom or euphoric state comprises for Minsky a fundamental instability in the markets' structure. These insights proved essential for the understanding of markets' behaviour in this book. Further, Minsky's notion of hedge versus Ponzi finance was critical to the comprehension of how and when an economy dominated by speculative and Ponzi units will have substantially lower margins of safety. The case of Brazil confirmed how a highly fragile financial structure proved critical for the escalation of financial crisis. Lastly, the work of Kindleberger on the cycle of financial crises has been presented as essential to understanding the implications of excess liquidity. Kindleberger's analysis of the cycle of credit expansion, speculative manias, excessive consumption, displacement, distress and ultimate panic reflects very accurately the manner in which financial volatility and consequent vulnerability evolved in Mexico, Brazil and Korea.

Chapters 3, 4 and 5 analysed the reasons behind the striking increase of capital flows in international markets since the early 1980s and identified the causes behind their redirection to the financial markets of middle-income economies. Both supply-push and demand-pull factors interacted in complicated dynamics, distinct in each case, to determine the causes of capital flows in the emerging markets of the period. The high levels and new sources of liquidity in international financial markets were a central push factor generating additional liquidity in emerging markets – mainly in the form of bonds and equities. An important finding was that the evolution in size and complexity of international financial markets, together with specific developments that are endogenous to the function of their economies, resulted in the direction of liquidity to emerging economies – which were seen as markets of last resort. In other words, the development of new institutional investors, the rise in the trading of new instruments and securities, the evolution of new financial conglomerates with larger portfolios and the increased needs for diversification made investment in developing countries more attractive than ever before. The economic stabilisation, together with financial liberalisation reforms, comprised the country-specific demand-pull factors attracting capital in the domestic economies. The stabilisation of macroeconomic indicators in all three economies together with the opening of their banking, bond and stock exchange markets, the privatisation of many state companies and the ratification of their membership in open market international organisations signalled their increased investment attraction.

Chapters 6, 7 and 8 provided a detailed analysis of each country's economic and financial route to crisis. It analysed the variables that were significant for each country's economic performance, capital attraction and eventual frenzied capital exodus.

The case of Mexico can be understood in the context of various factors. The Brady debt agreement, which re-inserted Latin America into the investment map, as well as other key developments, such as Mexico's formal rating by CRAs, the band exchange rate regime and the state guarantee of property rights on foreign capital, were crucial in reducing overall market uncertainty. Two main findings regarding the reasons behind the rapid exodus of capital from Mexico are identified: first, the large share of short-term portfolio investments in overall capital flows and, second, the large share of Tesobonos in public debt, which increased the difficulty of the authorities to defend the domestic currency once the initial displacement shook the confidence of investors.

In the case of Brazil, the full sterilisation policy is found to be a key factor in the understanding of domestic financial instability as a result of the high interest rate it necessitated and the consequent debt burden that had to be paid by the state. The importance of two specific findings is emphasised here. First, how the high interest rate burden further led to the collapse of the domestic private banking system, especially when combined with the high levels of non-performing private debt. Second, the additional problematic dynamic of public debt resulting from the misguided government rescue plans for these failing banks.

Korea's unique contribution to the understanding of financial markets is indicative of how volatility, and eventually turmoil, can be apparent even at times when private investment and industrial production are high. The additional finance created by inflows was used productively by the corporate sector, without the usual inflow side-effects of pronounced asset bubbles or consumer booms. Nevertheless, the economy still experienced a severe crisis as a result of the increase in corporate debt. In Korea, the collapse of profitability in the corporate sector was translated into a self-sustaining need for additional finance and higher volumes of credit. Key findings explaining the escalation of events in the case of Korea are: the accumulation of unsustainable levels of corporate debt to maintain the levels of investment needed; the corporate debt's asymmetric weight upon short-term maturity liabilities; and, on a national level, the low level of foreign exchange reserves held by the Central Bank at the apex of the crisis.

Chapters 6, 7 and 8 raise two important findings. First, despite the divergence of each country's liberalisation route, exchange rate stability played a key role in the attraction of finance in all three economies. Second, the rapid accumulation of debt and its short-term maturity structure in the cases of Korea and Brazil or foreign currency indexation in the case of Mexico were critical to the severity, speed and volatility of financial outflows.

Chapter 9 analysed the country-specific findings and linked the structural characteristics behind each economy's route and actual experience of financial crisis to key economic concepts. This chapter identifies the structural similarities between countries with regard to the manner in which they have experienced the crisis and finds systemic components of fragility in financial markets and volatility in investment behaviour similar to the ones described in the Keynesian literature. Parallels and differences are identified between the economies with regard to the channels of inflow absorption and how these were translated into private credit, higher consumption and a real estate boom. A fundamental similarity identified in all three economies is the prevalence of herding behaviour among international and domestic investors that spread rapidly following the deregulation of their markets. The deregulation of domestic markets, together with the increasing influence of CRAs and financial information dissemination firms, is found to work in a pattern similar to the mechanism identified in Keynes' beauty contests. The assumption of long-run investment decisions following the performance of financial indicators shaped by past performance is disturbed in precisely the manner that Keynes would have predicted: by animal spirits and the destructive effects of herding behaviour. A critical finding of this chapter is the clear link between the problematic dynamic of high levels of short-term bank lending prevalent in all three economies and the pro-cyclical nature of credit as described by Minsky. Minsky's identification of the upward fundamental instability of markets is found to persist in all economies studied. Pro-cyclical conventions transformed the markets' upward trends into speculative investment manias and were experienced at different times in the booming phases of all three economies: Mexico, Brazil and Korea. These booming phases were all associated with high and rapid prosperity, as well as increased levels of 'acceptable' debt burdens. The pro-cyclical character of finance was equally reflected in the ease with which short-term inflows were reversed.

An additional important finding of Chapter 9 should be emphasised. A structural difference between the Latin American and the East Asian regions is exposed with regard to the preceding period of credit inflows. The macroeconomic fundamentals in the majority of the Latin American region were largely problematic: exports were at historically low levels, there was a very inelastic demand for imported goods, investment was weak and exchange rates were rapidly appreciating. The picture in the East Asian region was different chiefly in the export and investment spheres. It was instead characterised by vulnerabilities stemming from the insufficient pool of foreign reserves in the regions' economies. Unlike Latin America, private consumption patterns did not distort the economies' macroeconomic equilibria. The region's exchange rates did not act against the economies' exports, current account deficits were almost negligible, and the share of savings and investment in GDP was large and growing. Notwithstanding, at the time of panic the concentration of foreign exchange reserves proved inadequate for maintaining investors' confidence and defending the national currencies – as it usually does in a Kindlebergian logic of manias, panics and crashes. This allowed speculative attacks to drive the countries into currency collapse and overall default.

Discussion on supply-push, demand-pull and liquidity generation

This book conducted a thorough analysis of the exogenous and endogenous variables that contributed to the significant jumps in capital flows into emerging markets in the 1980s and 1990s. The research finds that the complicated dynamics and relation between the supply-push and demand-pull factors that attract and allocate liquidity were critical in the shaping of financial crises in all three economies studied.

Generalised implications

Several common characteristics can be identified within the financial sectors of all three economies that point towards some general implications that are applicable to all of them.

Real economy: the opportunity cost of liquidity booms

The side-effect of the increase in the prices of financial and non-financial assets resulting from liquidity bonanzas was their transformation into highly liquid assets. Assets become more liquid, and this in turn increases their supply and relocates the supply of capital away from other less liquid uses. Particularly in the case of Mexico, where the real estate sector triumphed in capital attraction, the developments of less liquid investments with higher sunk costs, such as manufacturing, were the subject of this vast opportunity cost. The nature of liquidity in financial markets proved very problematic at times of both boom and bust. In times of euphoria, when the assets were highly liquid, the emphasis on credit allocated to them acted at the expense of the real economy in both Mexico and Brazil. On the other hand, at times when the assets became highly illiquid, panic spread to the markets and resulted in a downward spiral of capital outflows, contributing towards their enhanced vulnerability. The same herding behaviour that resulted in an upward spiral and eventual price bubble in all assets at times of euphoria resulted in a price slump at times of panic. While resource reallocation was regular but non-unsettling in the build-up to the bubble, the situation was significantly different when the bubble eventually burst. Resources were rapidly pulled out of the previously liquid markets making the markets highly illiquid and inducing shortages of finance.

Short maturity debt: a dynamic in need of control

In all the economies studied, the short-maturity structures of their private and public debt accounts were shown to create problematic dynamics. In the case of Latin America, the public debt profile that leaned towards short-term obligations, and, in the case of South Korea, the equivalent figures that were manifested in the high private debt profile of the economy, developed into highly destabilising forces. Short-term maturities in times of booms and euphoria might be easily bypassed, but during crises they developed into major disrupting factors. In cases of public debt, the same phenomenon can be equally applied to short-term profile liabilities – where investors holding short-term public sector securities can easily resort to capital flight, encouraging additional negative speculation. Mexico's move from CETEs to Tesoboonos was enabled by the short-term maturity of the CETEs. In the case of Brazil the absence of Korean-type high levels of private and especially short-term debt could be partly traced to the economy's history of hyperinflation. The financial sector of the economy was not well developed with regard to long-term maturities as domestic firms held little fixed interest debt. Banking institutions, on the other hand, were mostly operating on the basis of unproductive treasury operations and inflation arbitrage, so little debt was issued towards the private sector. Interestingly, however, despite the relatively small size of Brazilian private debt, its composition was distinctly problematic. Prior to the crisis a large and increasing share of private debt was non-performing (see Table 7.6, Chapter 7).

With reference to the size of private debt in Brazil, it is interesting to consider which factors contributed to the formation of the crisis based on the high burden of interest rates and their consequent erosion of the public sector balance sheets. Why was the crisis felt predominately in the public sector in Brazil? Why did it differ from the Asian private sector routes? And why was the eventual magnitude of the crisis much more constrained compared to Korea? The main crisis determinants in Korea, but also in the region in general, were that bank and corporate balance sheets were increasingly negative, while in Brazil no major bank or corporate failure took place. Brazilian firms had low levels of interest-fixed debt – an imbedded memory lesson from the economy's long history of hyperinflation. As outlined in Chapter 7, Brazilian banks prospered during the inflationary period as a result of the inflationary income they appropriated through inflation arbitrage and treasury operations. But after the introduction of the Real Plan Brazilian banks managed to advance only very slowly with regard to expanding lending directly to the private sector. As an immediate result of these peculiarities, the corporate sector in Brazil was not highly indebted to the banking system – in 1997 the average debt of the corporate sector was as low as 30% of the owner's equity (Kregel, 2000).

Volatile and short-term flows

Domestic macroeconomic and policy weaknesses can only explain part of the instability caused in the economies studied. In the 1990s and following the Mexican crisis, both the IMF (1995a) and the BIS (1995) explicitly documented the problems resulting from short-term capital flows. They even proposed government intervention to effectively manage inflows along with the development of sound macroeconomic fundamentals to reduce the likelihood of a crisis. One does not need to be radical to suggest that controls or taxes on short-term capital inflows should be part of a policy package following financial liberalisation (see Calvo and Goldstein, 1995). Especially in the case of Mexico, the crisis was completely out of proportion to the actual macroeconomic indicators as a result of the panic behaviour induced by the sudden exit of short-term capital. Subsequently, panic and speculative behaviour played a large role in the severity of the Mexican crisis but equally in the case of Korea where contagion and terror were spread among the entire region's markets. This Minskyan instability clearly associated with short-term capital flows has costly economic and social manifestations. In purely economic terms the volatility induced increases uncertainty and diminishes the efficiency of fixed capital investments. In Mexico and Brazil, this manifested itself predominately in the overall discouragement of private investment. As a result of the higher levels of uncertainty and lower rates of investment efficiency, economic agents leaned towards more cautious microeconomic strategies and avoided a major commitment of capital to the production process. In financial terms this further translated itself into financial investments of shorter maturity.

Withdrawal of funds

The swift exodus of funds that immediately followed the occurrence of the crises can be explained in terms of phenomena that have been previously analysed in this book: the contagious mania of market agents to place investments in emerging economies despite the customary absence of detailed and extensive information on the economies' public and private financial developments.[1] The scale of excessive credit provision in all three economies, far exceeding the production and productivity potentials of each, led to a Kindlebergian over-reaction – that is, panic – where flows not only eventually declined but, most importantly, were reversed in all of the cases studied. This withdrawal could be explained through the investor's pre-determined trade-off between information and investment diversification, as Stiglitz would suggest, or through a Keynesian rejection of the ergodic axiom – whereby investors could only but fail by making their investment decisions on what are assumed to be accurate predictions based on the markets' previous behaviour. The post-1980s diversification in the portfolios of institutional investors, founded upon the increase in the variation of investments in higher risk markets of last resort, induced lower incentives to obtain timely and detailed information. This was a result of the price premium associated with the higher risk of the new investment placements together with the lower marginal benefit associated with gathering individual market information when market diversification increases in general. In the absence of timely information and dominance of market expectations built upon the blueprint of their previous patterns, herding behaviour 'flourishes'. At the apex of market panic, market investors collectively respond to market news or rumours rather than to an informed or in-depth analysis of the markets' fundamentals.

Liberalisation and fall in performance of the real economy

Eatwell and Taylor identify the key channels through which liberalised financial markets can cause deterioration in overall economic perfor-mance (Eatwell and Taylor, 2002). These channels associate the opera-tion of liberalised finance with Keynes' analogy of 'beauty contest' as described in his *General Theory* (Keynes, 1936). In this 'beauty contest', the participants' objective is to guess the rest of the participants' average judgment on what average judgment regarding the prettiest participant would be. Accordingly, Eatwell and Taylor (2002) claim that, when lib-eralised, financial markets often function on the basis of 'conventions' regarding their behaviour and do not operate upon normal distributions typical of many physical phenomena. When market agents function on the basis of these perceived conventions, they may produce systemic changes in the public and private sectors as these ruling conventions get deeply embedded in their structure.

These propositions are very relevant to all three cases studied in the book. The prediction of Eatwell and Taylor on liberalised finance behav-ing in the manner of a beauty contest and ultimately harming overall economic performance was appropriate with regard to both the herding behaviour that evolved and the magnitude of the 'tails' that dominated the markets. The herding behaviour that was prevalent in all three markets is highly analogous to the domination of 'conventions' over the operation and the evolution of the markets that direct investment placements of their participants. Financial conventions were stable and optimistic for an extended period of time in all three economies. However, they all proved highly volatile and led to liquidity outflows once a displacement occurred and the 'average' opinion shifted in the same direction. This not only increased the cost of capital for all three but also induced severe financing shortages. The logic of the beauty contest further implies that fluctuations in asset prices and profitability do not follow the patterns of normal statistical distributions. Instead, in all three economies the phases of manias and panic confirmed the 'fat tails' hypothesis, where changes were concentrated on the extremes, which made volatility even higher.[2]

Liquidity lessons: summing up

The findings of the book provide strong support to the Kindlebergian proposition that sudden access to easy credit invariably results in a surge of buoyant expectations and animal spirits (Kindleberger 1978). This dynamic leads to the formation of a predicament where liquidity-demand always matches excesses in liquidity-supply and in a self-fulfilling way reaches a 'clearing level' in financial markets. This self-reinforcing procedure leads to what can be quickly described as over-lending, which results in over-borrowing. Easy and cheap access to credit stimulated expectations in all three economies so that optimism regarding future performance was fuelled and resulted in over-borrowing and over-spending. In an environment of cheap and excessive liquidity, Keynes' prediction of irrational market behaviour can thrive. Investors end up accumulating more risk than is individually efficient, shaping skewed investment incentives, where herding behaviour is always threatening capital outflows.

The contributions of Keynes and Minsky are critical in the analysis and interpretation of the three different routes to crisis. Price bubbles are often accompanied by rising debt. In the case of Brazil, this was reflected in mounting levels of public debt, in Korea through the unsustainable and short maturity structure of private debt, while in Mexico through a combination of increasing US dollar-indexed public debt and soaring consumption-induced private credit. Kindleberger's description of how price bubbles have historically been accompanied by debt frenzies has been critical throughout the book. It provides an all-encompassing historical account imperative for understanding how each crisis, despite being induced by different dynamics, had characteristics in common with the rest in the operation of 'convention'-dominated market behaviour. Kindleberger's analysis is key in the application of a theoretical framework where liquidity-induced price inflation is related to growing indebtedness in a self-reinforcing manner.[3]

The understanding of the complicated relationship and causal links between the determinants of supply-push demand-pull liquidity flows is critical when understanding and analysing the variables that drive changes in an economy's current and capital accounts.[4] Studies on this subject demonstrate how the two regions studied in this book followed different causal patterns. Ocampo and Palma (2007) use the Granger 'time-precedence' or 'predictability' test and find that in Latin America changes in the current account tend to follow developments in the capital account, whereas in East Asia the causal dynamic is the reverse.

The above finding can have very important implications, which are predominantly reflected in the use and the mode of implementation of capital controls. In the context of this research if, as in the case of East Asia, capital inflows indeed followed changes in the current account of the economy, then capital controls are not the most obvious and efficient tool to eliminate the volatility. Instead, policies devised to eliminate risks caused by or related to liquidity fluctuations could be dealt with changes in the domestic economy.

New financial products, institutions and practices

In the 1990s several of the characteristics of the evolving financial markets complicated the authorities' role and understanding of how the new products affected volatility in the markets. Similarly to the current crisis, flows of assets such as securities and, what is more relevant, mortgages contributed additional uncertainty to the markets. Some of the main variables, identified throughout this book, that this uncertainty can be attributed to are the following:

- The role, function and financing mode of Credit Rating Agencies was a key contributor to the asymmetry of risk reflection in times of euphoria versus times of panic. The fee-based model of CRAs, which attributed triple A ratings to ultimately problematic structured products, and their institutional and legal hardwiring into the operation of international financial markets, were the most important reasons for this asymmetry in risk depiction.
- Generally, regulatory and accounting standards allowed for liabilities to be removed from balance sheets. This resulted in banking institutions increasing their leverage with identical amounts of capital, which in turn contributed to greater rates of 'capital efficiency'.
- In some cases, especially in Latin American countries from the second half of the 1990s, the use of newly evolved Credit Default Swaps and products traded in increasingly 'sophisticated' insurance markets artificially enhanced the credit quality of their underlying assets. This concealed the risk involved and contributed towards higher risk and uncertainty.
- Equally, the securitisation of mortgages meant that on several occasions assets were moved off the balance sheets of banks and other financial institutions into special investment vehicles designed in a way that capital was not required to issue them. These liabilities

were, either directly or via further securitisations, often passed as liquidity inflows to emerging economies and therefore contributed to the weakening of their financial structures.[5]

The problematic dynamics of policy response

Given the fact that all economies chose to defend their currencies, their authorities failed to engage in a number of operations that could have shielded them from speculative attacks. The political authorities and Central Bank of all three economies were unable to defend the domestic currency, largely as a result of failing to construct a large pool of foreign exchange reserves,[6] and also because they did not devise alternative operations to defend their currency when under attack. None of the three Central Banks engaged in any forward interventions supplying domestic currency credit directly to short sellers or selling the long currency positions to balance the subsequent operation of buying.[7] The presence of a large pool of speculative attack investments was not tackled in advance in any of the three economies. The activity of market investors engaging in foreign exchange swaps with domestic banks was allowed to persist and no banning or heavy forward discounts were imposed upon them in order to secure the stability of the national currency and the returns of domestic consumers.

Relevance to the Great Recession

The current Great Recession and subsequent Eurozone debt crisis have brought to the forefront the discussion on necessary and effective regulation to limit markets' exposure to liquidity and foreign exchange fluctuations. The ongoing discussion examines a broad spectrum of different types and applications of controls. So far, there is a consensus among international financial institutions and organisations that 'light touch implementation' works best. The spectrum of different options considered by policy-makers and institutions includes discussion regarding the effectiveness of price-based versus quantity-based capital controls subject to the level of short-term capital flows, capital controls subject to country-specific characteristics (Magud, Reinhart and Rogoff, 2011), controls on curbing inflows versus discouraging outflows, and pro-active prudential regulations such as limiting private external borrowing in euphoric times. Capital controls are acknowledged to contribute towards the independence of domestic monetary policy, alter the composition of flows and, most importantly, decrease market pressures on real exchange rates. Specifically, some of the proposals recently discussed would require changes in the banking sector targeting the elimination of excessive risk taking and consequent capital flow volatility. These could include, among others: the banks imposing stricter reserve requirements to discourage foreign currency funding; matching maturities of foreign capital assets and liabilities; implementing taxation (such as Tobin taxes) that would ultimately reduce the volume of transactions seeking to benefit from short-term speculative gains; imposing more stringent minimum maturities on foreign currency funding. Additionally, such measures could include regulations to hedge foreign exchange risk exposure and guarantee that borrowers hedge their own exposure as a condition for loan issuance as well as developing a mechanism to attach foreign currency loans to a fixed share of the capital, thus lowering foreign exchange credit risk – or requiring banks to hold additional capital against the foreign exchange indexed loans (Financial Stability Forum, 2000).

The relevance of this book to contemporary markets and financial developments is high and clear. The current financial crisis and the policy responses to it have resurfaced two relevant topics. These are: the unsustainable levels of public and private debt in the economies of the Eurozone and the continued attractiveness of emerging economies as 'markets of last resort' for international financial flows. First, the need for further discussion regarding the spectrum of the proactive and reactive policy measures that can possibly be implemented in the developed economies' markets is apparent. Second, there is an need – which is further compounded by the crisis-induced quantitative easing policy of several developed countries – to deal with the new surges of liquidity into the emerging world. The post-2007 monetary policy in all of the G20 economies has been based on monetary easing mainly through a lowering of interest rates. This has consequently been followed by injections of liquidity. Benchmark interest rates have been reduced and are at historical lows in the US, the UK and the Eurozone countries. The post-2007 drop in US interest rates combined with policies such as the introduction of several financing and bailout projects (i.e., the US Banks Bailout Stimulus and the US Recovery Act) have generated vast volumes of liquidity. These new liquidity flows, when combined with the liberalised backgrounds of emerging economies and the financial markets' historical demand matching excess supply behaviour, lead to a surge in capital overflow in emerging markets.

Scope for further work

This book exposes two important and related avenues for further research. First, the great scope for additional discussion around policy design and implementation during both the pre-crisis liberalisation period and the post-crisis period. Second, the debate regarding the social implications of liberalisation and subsequent crisis with regard to the distribution of costs and benefits to individuals.

Following the 2007 crisis, a vast discussion on proposals and remedies to reform financial markets developed. The devastating dynamics of private and public debt accumulation in the US and the Eurozone have initiated a wide discussion about the current financial architecture and the urgent need to reform it. This discussion includes policy proposals on: reforming the exposure of the banking sector; narrowing to some degree the boundaries of the shadow banking system;[8] public debt profiles and the space of policy to alleviate problems stemming from fixed exchange rate parities – such as those in the Eurozone.

The present volatility of international capital flows in the Eurozone and emerging economies, together with the similar findings of this book, points towards a challenging but necessary area of research. How should financial architecture be shaped to ensure long-term stable capital flows in both emerging economies – which are traditionally more sensitive to large credit swings – and developed ones which have recently proved to be greatly exposed? When addressing this question, two key points need to be investigated. First, were the order and the procedure of market liberalisation performed in a manner that resulted in the dominance of short-term flows? And second, what are the structural factors discouraging the persistence of long-term capital flows? This needs to be looked at holistically and historically without omitting the specific characteristics of each economy. Research needs to focus on the characteristics of regions, or even countries, rather than the overall characteristics of finance, so that the design of instruments to shape the long-term composition of flows will suit the particularities of each market. The failure of the 'one size fits all' capital account liberalisation strategy that was applied indiscriminately to emerging economies can only but point to the need to tailor economic policy design to the economical, historical, political and social specifics of each case study.

The social cost of financial liberalisation and eventual financial collapse is a field not covered in this book, but it is of great interest, particularly at this point in time. The distribution of the benefits of financial liberalisation and the sharing of the costs of financial collapse is a question that has been largely ignored, even after the current crisis. It is important to determine who has been the winner during the upswing of the cycle and equally who has suffered the most during the bust. However, a growing discussion has been initiated in this field. This could induce some optimism because until recently academic interest in the relationship between economic inequality and economies that are over-reliant on finance was non-existent. The work of Palma (2009a, 2011b) has been increasingly influential in understanding the relative appropriations of additional wealth produced by the liberalisation of capital and the enabling role played by financialisation in this process. Palma suggests that there are two opposing forces at work with regard to increasing inequality of income: a centrifugal force and a centripetal force. The first induces an increased divergence in the shares of total national income appropriated by the top 10% and bottom 40%, while the second conforms to an increasing uniformity among the share of the income appropriated by the remaining population that forms the homogeneous middle classes. Palma discusses the evolution of what he calls the 'Robin Hood of the rich' – stealing from the rich to give to the very rich – as an evolving trend initiated by market liberalisation. The discussion regarding the increasing imbalances in income inequality in the tails of income distribution seems to be growing popular among the mainstream press. Piketty's latest book *Capital in the 21st Century* (Piketty, 2014) has been appraised by, among many others, the *Financial Times* and the *Economist* – (see Wolf, 2014, and *Economist*, 2014), while Krugman has been transformed into a staunch defendant of the French economist's portrayal of the wealth inequality trends (Krugman, 2014). The book argues that the increasing wealth appropriation of the top tier of the world population has far outstripped the unexceptional rates of economic growth. Accordingly, the concentration of this additional wealth is distributed to a very small group of rentiers and super-managers and does not significantly 'trickle-down' to the real economy. The role that the financial sector played after the 1980s in diverting resources away from the real economy and concentrating them among a few highly placed participants in financial markets has been paramount to this distributional outcome. A great share of popular – and historically conservative – media now seems to agree with this disequilibrating sentiment. Other than the extreme asymmetry in the income appropriation of the tails of the income distribution, discussion has been generated on the stagnation of the middle classes. The concerns regarding how the once forceful American middle classes are now stagnating in both absolute and relative terms[9] (Leonhardt and

Quealy, 2014) are not only challenging the once forceful notion of the American dream but also raise deeper concerns about the impact of financial markets and the wider evolution of capitalism itself.

The question of the social and consequently political impact of the disparities brought about by financialisation is still to be answered. Kaldor (1975) forcefully argues that manufacturing is more effective than every other mode of production in terms of growth, productivity and positive spillovers. It has become clear that having finance at the core of economic activity is structurally sub-optimal for the economy. What is more, there is growing evidence that having finance at the core of economic activity is structurally sub-optimal for society as whole. It is certainly not implausible to assume that the economic and social consequences of financialisation will be at the epicentre of political discourse for the foreseeable future.

Appendix

Scale of Ratings for Sovereign Debt

Moody's				S&P		FITCH-IBCA	
Rating	Number	Rating	Number	Rating	Number	Rating	Number
Aaa3SS	8.5	Ba2	5.1	AAA	8	AAA	8
Aaa3S	8.8	Ba1SS	5.3	AA+	7.33	AA+	7.33
Aaa3	8.7	Ba1S	5.5	AA	7	AA	7
Aaa2SS	8.9	Ba1	5.4	AA–	6.66	AA–	6.66
Aaa2S	9.2	Ba	5	A+	6.33	A+	6.33
Aaa2	9.1	B3SS	3.5	A	6	A	6
Aaa1SS	9.3	B3S	3.8	A–	5.66	A–	5.66
Aaa1S	9.5	B3	3.7	BBB+	5.33	BBB+	5.33
Aaa1	9.4	B2SS	3.9	BBB	5	BBB	5
Aaa	9	B2S	4.2	BBB–	4.66	BBB–	4.66
Aa3SS	7.5	B2	4.1	BB+	4.33	BB+	4.33
Aa3S	7.8	B1SS	4.3	BB	4	BB	4
Aa3	7.7	B1S	4.5	BB–	3.66	BB–	3.66
Aa2SS	7.9	B1	4.4	B+	3.33	B+	3.33
Aa2S	8.2	B	4	B	3	B	3
Aa2	8.1	Caa3SS	2.5	B–	2.66	B–	2.66
Aa1SS	8.3	Caa3S	2.8	CCC	2	CCC+	2.33
Aa1S	8.5	Caa3	2.7	CC	1	CCC	2
Aa1	8.4	Caa2SS	2.9			CCC–	1.66
Aa	8	Caa2S	3.2			CC	1.33
A3SS	6.5	Caa2	3.1			C	1
A3S	6.8	Caa1SS	3.3				
A3	6.7	Caa1S	3.5				
A2SS	6.9	Caa1	3.4				
A2S	7.2	Caa	3				
A2	7.1	Ca3SS	1.5				
A1SS	7.3	Ca3S	1.8				
A1S	7.5	Ca3	1.7				
A1	7.4	Ca2SS	1.9				
A	7	Ca2S	2.2				
Baa3SS	5.5	Ca2	2.1				
Baa3S	5.8	Ca1SS	2.3				
Baa3	5.7	Ca1S	2.5				
Baa2S	5.9	Ca1	2.4				
Baa2S	6.2	Ca	2				
Baa2	6.1	C3SS	0.5				
Baa1SS	6.3	C3S	0.8				

(*continued*)

Continued

	Moody's			S&P		FITCH-IBCA	
Rating	Number	Rating	Number	Rating	Number	Rating	Number
Baa1	6.5	C3	0.7				
Baa	6	C2S	0.9				
Ba3SS	4.5	C2	1.1				
Ba3S	4.8	C1SS	1.3				
Ba3	4.7	C1S	1.5				
Ba2SS	4.9	C1	1.4				
Ba2S	5.2	C	1				

Source: Bloomberg.

Notes

1 Introduction: Financial Crises – An Inter-Temporal, Inter-National and Endogenous Capitalist Problem

1. See Chapters 6, 15 and 17 of Keynes' General Theory (Keynes, 1936 and Bibow, 2009).
2. The manifestation of international liquidity will be proxied throughout this essay by the sum of global financial assets.
3. It needs to be acknowledged at this point that whereas a relative homogeneity on the adoption of liberalisation reforms was observed in the majority of Latin American countries, the economies of East Asia (predominantly the NICs I: South Korea, Taiwan, Singapore and Hong Kong) tailored the reforms to their industrialization needs.
4. The term was coined in 1989 by the British economist John Williamson to refer to the support of all IMF, WB and the American government to market liberalisation reforms particularly implemented in Latin American states. These prioritised ten-policy principles that can be summarised by: trade liberalisation; finance liberalisation; competitive exchange rates; tax reforms; fiscal prudence; labour market deregulation; privatization of state enterprises; no barriers to Foreign Direct Investment; infrastructure investment and protection of property rights (Williamson, 1990).
5. See: Rodrik on his early understanding of the failure of WC to engage and reinforce social and political institutions (Rodrik, 2000, and Rodrik and Velasco, 2000).

2 A Keynesian and Post-Keynesian Theoretical Brief: Selected Concepts

1. The large debate on the character of money supply among post-Keynesian economists is of high relevance. Accordingly, some economists follow strictly the Keynesian tradition of the General Theory, assuming money supply to be exogenous while others take money supply 'as given' (Dow and Earl, 1982, and Dow, 1996). The latter reach this conclusion as they reject the assumption that the economy always being in equilibrium.
2. At this point the whole debate between the rejection of the ergodic axiom versus the EMH and the classical economists' treatment of market externalities as a systemic endogenous limitation is highly relevant.
3. The third being the consumption function, influenced by expectations via any changes in the expected income flows.
4. For an extensive analysis of the supply shocks of liquidity, see Palma (2009a, 2013).
5. Grossman-Stiglitz (2010) put forward the 'Grossman-Stiglitz paradox', suggesting that in an informationally efficient market, no agent would have an

incentive to acquire information on which prices are based, as all this information would have been reflected in the assets' prices. However, as a result of costly information, agents would have an incentive to acquire it only if it had not been already fully incorporated into prices. Thus, agents could make a profit by acquiring the relevant information.

6. In the majority of cases in this book, investment decisions are not conceptualised in a purely Keynesian manner – that is, as a process of financing the creation of capital goods investment. Rather, investment decisions are often discussed as placements or savings in a variety of financial assets.

3 Post-1980 Global Liquidity Data: Exponential Flows

1. As mentioned before, this analysis has been drawn upon Palma's distinction of supply-push demand-pull factors when examining the causes behind the mobility of international capital flows (Palma, 2013).
2. Productive investment and capital formation are viewed throughout this book via adopting a Kaldorian perspective on growth. It is thus assumed that GDP growth is positively related to the growth of the manufacturing sector and that the latter is also positively related to the productivity of the manufacturing sector itself as well as the productivity of the remaining sectors of the economy (Kaldor, 1967).
3. According to JP Morgan's Emerging Market Bond Index (EMBI), the spread of emerging markets sovereign bonds over the US Treasury ones decrease from the level of over 15% in the late 1980s to 4–8% in the first half of the 1990s (IMF, 1999).
4. See the remarkable increase of Brazil's direct purchases of foreign exchange in domestic exchange markets from $171mn to $28bn for the 1990–1999 period cum the Real stabilisation Plan and the consequent sterilisation scheme implemented (Morvan, 2000).
5. Privatisations are relevant at this point as a potential source of profitable investment opportunity attracting foreign investment capital or credit.
6. See the relevance of the growing new instruments such as, among others, the Multi Option Facility (US Department of Treasury, 2009).
7. It is interesting at this point to think of the actual dimensions of such a change given the internal evolution in size and strength of institutional investors.
8. Here 'double causality' refers to the dynamic and complicated interplay of two phenomena that interacted with each other. This first is summarised by the rapid increase in size and sophistication of OECD countries' financial markets and the second by the opening of capital accounts in emerging markets.
9. This included, among others, cross-border arbitrage in yields of investments with identical risks.

4 Supply-Push: The Western-Induced Endogenous Generation and Proliferation of Liquidity

1. In possession of at least $100mn of securities.
2. 'Vanilla' mortgages usually refer to very low risk fixed interest mortgages with long maturities (commonly 30 years).

3. By shadow banking system this book refers to the investment banks and non-commercial bank and other financial institutions. According to B. Bernanke's the shadow banking system

> comprises a diverse set of institutions and markets that, collectively, carry out traditional banking functions – but do so outside, or in ways only loosely linked to, the traditional system of regulated depository institutions. Examples of important components of the shadow banking system include securitization vehicles, asset-backed commercial paper (ABCP) conduits, money market mutual funds, markets for repurchase agreements (repos), investment banks, and mortgage companies.
>
> (Bernanke, 2012)

4. The regulator of banks with national charters.
5. Fluctuations in the economies' terms of trade are considered critical here mainly through their effect on higher credit demand needed to finance more costly import consumption.
6. See the contribution of C. Schwab in the development of the industry (Subramani and Walden, 2001).
7. By Western generation of liquidity, mostly Western economies are considered. However, the generation of liquidity by the Chinese economy is definitely not considered negligible.

5   Demand-Pull: The Internally Induced Attractiveness of Emerging Markets

1. This perceived improvement in emerging economies' fundamentals is strongly related to the introduction of Brady bonds in the late 1980s. Brady bonds were Dollar-denominated bond instruments that were issued by the majority of Latin American countries. This allowed commercial banks to exchange and restructure their claims on developing economies that had defaulted on their debt and, consequently, remove a large stock of debt off the banks' balance sheets. As a result, this process heavily relieved a great share of US commercial banks. The function and historic evolution of Brady bonds is discussed again in this chapter.
2. The formal definition of Brady bonds according to the US Federal Reserve Trade and Capital Markets Activities Manual is the following: Brady bonds refer to restructured bank loans that comprised the most liquid market for below investment-grade debt and were at the time one of the largest debt markets of any kind. 'The Brady plan, named after then U.S. Treasury Secretary Nicholas Brady, was announced in 1989 to restructure much of the debt of developing countries that was not being fully serviced due to economic constraints. The plan provided debt relief to troubled countries and, in theory, opened access to further international financing. It also provided the legal framework to securitise and restructure the existing bank debt of developing countries into bearer bonds. Linking collateral to some bonds gave banks the incentive to cooperate with the debt reduction plan' (US Federal Reserve). What, however, this definition fails to capture is how the Brady Plan

effectively served in reducing the debt exposure and likely the failure of a vast number of American commercial banks. Prior to the Brady agreement several major US commercial banks' exposure to 'these troubled loans represented two to three times the banks' net worth' (Drainville, 2009). Thus, the Brady Plan through saving a great share of US banks resulted in liquidity spillovers received again by emerging markets.

3. Chile was a great exception here as it rapidly engaged into liberalisation immediately after the Pinochet coup of 1973.

4. It is interesting to note how other parts of the developing world such as Eastern European, Middle East and Sub-Saharan African countries' stock markets collectively shrunk by an average of 2.3% (IMF, 1997, p. 32).

5. Horizontal and vertical supply in manufacturing refers here to the structure of the manufacturing supply chain. Specifically, with regard to horizontal manufacturing supply or integration, manufacturing in the Latin American region did not develop in a way so as to specialise in the production of a wide range of alike units (with the exception of Mexico). Even more so, the manufacturing industry of the region did not operate in a vertical integration manner, whereby it would own the entire supply chain of its production.

6. It should be noted here that these three variables should also be understood under the following terms. The absence of domestic public investment should also be seen through the general framework of the sovereigns' fiscal policies trying to balance public finances in an attempt to boost the 'fundamentals' of the economies in the face of additional capital inflows. The over-valued currencies of the regions shaped the economies to be uncompetitive, in a large part as a result of financial inflows and consequently shifting demand towards international markets. Lastly, the high domestic interest rates were part of the economies' sound monetary policy, which again signalled strong and improving 'fundamentals' – with the special case of Brazil, where part of this 'stability signalling' included the economy's sterilisation plan and immense interest rate burden on public finances that this entailed.

6   Country Analysis

1. According to the IMF definition Real interest rate is the lending interest rate investors expect to receive adjusted for inflation as measured by the GDP deflator. The terms and conditions attached to lending rates differ by country, however, limiting their comparability.

2. The US dollar LIBOR interest rate is the

> average interbank interest rate at which a large number of banks on the London money market are prepared to lend one another unsecured funds indexed in US dollars. It is available in 7 maturities, from overnight to 12 months ... and serves as a base rate for all sorts of other products such as savings accounts, mortgages and loans.

> (Global Rates)

3. The use of immediate interest rate is applied here as a term to describe 'official discount rates and call-money rates' (Financial market trends definitions, OECD). Immediate interest rates are usually, as in this case, more volatile and reveal quicker responses to market developments.

4. By 'markets of last resort' the following dynamic should be understood: very high levels of liquidity were generated in Western financial markets; these markets were unable to absorb all of this liquidity; the surplus liquidity, combined with the increasing attractiveness of emerging market economies after the introduction of the Brady Bonds, was directed to emerging markets after a decade of capital inflow stagnation in the 1980s. The direction of excess liquidity in the emerging economies as 'markets of last resort' is also related to Stiglitz's information asymmetry theory. Accordingly, investors would place their savings in environments where information availability and transparency are higher – hence, in the 1990s, after exhausting the opportunities in their familiar domestic markets, their second best option was to direct their funds to emerging economies (for the original model on information asymmetry, see Stiglitz and Weiss, 1981).
5. See Calvo and Mendoza (1995) analysis on the overvalued Mexican Peso.
6. At this point it is crucial to mention the complex evolution of the three types of debt in the Mexican economy: public debt, private publically guaranteed debt and private not publically guaranteed debt. After the 1982 crisis, and with the IMF intervention to protect American banks and consequently prevent a collapse in the banking sector, the government gave an ex-post public guarantee on private non-publically guaranteed bonds. This resulted in the bloating of public debt not only as a result of the US interest hike but also because of the government acquisition of this publically guaranteed private debt (for a more detailed analysis, see Dornbusch and Werner, 1994, and Barkbu, Eichengreen and Mody, 2011).
7. Mexico's exchange rate policy was highly experimental during this period. It changed from a fixed to crawling peg in 1989 and then to an adjusted band in 1991. The work of Lustig (1995) gives a great insight into these developments.
8. The growing exposure of Mexican banks to foreign debt needs to be investigated together with the low-quality credit lines under which the banks were operating domestically. Specifically, Mexican banks increased their foreign exposure by borrowing cheaply from abroad and, subsequently, increasing their exposure to low-performing debt through supplying these funds domestically to under-performing borrowers.
9. At this point it is interesting to note how the Mexican Central Bank only enforced the band when the Peso was at risk of devaluation.
10. At this point it would be interesting to mention that the deregulation of FDI was not absolute. By 1993 investment in electricity, telecommunications and petroleum were still moderately regulated – making access simpler to Mexican investors, while for their international conglomerate counterparts legal loopholes were allowed, resulting in a remarkable manipulation of the law (Griffith-Jones, 1997).
11. The ratings of the economy were only downgraded after the December 1994 crisis.
12. This agreement took place at the nadir of the large decrease in the stock of foreign reserves that had fallen to US$10bn. There is a great body of literature criticising the delay of the authorities and emphasises the existence of several chances available prior to the given exogenous shocks of the same year – when the level of reserves was much higher and the authorities' ability to defend the currency was much stronger (see: Calvo and Reinhart, 1995; Calvo and Mendoza, 1996, and Ramiderez, 1995).

13. That is, the resignation of the Secretary of the Interior in June of the same year.
14. There are several suggestions with regard to how business participants benefited from the information themselves and immediately purchased US dollars. For a detailed overview, see Griffith-Jones, 1997.
15. NAFTA's initial objectives, as outlined in Article 102 of the Agreement, were to:

> Eliminate barriers to trade in, and facilitate the cross-border movement of, goods and services between the territories of the Parties; promote conditions of fair competition in the free trade area; increase substantially investment opportunities in the territories of the Parties; provide adequate and effective protection and enforcement of intellectual property rights in each Party's territory; create effective procedures for the implementation and application of this Agreement, for its joint administration and for the resolution of disputes; and establish a framework for further trilateral, regional and multilateral cooperation to enhance and expand the benefits of this Agreement.
>
> (Organisation of American States)

16. The transportation equipment industry was initially protected by the Mexican government as the industry's investment decisions were made on the basis of state-led industrial programs guaranteeing protection in exchange for achieving trade balance-related performance targets (Moreno and Ros, 2009).
17. At this point the proposition of Sachs et al. regarding the underreporting of the economy's deficit could be highly relevant. Their research suggests a current account deficit of 7.6% (instead of 6.3%) for 1994 as a result of the real exchange rate appreciation (20–25%) in the beginning of 1994 (Sachs, Tornell and Velsaco, 1995).
18. A member's quota in the IMF 'determines the amount of its subscription, its voting weight, its access to IMF financing, and its share in the allocation of SDRs' (IMF, 1995c).
19. The IMF only tried to factor in this problem and improve data standards amongst members *after* the Mexican crisis. The Special Data Dissemination Standard and the General Data Dissemination Standard in 1995 were initiated for this reason (IMF, 2007).

7 Brazil: The Anti-Mexican Public Debt Failure

1. The 1988 debt agreements with foreign creditor banks provided $5.2 billion in new loans and restructured $62 billion worth of medium- and long-term bank debt at lower interest rates (*New York Times*, 1988).
2. The mounting public debt, other than the external obligations of Brazil, could be partly attributed to the 1988 Constitution changes, which reduced the revenue of Federal Government and directed it to states and municipalities without equally reducing the government's financial obligations to the latter (Cardoso and Helwege, 2001).
3. Under the Presidency of Itamar Franco, Cardoso was the Minister of Finance, designer and initiator of the Real Plan.

4. Manufacturing exports were the first to be exempted from taxation – even before the currency appreciation became evident.
5. This was allowed through Resolution 63, which allowed banks to hold foreign resources and transfer them to clients in Brazil (BNDES). Resolution 63 was passed in 1978 but rapidly grew in influence in the 1990s.
6. See the following paragraphs for an analytical description of both programmes.
7. Programa de Incentivo à Redução do Setor Público Estadual na Atividade Bancária, which was similar to PROER but for the state-owned banking system.
8. 'The "good bank" is constituted from the good assets and deposits of the troubled bank. The acquiring bank is free to select the assets from the troubled bank (due diligence), but it is compelled to assume all troubled bank deposits. The "bad bank" is made up of the remaining troubled bank assets (i.e., the impaired assets) and liabilities' (BIS, 1999, p. 112).
9. The number of domestic capital relying banks decreased from 144 to 108, the number of public banks from 30 to 24 and state banks' share of overall deposits shrunk from 19.35% in 1996 to 6.5% in 1998 (Baer, 2008).
10. In addition, the Brazilian economy was highly exposed to exchange rate fluctuations and their relation to potential debt escalations through the issue of Dollar indexed debt to mainly banking institutions (using it to hedge their exposure when offering forward cover to their customers, see IMF, 1995a).
11. For a comprehensive analysis of the impact of state-government finances on overall public debt, see Palma, 2002b.
12. Inflation revenue is used to describe the erosion of deposits' value (effectively the negative interest paid by domestic deposits minus the reserve requirements).
13. See how commercial banks' credit to the private sector increased from R$1bn in 1994 to R$500bn in 1998 – 60% of Brazil's GDP at the time (Ocampo, Kregel and Griffith-Jones, 2007).
14. Middle markets' borrowers refer to companies with revenues between US$100mn and US$3bn per year (US Census Bureau).
15. At this point it needs to be emphasised that though significant, the size of Brazil's consumer credit boom relative to Mexico or the rest of Latin American countries was small.
16. It is interesting to note how under such conditions portfolio investment can be easily liquidated and transferred in different markets.
17. Ponzi finance refers to what Minsky described as a speculative financing unit for which the interest portion of its attached cash payment commitments exceeds its net income cash receipts. Such a unit has to increase its debt in order to meet commitments on outstanding instruments. See Chapter 2 of the book for more information.
18. High interest rates should be seen as way to both increase investors motivations to buy Brazilian bonds and reflect the authorities' need to establish some kind of credibility in international markets.
19. See how in 1992, before the Real Plan was implemented, financial flows were still entering the economy as the interest rate differential between the Brazilian currency and the US dollar exceeded the depreciation expectations

of the time. At the time, however, the authorities used some capital controls to differentiate between productive investment inflows and short-term speculative ones (Cardoso and Helwege, 2001).

20. At this point it would be interesting to incorporate the relevant discussion on real interest rates being even higher than the published official rates, given the fall of the inflation rate. The International Financial Statistics of the IMF only started calculating Brazil's real interest rates in 1997 and the corresponding value for the year was 65.5%, while 78.7% in 1998 (IMF, 1998).

21. Net public debt refers to the total national debt minus the foreign exchange reserves and other public sector assets.

22. The interest portion of Brazil's cash payment commitments was mostly used to finance the government's various macroeconomic policy schemes.

23. See how in September 1998 the interest rate reached the level of 50% in annualised real terms (Cysne, 2005).

8   South Korea: The Private Debt Story

1. It should be noted here that the Korean case was chiefly different as the majority of dominant corporations were Korean.

2. For the early 1970s' Korean crisis and the specific developments in the state's post-crisis abandonment of the late 1960s' pilot liberalisation policies (mainly via the suspension of all 'curb market loan' servicing), see Chang (1993) and Harris (1987).

3. In 1961 a 'temporary law' was introduced whereby the shareholders' voting rights were limited in banks in which the government did not have the majority stake. To complement that the 1981 Banking Act amendments replaced the 'temporary law' establishing an 8% ceiling to the non-state individual banking ownership (Park, 1996).

4. At the time, there was so much institutional resentment to capital flight that even the death sentence was possible for individuals engaging into capital flight (Chang, 2005).

5. At this point it is interesting to incorporate Chang's (2005) analysis on the role of deregulation and the demise of industrial policy in the shaping of Korea's financial crisis (through channels such as duplicative investments and enhanced cronyism).

6. Memory-chips were one of Korea's main exports. 'The D-Ram price per megabyte fell from US$26 (1995) to US$10 (1996), US$4 (1997), and less than US$1 (1998)' (Palma, 2013, p. 21).

7. Palma (2013) suggests that the collapse of profitability in microelectronics was significantly explained by the new bulk of Taiwanese investment coming into fruition (in 1995) at the wrong time – when microelectronics prices were already declining as a result of the quickly growing supply.

8. Overall, the work of Palma (2013, 2003a, 1998) is particularly important when studying the reasons behind the fall in profitability of Korean technology-intense enterprises.

9. The equivalent foreign debt growth rates in the period from 1976 to 1983, which encompassed the build-up to the crisis and actual crisis (see 1980

negative growth rate of the economy, Chang 1993), were almost half (17.8%) (BIS, 1999. See also Dollar, 1992).
10. Short-term debts are defined as those maturing in less than a year.
11. This was mainly the result of the authorities considering short-term debt to be financing working capital and long-term debt to finance overall invest-ment. However, the authorities gradually mixed up the two and the approval procedure of the investment that targeted long-term debt became more complicated.

9 Deregulation and Volatility: Where the Three Economies Meet

1. Bloomberg and Thomson Reuters are among the largest financial informa-tion dissemination firms.
2. Credit Rating Agencies (CRAs) are considered to

> provide an independent evaluation and assessment of the ability of issu-ers to meet their debt obligations. In this way, CRAs provide 'information services' that reduce information costs, increase the pool of potential borrowers, and promote liquid markets. This implies that market prices are influenced by rating actions, and that CRA opinions can be important from a financial stability perspective.
>
> (IMF, 2010)

3. In Korea, the post-1997 jump in stock market capitalisation observed in Figure 9.3 should be understood through the IMF conditionality to eliminate any remaining regulations in the domestic financial markets after the crisis.
4. See the 'strong version' of EMH as described by Fama (1970 and 1991) ana-lysed in Chapter 2.
5. The work of Persaud (2000) on the herding and volatility dynamics of pub-lic versus private bond investment in emerging economies in the 1990s is highly relevant in this respect.
6. On this point it is interesting to see how equity investment overshadowed FDI for both Mexico and Brazil (Ocampo, Kregel and Griffith-Jones, 2007).
7. Mexican and Brazilian private bonds grew by a factor of 4.7 and 2.6, respec-tively, between 1992 and 1993 as previously seen in Figures 6.3 and 7.6 (WB data).
8. Short-term international debt is defined here as cross-border debt with matu-rity of one year or less. The institutional definition used in this book is that of the Bank for International Settlements (BIS, see BIS *Guidelines for report-ing the BIS international banking statistics*). The World Bank (WB) provides a definition very similar to the BIS, which only diverges in one parameter. According to the WB (see WB *Global Development Finance)* short-term debt comprises only cross-border liabilities with original maturities of one year or less. BIS disregards the original maturity of debt. Instead it proposes the concept of 'remaining maturity' implying all international debt falling due within a year's time.
9. Monthly and quarterly data would be even more revealing as to their equiva-lent volatilities here.

10. See the previous detailed analysis on Korea.
11. See at this point how the only two Asian Tiger economies that managed to avoid a financial crisis were the financially independent Hong Kong and Singapore.
12. Differences throughout the three economies in real money growth (and especially *vis-a-vis* the case of Brazil) can be partly explained through Brazil's inflow sterilisation policy.
13. The case of South East Asian economies is different with regard to this point. Private investment, through the channels of external finance and exogenous liquidity injections, was not crowded out in the region but on the contrary increased to considerably high levels. The financing of private investment was, however, opaque and proved highly problematic. In South East Asia the route to financial collapse was one of debt deflation where the domestic private sector sold stocks and capital to repay debt and domestic currency to service its foreign loans (IMF, 1995a).
14. Liquidity preference is considered here in terms of the way in which investors decided to hold particular forms of monetary wealth.
15. Other than in Latin American economies, this was also the case for South Korea where by 1989 after the first wave of market liberalisation, the average price over earning ratios of debt finance had risen to 14, thereby reducing the cost of equity capital to 7.1% (Singh, 1997).
16. As share of the countries' GDP.
17. The imbalances are considered modest here mostly in relative terms – when compared to their Latin American counterparts.
18. Shortages in foreign exchange reserves and excessive levels of public debt are understood at this point as potential deeper imbalances.
19. See how this compared to an equivalent 37% for the 1990–1993 period.
20. The high financial multiplier of the Asian region is associated with a high covariance of high trade and investment flows (Stiglitz and Uy, 1996).
21. Financial conglomerates are closely intertwined with industrial conglomerates.
22. The work of A. Diaz gives a great insight to this (Diaz, 1984)
23. See how devaluation generally acts like an increasing function of debt and contributes towards resource depletion.
24. The discussion and estimates of Mexico's domestic consumption are highly relevant here. Within the first part of the 1990s just the imports of consumption goods in Mexico were half the value of the economy's total exports – illustrating that the contribution of private consumption to the country's GDP growth was much greater than the equivalent one of exports. Specifically, it has been estimated that in the first years of financial reforms Mexico doubled its consumer imports, whereas six years after the implementation of the reforms the initial levels of consumer imports had grown by a factor of 11 (see Calvo and Mendoza, 1995). Figure 9.13 shows not only the enormous difference between Mexico and Korea's consumption as a share of GDP but also the largely increasing consumption pattern adopted by the former in the period between the liberalisation of its markets and its financial crisis.
25. See the higher interest spreads of the region *vis-à-vis* the OECD countries and the East Asian region.

26. At this point the significant role played by speculative investment in real estate finance should be considered.

10 An Endogenous Conclusion

1. The delusion of investors' conviction that they will be the first to leave the markets and secure their funds is crucial when understanding the mania dynamic.
2. For a clear and succinct analysis of the 'fat tails' hypothesis and its application to financial markets, see Ormerod (2001).
3. At this point it needs to be acknowledged that Kindleberger could be considered the key scholar when explaining this relationship, as Keynes did not make a direct connection but instead strongly implied a link between asset price increases and price bubble formations.
4. See discussion in Palma (2013) on distinction and determinants of 'endogenous pull' where the current account is found to be pulling the capital account, while in an 'exogenous push' the opposite holds.
5. This practice was further exacerbated and was performed in larger magnitude in the 2000s when mortgages – among other lines of credit – were sliced into different credit quality instruments and then were each collaterised with assets or guarantees from Collaterised Debt Obligations with triple A ratings.
6. See how even in the case of Brazil, which had a large pool of foreign reserves as a result of its sterilisation policy, US dollar reserves were rapidly exhausted.
7. A traditional solution to the maturity mismatch that long selling would cause is the transaction of foreign exchange swaps entailing the delivery of US dollars for domestic currency much quicker than the delivery of domestic currency for Dollars (IMF, 1997).
8. Discussion on this is mostly held at the European level.
9. It is interesting to note how the relative performance of the middle classes in other countries such as Canada or the Netherlands has been surprisingly stronger (Leonhardt and Quealy, 2014).

References

Acemoglu, D. and F. Zilibotti (1997). "Was Prometheus Unbound by Chance? Risk, Diversification, and Growth", *Journal of Political Economy*, Vol. 105, pp. 709–751.

Amsden, A. H. (1992). *Asia's Next Giant: South Korea and Late Industrialization*, Oxford, UK: Oxford University Press.

Amsden, A. H. and Y-D. Euh (1990). "Republic of Korea's Financial Reform: What are the Lessons?", *UNCTAD Discussion Paper*, No. 30, April.

Arestis, P. and P. Demetriades (1997). "Financial Development and Economic Growth: Assessing the Evidence", *The Economic Journal*, Vol.107, No.442, pp. 783–799.

Baer, W. (2008): *Brazilian Economy: Growth and Development*, Boulder, CO: Lynne Rienner Publishers.

BAI (Board of Audit and Inspection). (1998). *The Analysis and Evaluation of the 1997 Foreign Exchange Crisis*, Seoul, Board of Audit and Inspection, Government of Korea.

Baig, T. and I. Goldfajn (2000). "The Russian Default and the Contagion to Brazil", LACEA (Latin American and Caribbean Economic Association). Bogota, [online]. Available at: http://www.lacea.org/meeting2000/TaimurBaig. PDF [Accessed on August 2013].

Balassa, B. (1989). "The Effects of Interest Rates on Savings in Developing Countries,"Working Paper, World Bank, Washington D.C.

Balassa, B., Gerardo, M., Kuczynski P. P. and M. H. Simonsen (1986). *Toward Renewed Economic Growth in Latin America*, Washington DC, Institute for International Economics.

Baldacci, E., De Mello, L., andInchauste, G. (2002). "Financial Crises, Poverty, and Income Distribution", International Monetary Fund, Working Paper, No. 2002–2004.

Basel Committee on Banking Supervision, (1997). *Core Principles for Effective Banking Supervision*, Basle: Bank for International Settlements, April.

Barkbu, B., Eichengreen, B. and Mody, A. (2011). "International Financial Crises and the Multilateral Response: What the Historical Record Shows", *NBER Working Paper*, No 17361.

BCB (Brazilian Central Bank). (1987). *Resolution 1289* [online]. Available at: http://www.bcb.gov.br/?WORKINGPAPERS [Accessed October 2011].

BCB (Brazilian Central Bank). (1995). *PROER – Program of Incentives to the Restructuring and Strengthening of the National Financial System* [online]. Available at: http://www.bcb.gov.br/?PROEREN [Accessed February 2013].

BCB (Brazilian Central Bank). (2012a). "SériesTemporais" [online]. Available at: http://www.bcb.gov.br [Accessed on various dates between 2012–2014].

BCB (Brazilian Central Bank). (2012b). "BoletimMensal" [online]. Available at: http://www.bcb.gov.br/?boletim [Accessed on various dates between 2012–2014].

Beck, T., Lundberg, M. and G. Majnoni (2006). "Financial Intermediary Development and Growth Volatility: Do Intermediaries Dampen or Magnify Shocks?", *Journal of International Money and Finance*, Vol.25, No. 7, pp. 1146–1167.

Bernanke, B. (2012). "Some Reflections on the Crisis and the Policy Response", Paper Presented at the Russell Sage Foundation and The Century Foundation Conference on "Rethinking Finance," New York, April [online]. Available at: http://www.federalreserve.gov/newsevents/speech/bernanke20120413a.htm [Accessed on February 2014].

Bibow, J. (2009). *Keynes on Monetary Policy, Finance and Uncertainty: Liquidity Preference Theory and the Global Financial Crisis*, London, Routledge.

BIS (Bank of International Settlements) Statistics. Available at: https://www.bis.org/statistics/index.htm

BIS (Bank for International Settlements). "Guidelines for Reporting the BIS International Banking Statistics" [online]. Available at: http://www.bis.org/statistics/bankstatsguide.htm [Accessed May 2012].

BIS (Bank for International Settlements), (1995). *Annual Report*, Basel, Switzerland.

BIS (Bank for International Settlements), (1997). "Group of Ten – Financial Stability in Emerging Market Economies", [online]. Available at: http://www.bis.org/publ/gten02.htm [Accessed June 2013].

BIS (Bank for International Settlements), (1999a). "A Review of Financial Market Events in Autumn 1998", Committee on the Global Financial System, Bank for International Settlements, Basel, Switzerland.

BIS (Bank for International Settlements), (1999b). "Bank Restructuring in Practice", BIS Policy Papers, No.6, Bank for International Settlements, Basel, Switzerland, August.

BIS (Bank for International Settlements). (2013). "Basel Committee on Banking Supervision", [online]. Available at: http://www.bis.org/bcbs/history.pdf [Accessed August 2013].

BNDES (Brazilian Development Bank). "Data on Inflationary Bank Reserves", [online]. Available at: http://www.bndes.gov.br/SiteBNDES/bndes/bndes_pt/Institucional/Publicacoes/Consulta_Expressa/ [Accessed on various dates between 2012–2014].

BNDES (Brazilian Development Bank), (2002). "Privatisation in Brazil" [online]. Available at: http://www.bndes.gov.br/SiteBNDES/export/sites/default/bndes_en/Galerias/Download/studies/priv_brazil.pdf [Accessed on January 2014].

BOM (Bank of Mexico). (1992). *The Mexican Economy*, Mexico City, Bank of Mexico.

BOM (Bank of Mexico). (1995). *InformeAnual 1994*, Mexico City, Bank of Mexico.

BOM (Bank of Mexico). Various years, *Public Finance Statements*, Mexico City, Bank of Mexico.

Calvo, G. and M. Goldstein (1995). "*Crisis Prevention and Crisis Management after Mexico*", Paper Presented at the September Conference on Private Capital Flows after the Mexican Crisis, Vienna, Institute for International Economics.

Calvo, G. and E. G. Mendoza (1995). "*Reflections on Mexico's Balance of Payments Crisis*", Mimeo, University of Maryland, October.

Calvo, G.A. and E. G. Mendoza (1996). "Mexico's Balance-of-Payments Crisis: A chronicle of a Death Foretold", *Journal of International Economics*, Vol. 41, pp. 235–164.

Calvo, G. A. and E. G. Mendoza (2000). "Capital-Markets Crisis and Economic Collapse in Emerging Markets: An Informational-Frictions Approach", *American Economic Review*, Vol.90, No.2, pp. 59–64.

Calvo, G. A. and C. Reinhart (1995). "Capital Inflows to Latin America: Is there Evidence of Contagion Effects?", Mimeo, World Bank and International Monetary Fund.

Calvo, G. A., Leiderman, L. and C. M. Reinhart (1996). "Inflows of Capital to Developing Countries in the 1990s", *The Journal of Economic Perspectives*, Vol. 10, No. 2., pp. 123–139.

Cantor, R. and F. Packer (1995). "Sovereign Credit Ratings", *Current Issues in Economics and Finance*, Federal Reserve Bank of New York, Vol.1, No.3, June, pp. 37–53.

Cardoso, E. and A. Helwege (2001). "The 1990s Crisis in Emerging Markets: The Case of Brazil", pp. 161–181 in D. Dasgupta, M. Uzan and D. Wilsom (Eds) *Capital Flows Without Crisis? Reconciling Capital Mobility and Economic Stability*, New York, Routledge.

Chang, H. J. (1993). "The Political Economy of Industrial Policy in Korea", *Cambridge Journal of Economics*, Vol.17, No.2, pp. 131–157.

Chang, H-J. (1994). *The Political Economy of Industrial Policy*, London and Basingstoke, MacMillan.

Chang, H-J. (1998a). "Korea: The Misunderstood Crisis", *World Development*, Vol.26, No.8., pp. 1555–1561.

Chang, H.-J. (2005). *The East Asian Developmental Experience*, London, Zed Press.

Chang, H-J., J. G. Palma, and H. Whittaker (2001). *Financial Liberalisation and the AsianCrisis*, London, Palgrave.

Chang, H.-J., Park, H.-J. and C. G. Yoo (1998b). "Interpreting the Korean Crisis: Financial Liberalisation, Industrial Policy and Corporate Governance", *Cambridge Journal of Economics*, Vol.22, pp. 735–746.

Chang, R., and Velasco, A. (1998). "The Asian liquidity Crisis", *NBER Working Paper*, No 6796.

Chang, S.-J. (2003). *Financial Crisis and Transformation of Korean Business Groups: The Rise and Fall of Chaebols*, Cambridge, Cambridge University Press.

Chenery, H. B., Robinson, S. and M. Syrquin (1986). *Industrialization and Growth*, Washington DC, World Bank.

Claessens, S., Djankov, S. and L. H. Lang (2000). "The Separation of Ownership and Control in East Asian Corporations", *Journal of Financial Economics*, Vol. 58, No.1, pp. 81–112.

Cosh, A., Hughes, A. and A. Singh (1989). "Openness, Finanncial Innovation, Changing Patterns of Ownership and the Structure of Financial Markets", Discussion Paper, Helsinki, World Institute for Development Economics Research.

Cosh, A., Hughes, A., Lee, K. and A. Singh (1989). "Institutional Investment, Mergers and the Market for Corporate Control", *International Journal of Industrial Organisation*, March.

Crotty, J. (1994). "Are Keynesian Uncertainty and Macrotheory Incompatible? Conventional Decision Making, Institutional Structures and Conditional Stability in Keynesian Macromodels", in Dymski and Pollin (Eds) *New Perspectives in Monetary Macroeconomics: Explorations in the Tradition of Hyman Minsky*, Ann Arbor, University of Michigan Press, pp. 105–142.

Crotty, J. (2009). "Structural Causes of the Global Financial Crisis: A Critical Assessment of the 'New Financial Architecture'," *Cambridge Journal of Economics*, Vol.33, No. 4, pp. 563–580.

Cuevas, A., Messmacher, M., and Werner, A. (2002). Changes in the Patterns of External Financing in Mexico since the Approval of NAFTA. *Documento de trabajo del Banco Central de México (Ciudad de México)*.

Cysne, R. P. (2005). *An Overview of some Historical Brazilian Macroeconomic Series and Some Open Questions*, FundaçãoGetulio Vargas, Rio De Janeiro.

Dadush, U., Dasgupta, D. and D. Ratha (2000). "The Role of Short-Term Debt in Recent Crises", *Finance and Development Quarterly Magazine*, IMF, Vol. 37, No. 4, December.

Davidson, P. (2007). *John Maynard Keynes*, New York, Palgrave MacMillan.

Datastream (2014). *Thomson Reuters DataStream* [Online]. Available at: Subscription Service [Accessed on various dates between 2011–2013].

Deb, P., Manning, M., Murphy, G. Penalver, A. and A. Toth (2011). "Whither the Credit Ratings Industry?", *Financial Stability Paper* No. 9, Bank of England. London.

Díaz, A. (1984). "Latin American Debt: I Don't Think we are in Kansas Anymore", *Brookings Papers on Economic Activity*.

Dollar, D. (1992). "Outward-Oriented Developing Economies Really Do Grow more Rapidly: Evidence from 95 LDCs, 1976–1985", *Economic Development and Cultural Change*, pp. 523–544.

Dornbusch, R. and I. M. Werner (1994). "Mexico: Stabilisation, Reform and No Growth", *Brookings Papers on Economic Activity*, Washington DC, The Brookings Institute.

Dow, S. C. and P. E. Earl, (1982). *Money Matters,,* New York, Robertson Press.

Dow, S. C. (1996). "Horizontalism: A Critique", *Cambridge Journal of Economics*, Vol. 20, No.4, pp. 497–508.

Drainville, B. (2009). "Emerging Market Debt – A Primer", Pyramis Global Advisors Investments Company. [online]. Available at: http://www.pyramis.com/fileadmin/templates/pyramis_public/downloads/us/Emerging_Mkt_Debt_A_Primer_4.pdf [Accessed March2014].

Eatwell, J. and L. Taylor (2002). *International Capital Markets: Systems in Transition*, New York, Oxford University Press.

ECLAC (Economic Commission for Latin America and the Caribbean). (1994). *Polices to Improve Linkages with the Global Economy*, Santiago, United Nations, Cepal.

ECLAC (Economic Commission for Latin America and the Caribbean). (2002). *Developing Countries' Anti-Cyclical Policies in a Globalized World*, Santiago, CEPAL.

Economist (4.07.2007). "Ten Years on: How Asia Shrugged off its Economic Crisis",[online]. Available at: http://www.economist.com/node/9432495 [Accessed March2012].

Economist (4.01.2014)."All Men are Created Equal; Free Exchange".

Eichengreen, B. (1991). "Trends and Cycles in Foreign Lending", in H. Siebert (Ed) *Capital Flows in the World Economy*, Mohr, Tdbingen.

Eichengreen, B. (1999). *Toward a New International Financial Architecture: A Practical Post–Asia Agenda*, Washington, DC, Institute for International Economies (IIE).

Eichengreen, G. (2004). *Capital Flows and Crises*, Cambridge, MA, MIT Press.

Eichengreen, B. and R. Hausmann (1999). "Exchange Rates and Financial Fragility", NBER Working Paper, No. 7418.

Eisner, R. (1997). "Marginal Efficiency of Capital and Investment", pp. 185–197, in G. Harcourt and P. Riach (Eds) *A Second Edition of the General Theory*, Vol. 1, London, Routledge.

Fama, E. (1970). "Efficient Capital Markets: A Review of Theory and Empirical Work", *The Journal of Finance*, Vol. 25, No.2, pp. 383–417.

Fama, E. (1985). "What's Different About Banks?", *Journal of Monetary Economics*, Vol. 15, January.

Fama, E. (1991). "Efficient Capital Markets: II", *Journal of Finance*, Vol. 46, No.5, pp. 1575–1617.

FDIC (Federal Deposit Insurance Corporation). Statistics [online]. Available at: http://www2.fdic.gov/SDI/SOB/ [Accessed on March 2013].

Ferrari-Filho, F., (2001). "The Legacy of the Real Plan: AStabilization without Economic Growth", *University of Oxford's Centre for Brazilian Studies*, Oxford, UK.

Financial Stability Forum (2000). *Report of the Working Group on Capital Flows*, Financial Stability Board, April.

Flood, R. and N. Marion (1998). "Self-Fulfilling Risk Predictions: An Application to Speculative Attacks", IMF Working Paper, WP98/124, IMF, Research Department, IMF, August.

Fonseca, P. C. D. (1998a). "Brazilian Regional Development Bank: A regional Pro-development Institution", *Business and Economic History*, Vol.27, No. 2., pp. 112–131.

Fonseca (Da), M. A. R. (1998b): "Brazil's Real Plan", *Journal of Latin American Studies*, Vol. 30, No.3, pp. 619–639.

Friedman, M. (1998). "Markets to the Rescue", *Wall Street Journal*, 12 October.

Friedman, M. and K. Kuttner (1996). "A Price Target for US Monetary Policy? Lessons from the Experience with Money Growth Targets", *Brookings Papers on Economic Activity*, Vol. 1, pp. 77–125.

Galbraith, J. K. (1998). "The Legacy of the HCI: An Empirical Analysis of Korean Industrial Policy", *Journal of Economic Development*, Vol. 23, No. 1, pp. 1–20.

Global Rates (2014). "US LIBOR Interest Rate". [online]. Available at: http://global-rates.com/interest-rates/libor/american-dollar/american-dollar.aspx [Accessed on May 2014].

Goldfajn, I., and R. O. Valdés (1997). "Capital Flows and the Twin Crises: The Role of Liquidity," IMF Working Paper 97/87, IMF, Washington D.C.

Griffin, K. (1970). "Foreign Capital, Domestic Savings and Economic Development", *Bulletin of the Oxford University Institute of Economics & Statistics*, Vol. 32, No.2, pp. 99–112.

Griffith-Jones, S. (1994). "European Private Flows to Latin America", in R. French-Davis and S. Griffith-Jones (Eds) *Coping with Capital Surges: The Return of Finance to Latin America*, Boulder, LynneRienner.

Griffith-Jones, S. (1997). "Causes and Lessons of the Mexican Peso Crisis", Working Paper No 132, World Institute for Development Economics Research, The United Nations University, WIDER.

Griffith-Jones, S. and A. Bhattacharya (2001). *Developing Countries and the Global Financial System*, London, The Commonwealth Secretariat, Marlborough House.

Gross, B. (2008). "Pyramids Crumbling", *PIMCO Investment Outlook*, January, [online]. Available at: www.pimco.com [Accessed on May 2013].

Grossman, S. J. and J. E. Stiglitz (1980). "On the Impossibility of Informationally Efficient Markets", *The American Economic Review*, Vol.70, No.3, pp. 393–408.

Gurria, A. (1995). "Capital Flows: The Mexican Case", in R. French-Davis and S. Griffith-Jones (Eds) *Coping with Capital Surges: The Return ofFinance to Latin America*, Boulder, Lynne Rienner.

Harcourt G. C. (2001) "Investment Expenditure, Unrealised Expectations and Offsetting Monetary Policy", in G. C. Harcourt (Ed) *50 Years a Keynesian and other Essays*, Houndmills, Palgrave.

Harcourt, G. C. (2010). "The Crisis in Mainstream Economics", *Real-World Economics Review*, Vol. 53, No. 26, pp. 47–52.

Harcourt, G. C., Kriesler P. and J. W. Nevile (2013b). "Why Myths in Neoclassical Economics Threaten the World Economy: APost- Keynesian Manifesto", Australian School of Business, Research Paper No. 2013, ECON 36.

Harris, L. (1987). "Financial Reform and Economic Growth: A New Interpretation of South Korea's Experience", in L. Harris, J. Coakley, M. Croasdale, T. Evans (Eds) (1988). *New Perspectives on the Financial System*, London, Croom Helm.

IMF (International Monetary Fund), Various issues, *World Economic Outlook Database*, Washington, DC.

IMF, Various issues, *International Capital Markets: Developments, Prospects and Policy Issues*, Washington, DC.

IMF (1995a). *International Capital Markets, Developments, Prospects and Policy Issues*, Edited by D. Folkerts Landau and T. Ito et al. August.

IMF (1995b). *Mexico: Recent Economic Developments*, Washington DC, IMF, June.

IMF, (1995c). "IMF Approves US$17.8 Billion Stand-By Credit for Mexico", Press Release No. 95/10, Washington DC, IMF, February. [online]. Available at: https://www.imf.org/external/np/sec/pr/1995/pr9510.htm [Accessed on May 2014].

IMF, (1997). "International Capital MarketsDevelopments, Prospects, and Key Policy Issues", *World Economic and Financial Surveys*, Washington DC, IMF, November.

IMF, (1998). *Brazil – Recent Economic Developments*, Washington DC, IMF, January.

IMF, (1999). "Moderating Fluctuations in Capital Flows to Emerging Market Economies", *Finance and Development Quarterly*, Vol.36, No.3, Washington DC, IMF, September.

IMF, (2007). *The Special Data Dissemination Standard: Guide for Subscribers and Users*, Washington DC, IMF.

IMF, (2009). *Global Financial Stability Report*, Washington DC, IMF, April.

IMF, (2010). *"The Uses and Abuses of Sovereign Rating Agencies"*, Washington DC, IMF, February. [online]. Available at: https://www.imf.org/external/pubs/ft/gfsr/2010/02/pdf/chap3.pdf [Accessed on May 2014].

Kaldor, N. (1967). *Strategic Factors in Economic Development*, Ithaca, NY: Cornell University Press.

Kaldor, N. (1975). "What is Wrong with Economic Theory?", *Quarterly Journal of Economics*, Vol.89, pp. 347–57.

Kaminsky, G. and S. Schmukler (2001). "Emerging Markets Instability: Do Sovereign Ratings Affect Country Risk and Stock Returns?", *World Bank Policy Research Working Papers Series*, No. 2678, September.

Keynes, J. M. (1933). A Monetary Theory of Production, reprinted in *The Collected Writings of John Maynard Keynes*, Vol.13, (1973). Edited by D. Moggridge, London, MacMillan.

Keynes, J. M. (1936). The General Theory of Employment, Interest and Money, reprinted in *The Collected Writings of John Maynard Keynes*, Vol.7, (1973). Edited by D. Moggridge, London, MacMillan.

Keynes, J. M. (1939a). The Process of Capital Formation, Economic Journal, reprinted in *The Collected Writings of John Maynard Keynes*, Vol.14, (1973). Edited by D. Moggridge, London, MacMillan.

Keynes, J. M. (1939b). The Ex Ante Theory of the Rate of Interest, reprinted in *The Collected Writings of John Maynard Keynes*, Vol.14, (1973). Edited by D. Moggridge, London, MacMillan.

Kim, E. M. (1988). "From Dominance to Symbiosis: State and Chaebol in Korea", *Pacific Focus*, Vol.3, No. 2, p. 105–121.

Kim, K. (2006). *1997–98 Korean Financial Crisis: Causes, Policy Response, and Lessons*, The High-Level Seminar on Crisis Prevention in Emerging Markets, IMF and Government of Singapore, Singapore.

Kim, L. (1993). "National System of Industrial Innovation: Dynamics of Capability Building in Korea", pp. 357–383 in R. R. Nelson (Ed) *National Innovation Systems: A Comparative Analysis*, Oxford University Press.

Kindleberger, C. (2000). *Manias, Panics and Crashes: A History of Financial Crises*, New York, Palgrave Macmillan.

Kindleberger, C. and Aliber, R. (2005). *Manias, Panics and Crashes: A History of Financial Crises*, New Jersey, Palgrave Macmillan.

Kindleberger, C. and Laffargue, J. P. (1982). *Financial Crises: Theory History and Policy*, New York, Cambridge University Press.

Kregel, J. A. (2000). "The Brazilian Crisis: From Inertial Inflation to Fiscal Fragility", Working Paper 294, Levy Institute, New York.

Krueger, A. O. (1997). "Trade Policy and Economic Development: How We Learn", National Bureau of Economic Research, Working paper No. 5896.

Krueger, A. O., and J. Yoo, (2002). "Falling Profitability, Higher Borrowing Costs, and ChaebolFinances during the Korean Crisis", *Korean Crisis and Recovery*, IMF and KIEP, Washington DC and Seoul, pp. 157–196.

Krugman, P . (1995). "Dutch Tulips and Emerging Markets", *Foreign Affairs*, Vol. 74, No. 4, July/August.

Krugman, P. (2014). "Why We're in a New Gilded Age", *The New York Review of Books*, May 8, 2014 Issue.

Leonhardt, D. and K. Quealy (2014). "The American Middle Class is No Longer the World's Richest", *The New York Times*[online], 22 April 2014. Available at: [Accessed on April 2014].

Lora, E. (2001). *Structural Reforms in Latin America: What has been Reformed and how to Measure it*, Inter-American Development Bank, Research Department, Working Paper, No. 466.

Lustig, N. (1995). "The Mexican Peso Crisis: The Foreseeable and the Surprise", *Brookings Discussion Paper in International Economics*, Washington, DC, June.

Maia, G. (1999). "Restructuring the Banking System: The case of Brazil", BIS Policy Papers, BIS.

Magud, N., Reinhart, C. and K. Rogoff (2011). "Capital Controls: Myth and Reality – A Portfolio Balance Approach", NBER Working Paper, No. 16805, February.

McKinnon, R. (1973). *Money and Capital in Economic Development*, Washington DC, Brookings Institute.

McKinnon, R. (1993). *The Order of Economic Liberalization: Financial Control in the Transition to a Market Economy*, Baltimore, Johns Hopkins University Press.

McKinsey, (2008). *Mapping Global Financial Markets: Fifth Annual Report*, McKinsey Global Institute, October.

Minsky, H. (1982a). The Financial Instability Hypothesis: A Restatement, in H. Minsky (Ed) *Can "It" Happen Again? : Essays on Instability and Finance*, New York, Armonk

Minsky, H. (1982b). Financial Instability Revisited: The Economics of Disaster, in H. Minsky (Ed) *Can "It" Happen Again? : Essays on Instability and Finance*, New York, Armonk.

Minsky, H. (1986). *Stabilising and Unstable Economy*, New York, McGraw-Hill.

Moreno-Brid, J. C. andJ. Ros (2009). *Development and Growth in the Mexican Economy: A Historical Perspective: A Historical Perspective*, Oxford University Press, USA.

Morvan, T. S. A. (2000). "Financial Liberalisation and Financial Crises", Economics Division, Heriot-Watt University, Edinburgh, Scotland.

Nam S.-W. and S.-J. Kim (1999). "Evaluation of Korea's Exchange Rate Policy", NBER (National Bureau of Economic Research), NBER Book Series East Asia Seminar on Economics, Cambridge, MA.

New York Times (1988). "Brazil and Its Creditors Sign Debt Agreement", *The New York Times Archive*, 23rd September [online]. Available at: http://www.nytimes.com/1988/09/23/business/brazil-and-its-creditors-sign-debt-agreement.html[Accessed on March 2014].

Ocampo, J. A. (2002) "Developing countries' anti-cyclical policies in a globalized world", *Informes y EstudiosEspeciales series*, No. 4 (LC/L.1740-P), Santiago, Chile, Economic Commission for Latin America and the Caribbean (ECLAC), June 2002, figure 1. United Nations publication, Sales No. E.02. II.G.60.

Ocampo, J. A. (2003). *Capital-Account and Counter-Cyclical Prudential Regulations in Developing Countries*, United Nations Publications, ECLAC, Vol.6.

Ocampo, J. A (2004). "Latin America's Growth and Equity Frustrations During Structural Reforms", *Journal of Economic Perspectives*, Spring, Vol. 18, No.2, pp. 67–88.

Ocampo, J. A. (2006). "Latin America and the World Economy in the Long Twentieth Century" pp. 44–93, in K. S. Jomoed. *The Long Twentieth Century: The Great Divergence: Hegemony, Uneven Development and Global Inequality*, Oxford University Press, New Delhi.

Ocampo, J. A (2009). "Latin America and the Global Financial Crisis", *Cambridge Journal of Economics*, Vol.33, No.4, pp. 703–724.

Ocampo, J. A. and J.G. Palma (2007). "Dealing with Volatile External Finances at Source: The Rôle of Preventive Capital Account Regulations", in J. E. Stiglitz and J. A. Ocampo (Eds) *Capital Market Liberalization and Development*, Oxford: Oxford University Press.

Ocampo, J. A., Kregel, J. and S. Griffith-Jones (2007). *International Finance and Development*, London, Zed Books.

OECD (Organisation for Economic Co-operation and Development). Financial Market Trends, *OECD Journal*, Various Issues [online]. Available at: http://www.oecd-ilibrary.org/finance-and-investment/oecd-journal-financial-market-trends_19952872 [Accessed at various dates between 2010–2014].

OECD (2002), *OECD Economic Surveys: Mexico*, Paris: OECD

Organisation of American States (OAS), "North American Free Trade Agreement", Foreign Trade Information System, [online]. Available at: http://www.sice.oas.org/trade/nafta/chap-01.asp [Accessed on July 2013].

Ormerod, P. (2001). *Butterfly Economics: A New General Theory of Social and Economic Behaviour*, Pantheon Books, New York.

Paiva, C. (2006). "External Adjustment and Equilibrium Exchange Rate in Brazil", IMF Working Paper, No. 221. International Monetary Fund, October.

Palma, J. G. (1998). "Three and a Half Cycles of 'Mania, Panic and [Asymmetric] Crash': East Asia and Latin America Compared", *Cambridge Journal of Economics*, Vol.22, No.6., pp. 649–652

Palma, J. G. (2000). "The Three Routes to Financial Crises: The Need for Capital Controls", *CEPA Working Paper Series III*, Working Paper No.18.

Palma, J. G. (2002a). "The Three Routes to Financial Crises: The Need for Capital Controls", in J. Eatwell and L. Taylor (Eds) (2002). (297–314) *International Capital Markets: Systems in Transition*, Oxford: Oxford University Press.

Palma, J. G. (2002b). "The Magical Realism of Brazilian Economics: How to Create a Financial Crisis by Trying to Avoid One", in J. Eatwell and L. Taylor, (2002) *International capital markets: Systems in transition*. Oxford: Oxford University Press, 2002. , pp. 391–342.

Palma, J. G. (2003a). "The 'Three Routes' to Financial Crises", in Chang (2003). *Rethinking Development Economics*, London, Anthem Press, pp. 125–152.

Palma, J. G. (2003b). "Latin American During the Second Half of the 20th Century: From the 'Age of Extremes' to the Age of 'End-of-History' Uniformity", in Chang (2003).

Palma, J. G. (2006). "The 1999 Financial Crisis in Brazil: 'Macho-Monetarism' in Action", *Economic and Political Weekly*, Vol. 41, No.9.

Palma, J. G. (2009a). "The Revenge of the Market on the Rentiers. Why Neo-Liberal Reports of the End of History Turned out to be Premature", *Cambridge Journal of Economics*, Vol. 33, pp. 829–869.

Palma, J. G. (2009b). "Why did the Latin American Critical Tradition in the Social Sciences Become Practically Extinct?", in M. Blyth (Ed) *The Handbook of International Political Economy*, Routledge, New York.

Palma, J. G. (2011a). "Why has Productivity Growth Stagnated in most Latin American Countries since the Neo-Liberal Reforms?", in J. A. Ocampo and J. Ros (Eds) *The Oxford Handbook of Latin American Economics*, Oxford University Press, Oxford.

Palma, J. G. (2011b). "Homogeneous Middles vs. Heterogeneous Tails, and the End of the 'Inverted-U': The Share of the Rich is What it's All About", *Development and Change*, Vol. 42, No.1., pp. 87–153.

Palma, J. G. (2013). "How the Full Opening of the Capital Account to Highly Liquid and Unstable Financial Markets Led Latin America to Two and a Half Cycles of Mania, Panic and Crash", in M. Wolfson and G. A. Epstein (Eds) *The Handbook of the Political Economy of Financial Crises*, Oxford University Press, Oxford.

Park, W. A. (1996). "Financial Liberalisation: The Korean Experience" in T. Itoand A. Krueger (Eds) *Financial Deregulation and Integration in East Asia*, Chicago, University of Chicago Press, pp. 735–746.

Park, Y. C. (1990). "Development Lessons from Asia: The Role of Government in South Korea and Taiwan", *The American Economic Review*, Vol. 80, No.2, pp. 118–121.

Park, Y. C. (1994). "Korea: Development and Structural Change of the Financial System", in H. T. Patrick and Y. C. Park (Eds) *The Financial Development of Japan, Korea and Taiwan*, Oxford: Oxford University Press, pp. 129–187.

Park, Y. C. and C. Y. Song (2001). *Financial Contagion in the East Asian Crisis: With Special Reference to the Republic of Korea*, pp. 241–265, Springer US.

Peretz, D. (2010). "Bilateral Surveillance of the United Kingdom," IEO Background Paper No. BP/10/05, IMF, Washington D.C.

Persaud, A. (2000). "Sending the Herd off the Cliff Edge: The Disturbing Interaction between Herding and Market-Sensitive Risk Management Practices", *Journal of Risk Finance*, Vol.2, No.1., pp. 59–65.

Piketty, T. (2014). *Capital in the Twenty First Century*, Massachusetts, Harvard University Press.

Pringle, R (1989). *"Financial Markets and Governments"*, Working Papers, UNU WIDER, No.57, June.

Ramiderez de la O. R. (1995). *"Special Report on Mexico"*, Ecanal, September

Rodrik, D. (1994). "The Rush to Free Trade in the Developing World: Why so Late? Why Now? Will it Last?", in S. Haggard and S. B. Webb (Eds) *Voting for Reform: The Politics of Adjustment in New Democracies*, New York, Oxford University Press.

Rodrik, D. (2000). "Institutions for High-Quality Growth: What They are and How to Acquire Them", NBER Working Paper No. 7540, February.

Rodrik, D. (2014). "Death by Finance", Project Syndicate, Project Syndicate, [online]. Available at: http://www.project-syndicate.org/commentary/dani-rodrik-reviews-the-fundamental-lessons-about-emerging-economies-that-economists-have-refused-to-learn [Accessed on February 2014].

Rodrik, D. and A. Velasco (2000). "Short-Term Capital Flows", Annual World Bank Conference on: Development Economics 1999, Washington, DC, The World Bank.

Ros, J. (1991b). "The Effects of Government Policies on the Incentives to Invest, Enterprise Behaviour and Employment: A Study of Mexico's Economic Reform in the Eighties", Working Paper. No.53, World Employment Programme Research, Geneva: ILO.

Ros, J. (1995). "Trade Liberalization with Real Appreciation and Slow Growth: Sustainability Issues in Mexico's Trade Policy Reform", in G. Helleiner (Ed) *Manufacturing for Export in the Developing World*, London and New York, Routledge.

Sachs, J., Tornell, A. and A. Velsaco (1996). "Financial Crises in Emerging Markets: The Lessons from 1995", NBER Working Paper No. 5576, May.

Sachs, J., Velasco, A. and A. Tornell (1995). "The Collapse of the Mexican Peso, What Have we Learned?", NBER Working Paper, No 5142. June.

Sheng, A. (2009). *From Asian to Global Financial Crisis: An Asian Regulator's View of Unfettered Finance in the 1990s and 2000s*, New York: Cambridge University Press.

Singh, A. (1997). "Financial Liberalisation, Stock Markets and Economic Development", *The Economic Journal*, Vol. 107, pp. 771–782.

Singh, A. (2003). "Capital Account Liberalization, Free Long-Term Capital Flows, Financial Crises and Economic Development", *Eastern Economic Journal*, Vol.29. No.2, pp. 191–216.

Solow, R. M. (1985), "Economic History and Economics", *American Economic Review*, Vol. 75, No.2, pp. 328–331.

Standard & Poor's, "Stock Market Review", [Several issues, online]. Available at: http://www.standardandpoors.com/en_EU/web/guest/home[Accessed on various dates between 2010–2012].

Standard& Poor's (2011). "Sovereign Defaults And Rating Transition Data, 2010 Update". Available at: http://www.standardandpoors.com/ratings/articles/en/us/?assetID=1245302231824 [Accessed on May 2013].

Stiglitz, J. E. and J. A. Ocampo (Eds) (2007). *Capital Market Liberalization and Development*, Oxford: Oxford University Press.

Stiglitz, J. E. and M. Uy (1996). "Financial Markets, Public Policy and the East Asian Miracle", *World Bank Research Observer*, No. 11, pp. 249–276, August.

Stiglitz, J. E. and A. Weiss (1981). "Credit Rationing in Markets with Imperfect Informtion", *American Economic Review*, Vol. 71, pp. 393–410.

Subramani, M. and E. Walden (2001). "The Impact of E-Commerce Announcements on the Market Value of Firms", *Information Systems Research*, Vol. 12, No. 2, pp. 135–154

Taylor, L. (1999). *After Neoliberalism: What Next for Latin America*, Ann Arbor, University of Michigan Press.

Tobin, J. (1984). "On the Efficiency of the Financial System", *Lloyds Bank Review*, Vol.87, No.153, pp. 1–15.

Tomlinson, R. and D. Evans (2007). "CDO Boom Masks Subprime Losses"[online]. Available at: http://www.bloomberg.com/news/2007-05-31/cdo-boom-masks-subprime-losses-abetted-by-s-p-moody-s-fitch.html [Accessed November 2013].

US Census Bureau (2014). "Statistics About Business Size" [online]. Available at: http://www.census.gov/econ/smallbus.html#RcptSize [Accessed on May 2014].

US Department of Treasury, "Data and Charts Centre" [online]. Available at: http://www.treasury.gov/resource-center/data-chart-center/Pages/index.aspx [Accessed on various dates between 2013–2014].

US Department of Treasury (2009). *Financial Regulatory Reform, A New Foundation: Rebuilding Financial Supervision and Regulation*, Washington DC, US Treasury.

US Federal Reserve (1998). *Trade and Capital Markets Activities Manual* [online]. Available at: http://www.federalreserve.gov/boarddocs/supmanual/trading/4000p2.pdf [Accessed on February 2012].

US Government Printing Office (2011). *The Financial Crisis Inquiry Report*[online]. Available at: http://www.gpo.gov/fdsys/pkg/GPO-FCIC/pdf/GPO-FCIC.pdf[Accessed on various dates within 2013].

Wade, R. (1998). "The Asian Debt and Development Crisis of 1997: Causes and Consequences", *World Development*, Vol. 26, No. 8., pp. 1535–53.

Watson, Farley and Williams (December 2012). "Debt Capital Markets Briefing", [online]. Available at: http://www.wfw.com/Publications/Publication1175/$File/WFW-MaritimeDebtCapitalMarkets.pdf [Accessed on various dates between 2013–2014].

WB (World Bank). "World DataBank" [online]Available at: http://databank.world-bank.org/data/home.aspx [Accessed on various dates between 2009–2013].

WB (World Bank). "World Development Indicators" [online]Available at: http://data.worldbank.org/data-catalog/world-development-indicators [Accessed on various dates between 2009–2014].

WB (World Bank). "Global Financial Development" [online]Available at: http://data.worldbank.org/data-catalog/global-financial-development[Accessed on various dates between 2009–2013].

WB (World Bank), (1993). *The East Asian Miracle*, New York, Oxford University Press.

WB (World Bank), (1997). *Global Development Finance*, Washington, DC, World Bank.

Whittome, A. (1995). "Report on Fund Surveillance 1993–4 – Mexico" IMF, Washington D.C., March.

Williamson, J. (1990). *Latin American Adjustment: How Much Has Happened?*Washington, Institute for International Economics.

Wolf, M. (2014), "Capital in the 21st Century by Thomas Piketty", *The Financial Times*, Available at: http://www.ft.com/cms/s/2/0c6e9302-c3e2-11e3-a8e0-00144feabdc0.html#axzz30SkLWmdd [Accessed on April 2014].

Index

access
  to bonds, 72
  to capital *or* capital markets, 70,
    84, 140
  to credit, 31, 40, 41, 60, 87, 94,
    109, 145, 162
  to finance, 31, 47, 59, 171, 174
  to investment, 72, 173
  to liquidity, 30
  to stock markets, 89
Amsden, Alice, 109, 110
animal spirits, 30, 145, 156, 162

banks
  Brazilian Development Bank
    (BNDES), 88, 91, 96, 175
  Central Bank, 17, 57, 164
  commercial, 44, 50, 51, 69,
    70, 80, 88, 91, 117, 144, 171, 172,
    175
  deposits, *see under* deposits
  development, *see under individual*
    names
  Federal Reserve Bank, 51,
    73, 171
  Korea Exchange Bank, 108
  Korea Housing Bank, 108
  Korean Bank for Small and
    Medium-Sized Firms, 108
  Korean Development Bank, 108
  of Brazil, 7, 86, 87, 90, 91, 92, 95,
    99, 102, 135
  of Korea, 8, 108, 111, 112
  of Mexico, 7, 69, 76, 147, 173
  private banks, 7, 29, 66, 98, 155
  shadow banking system, 20, 50,
    166, 171
  system, banking, 7, 18, 20, 21, 50,
    69, 70, 73, 92, 93, 96, 98, 101,
    104, 106, 110, 113, 139, 143, 153,
    155, 175
Basel Committee on Banking
  supervision, 54, 56

bonds, 23, 41, 43, 49, 90, 95, 96, 155
  Brady, *see under* Brady debt
    agreement
  corporate, *see under private bonds*
  Eurobonds, 54
  Fixed-interest, 141
  government, *see under* public bonds
  private, 3, 42, 56, 72, 89, 90, 100,
    115, 127, 173, 177
  public, 7, 57, 58, 66, 71, 72, 73, 79,
    88, 89, 94, 97, 102, 125–7, 140,
    170, 175
  sovereign, *see under* public bonds
  US Treasury, 3, 19, 50
  variable-interest, 141
borrowing, 26, 41, 74, 102, 108, 115,
    173
  external *see* international borrowing
  domestic, 133
  foreign *see* international borrowing
  international, 76–77, 82, 90, 108,
    115, 119, 164
  over-borrowing, 162
  short-term, 106, 143
  see also loans
Brady debt agreement *or* Plan, 84, 86,
    155, 171–3
  Brady bonds, 57, 66–67, 70, 72, 85,
    95, 171, 173
Brazil, 84–105
  see also individual variables
Brazilian Real, 86–7, 90–98, 103, 133
  see also Real Plan
  capital account, 87, 162, 179
  deregulation, 6, 134
  liberalisation, 2–4, 66, 67, 84, 110
  open, 2, 7–11, 14, 121, 170

capital flows
  excessive, 87
  exodus, 87
  foreign, *see under* interantional
  increases, 3, 8, 38, 52, 86, 154, 157

international, 10, 107, 122, 139, 166, 170
long-term, 166
portfolio, 88, 94
restrictions, 13, 151
short-term, 68, 73, 159, 164
sterilisation, *see under* sterilisation
to emerging economies, 52, 154
volatility, 3, 61, 146
capital markets, 15, 19, 42, 57, 62, 129
Brazilian, 88
deregulation, 48, 72
emerging, 129
international, 42, 44, 49, 62, 74, 82–4, 86, 94
liberalisation, 1, 60, 110, 144, 153
securitization, 45
Western, 47
Capitalism, 12, 14–5, 13, 22–3, 24–7, 30, 147, 149, 154, 168
crony capitalism, 117
financial system, 1–2
financial markets, 11, 15
CETES, 73, 79–81, 141, 158
chaebols, 108–110, 144
Chang, Ha-Joon, 106, 109, 111–2, 116–9, 144, 150, 176
Chiapas, 74, 77
Chile, 58, 166, 128, 185, 172
Collor de Melo, 85
Collor Plan, 86
Colosio, Luis Donaldo, 74, 80
commodity, 32, 59–61, 90, 109
prices, 31
competition, 45, 63, 72, 84, 94, 144, 174
construction sector, 109
Consumer Price Index, 84, 95
see also inflation
consumption, 40–1, 68, 73–4, 90, 133, 137, 139, 140, 147, 149–50, 154, 156–7, 162, 169, 171, 178
boom, 7, 66, 100
bubbles, 149
credit, 70
mania, 154
contagion, 36–7, 95, 102, 117, 120, 122, 136, 139, 160,

crash, 21, 34, 100, 120, 147, 157
Credit Rating Agencies (CRAs), 49, 50, 54–55, 112–3, 122, 155–5, 163, 177
creditors, 44, 66, 84, 174, 189
crises
financial, 1–5, 8–10, 12, 15, 22, 24, 26, 30, 32, 34, 36, 46, 64, 67, 80, 103, 121–3, 130, 151–4, 156–7, 165, 176, 178
prevention of, 151, 173
systemic, 1–3, 24, 122, 132, 133
Cruzado currency, 84–5
Cruzeiro currency, 84–7
currency crises, 67, 120
current account, 69, 74, 87, 111, 162–3, 179
balance, 67, 78, 87, 88
deficit, 67, 76–7, 82, 84–5, 98, 105–7, 111, 143, 148–9, 157, 174

decentralization, 25
debt
accumulation, 119, 126
crises, 2, 9, 43, 68, 82, 120, 164
debt-equity ratios, 26, 127, 150
maturity mismatch, 101–2, 119, 179
non-performing, 7, 66, 98, 101, 155, 159
service, 98, 119
demand pull, 3, 38–9, 40–1, 56–63, 133, 150, 154–5, 160, 162, 170–1
deregulation, 2–9, 32, 36, 38, 40–1, 44–6, 48–52, 57, 59, 61, 68, 71–2, 88, 110, 112, 114–5, 119, 121–5, 127, 129, 150, 152, 156, 169, 173, 176, 177, 191
derivatives, 40, 48–9, 51, 57, 59, 88, 94
deposits, 3, 49, 57, 60, 82, 85, 90–3, 96, 115, 138, 141, 171, 175

East Asia, 43, 58, 60–1, 66, 105, 107, 131, 134, 136–7, 142–6, 148, 150, 157, 162, 169, 178
East Asian crisis, 59, 130, 131
economic growth *see* growth

economies:
  developed, 38, 165
  developing, 4, 6, 41, 77, 121, 133,
    171
  emerging, 1, 10, 38, 40–1, 47–8,
    52, 54–64, 69, 122, 127–30, 135,
    138–42, 151–4, 160, 164–6, 171,
    173, 177
  middle-income, 1, 20, 46, 67, 131,
    152, 154
  OECD, 44, 133
  Western, 5, 171
Efficient Market Hypothesis (EMH),
  18, 32, 35–6, 63, 122, 125, 152–3,
  169, 177
endogenous, 1, 5, 13, 22, 24–6, 30–2,
  49, 63, 103, 133, 154, 157, 159,
  179
Ergodic Axiom, 16–8, 21, 23, 32, 125,
  129, 154, 160, 169
exchange rate, 32, 51, 59, 67–8, 70,
  74, 76, 80, 85–7, 99, 102–3, 114,
  116, 141, 143–4, 146, 148–9,
  155–7, 166, 169, 173
  changes, 45
  controls, 48
  effective, 95
  fixed, 45, 97, 102
  floating, 45, 94
  fluctuations, 10, 37, 43, 51, 175
  nominal, 69
  official, 79
  real, 61, 68, 78, 87, 95, 106, 165,
    174
  risk, 41
  stability, 68
  volatility, 43
exogenous, 22, 31, 37, 117, 157, 169,
  179
  changes, 20, 63
  liquidity, 2, 5, 21, 178
  shocks, 103, 173
exports, 60, 68
  Brazilian, 88, 141
  commodity, 59
  East Asian, 143, 148
  industrial, 59, 116, 175
  Korean, 176
  Latin American, 59, 146, 149, 157

manufacturing, *see* industrial
  exports
  Mexican, 77, 178
external, 12, 44, 57, 58, 61, 63, 68,
  80, 85, 96, 113, 134, 146, 153,
  164, 174
  debt, 68, 76, 82, 96, 117–20, 121, 134
  direction, 5, 63
  factors, 3, 11, 37, 52
  financing, 80, 121, 178
  inflows, 36, 97
  investment, 96, 150
  liquidity, 10

financial crises *see* crises
financial deepening, 2, 11, 40, 94
financial flows, 1, 10–12, 38–45, 62,
  73, 86, 88, 129, 134, 138–9, 152,
  165, 175
Financial Instability Hypothesis (FIH),
  24–5, 30, 129
financial institutions, 21, 26, 41, 44,
  48, 62, 82, 89, 92, 110, 113, 115,
  133, 138, 144, 163–4, 171
financial liberalisation, 1, 6, 9, 10, 39,
  60, 94, 110–6, 119, 140, 145, 147,
  152, 155, 159, 166
financial products, 6, 40, 43, 46, 52,
  59, 90, 94, 122, 163
financialisation, 46, 83, 145, 167–8
fiscal
  changes, 56–7, 80
  deficit, 98
  imbalances, 98
  policy, 9, 38, 45, 57, 82, 86, 97,
    127, 141, 146, 148, 172
  position, 93
  surplus, 68
float, the, 90, 93–4
Foreign Direct Investment (FDI), 42, 59,
  60, 77, 105, 115, 131, 144, 173, 177
foreign exchange
  accumulation, 113
  Brazilian direct purchases, 170
  fluctuations, 164
  inflows, 7, 108, 111
  Korean Foreign Exchange
    Concentration System, 108,
    111–2, 116

Korean Foreign Exchange
    Management Act, 108, 111
Korean Foreign Exchange Reform
    Plan, 116
    liberalisation, 116
    markets, 116
    products, 51
    regulation, 111
    reserves, 67, 74–6, 79, 80, 86,
        97, 112, 117, 120, 132–6,
        156–7, 164, 176,178
    revenues, 94
    risk, 164–5
    shortage, 108
    swaps, 164, 179

GDP, 60, 64, 71, 123, 127, 170
    Brazil, 88–9, 91, 93, 96, 98, 102, 175
    deflator, 85, 172
    emerging world, 69
    East Asia, 137
    global, *see* world
    Korea, 109, 111, 123, 127
    Latin America, 140, 145
    Mexico, 76–9, 123, 127, 129, 178
    world, 39, 48
    see also growth
GNP, 116, 119
globalization, 45
government bonds, *see under* bonds,
    public
growth
    credit, 31, 47, 59, 71, 77, 87, 149
    economic, 3, 9, 11–3, 19, 23, 30–1,
        39, 59–61, 68, 103, 105, 133, 149,
        167
    export, 59–60
    financial, 11, 39, 51, 110, 139
    liquidity, 56
    long-term, 99
    manufacturing, 61, 110
    mortgages, 69
    non-inflationary, 89

Heavy and Chemical Industrialisation
    (HCI), 108
hedge funds, 127
herd behavior, 61, 122, 125, 127,
    139–40, 156, 158, 161–2, 177

heterodox economics, 10–11

imports, 37, 46, 108, 171
    consumption goods, 148, 178
    Import Substitution
        Industrialisation (ISI), 60
    intermediate, 146
    manufacturing, 59, 61
    tariffs, 66, 77, 84, 108
industry
    Brazilian, 84, 90
    economies, 52
    exports, 59
    goods, 20
    Korean, 105, 108–117, 150, 153,
        155, 169, 176
    Mexican, 59–60, 77, 174
    policy, 108–117, 141
    sector, 144, 150, 172
inequality, 167
inflation, 10, 45, 162, 172
    arbitrage, 159
    Brazil, 84–7, 90, 93–4, 125, 176
    hyperinflation, 85, 159
    income, 159
    Mexico, 67–8, 76–7, 82–3, 121, 153
    revenue contribution, 90, 91, 94,
        99, 102, 175
    stock price, 123
    USA, 43
    see also GDP deflator
information, 34–6, 82, 97, 119,
    122–3, 128–9, 138, 156,
    160, 173–5
    asymmetry, 11–2, 22, 36, 54, 125,
        169–70
    price, 34
    symmetry, *see under* information
        asymmetry
    technology and IT progress, 40, 47,
        53–4
instability
    financial, 2, 7, 9, 12–3, 24, 27, 30,
        36, 66, 97, 129, 131, 151, 155
    fundamental, 25, 147, 154, 156
    inherent, 11, 15, 22, 153
institutions
    banking, 42, 44, 45, 46, 90–92, 110,
        144, 159, 163, 175

institutions – *continued*
  financial, 21, 26, 41, 44, 48, 62,
    82, 89, 92, 110, 113, 115, 133,
    138, 144, 163, 164, 171
  political, 169
  Western, 54
insurance, 42, 44, 48, 50, 51, 54, 94,
    115, 151, 163
integration, 36, 38, 43, 59, 66, 84,
    94, 172
interest rates, 19, 20, 29
  Asian, 106
  Brazilian, 90, 93–4, 96–102, 159,
    175–6
  developed countries, 64, 165
  emerging economies, 138,
    142, 144
  immediate, 65, 140, 172
  international, 115
  Latin American, 61
  Korean, 110
  LIBOR, 65
  long-term, 29
  Mexican, 69, 75
  short-term, 52–3, 94, 96, 142
  USA, 19, 43, 52–3, 65, 67, 103,
    133–4, 138, 165
  world, 52
international financial markets, 29,
    38, 40, 59, 62, 80, 94, 103, 123,
    136, 146, 148, 154, 163
international financial system, 80
International Monetary Funds (IMF),
    12, 61–2, 80, 82, 95, 97, 130, 159,
    169, 172–4, 176
international reserves, *see under*
  foreign exchange reserves

Japan, 37, 105–6, 143–4

Kaldor, Nicholas, 168, 170
Keynes, John Maynard, 1, 2, 4–5, 9,
    11–24, 32, 34, 37–8, 122, 125,
    129, 139, 149, 153–4, 156, 160,
    169, 170, 179
Kim, Young Sam, 110, 117, 119
Kindleberger, Charles, 9, 11–3, 30–7,
    100, 122–3, 138–9, 145–7, 154,
    162, 179

Korea, Republic of, 105–121
  See also individual variables
Korean Won, 116

Latin American
  See under individual variables
lender of last resort principle, 26, 34,
    80, 100, 102
liabilities, 24–9, 45, 50, 57–8, 73, 76,
    92, 96, 101–2, 134, 143, 146–7,
    153, 156, 158, 163, 165, 175
liberalisation *see* financial
  liberalisation
loanable funds theory, 12, 16,
    18–20, 149, 154

macroeconomic
  fundamentals, 3, 9, 68,
    157, 159
  imbalances, 105, 121, 143
  indicators, 10, 32, 155, 160
  policy, 1, 12, 76, 82, 114, 134,
    176
mainstream economics, 2, 9–12, 34–6,
    152, 167
manias, 31–5, 100, 134, 139,
    146–7, 149, 154, 156–7, 159,
    161, 179
  investment, 30, 31, 83, 100, 156
  manufacturing, 59–61, 88, 109,
    116–7, 117, 143–4, 149–50, 158,
    168, 170, 172, 175
  speculative, 34, 154
  see also industry
Maturity mismatch, 101–2, 119, 179
Mexican Peso, 67, 69, 72–5, 77, 79,
    82, 148, 173
Mexico
  See under individual variables
Microelectronics industry, 116–7,
    150, 176
Middle-income countries, 1–6, 9–10,
    13, 20, 30, 38, 46, 51, 62, 64,
    66–7, 79, 94, 121–2, 130–1, 138,
    151–2, 154, 167, 172, 175, 179
Minsky, Hyman, 9, 11–5, 22, 24–30,
    32, 36–7, 54, 66, 102, 122,
    129–30, 147, 151, 153–6, 160,
    162, 175

money neutrality, 16–17
moral hazard, 29, 35, 54
multilateral cooperation, 174
multinational companies, 60

national currencies
   See under individual variables
neo-classical economics, 5
New Financial Architecture (NFA), 36,
   38, 40
Newly Industrialised Countries
   (NICs), 12, 169
Non-Bank Financial Institutions
   (NBFIs), 92, 110, 144
non-performing loans, 7, 66, 70, 74,
   82, 98, 101, 106, 155
North Atlantic Free Trade Agreement
   (NAFTA), 59, 77, 148, 174–97,
   102–3

Opening up of markets, 64, 66, 84, 145
   see also deregulation
Organisation for Economic
   Cooperation and Development
   (OECD), 44, 52, 62, 77, 114, 119,
   133, 138, 170, 172, 178

Palma, Jose Gabriel, 6, 40, 41, 59,
   64, 66, 97, 162, 167, 169, 170,
   175–6, 179
Panics, 26, 31, 34, 74, 80, 83, 96, 106,
   117, 12–1, 129, 136, 147, 154,
   157–63
Piketty, Thomas, 167
Ponzi
   finance, 7, 28–30, 66, 97, 102–3,
      154, 175
   scheme, 29
poverty, 146
private debt, *see under* debt
private sector
   Brazil, 90–6, 101, 159, 175
   Korea, 121
   Mexico, 70–1, 76, 140
privatization, 41–2, 57, 60–1, 64, 68,
   70, 85, 90, 92, 94, 96, 102, 121,
   127, 150, 155, 169, 170
pro-cyclical capital flows, 24, 31, 127,
   133, 138–9, 145, 156–7

productivity, 13, 45, 83, 105, 144,
   150, 160, 168, 170
PROER, 91–3, 103, 175
PROES, 91–3, 103
public debt, *see under* debt
public sector, 7, 29, 66, 76, 82, 97,
   102–3, 134, 142, 148, 158–9, 176

real estate, 7, 31–2, 37, 66, 100, 111,
   147, 153, 156, 158, 179
Real Plan, 86–7, 90–8, 141–2, 159,
   170, 174
regulation, 1, 13, 37–41, 47, 51–4, 57,
   59, 62, 70, 72–3, 90, 94, 96, 107,
   110–3, 119, 128, 134,
   144–7, 163–5, 173, 177
   see also deregulation
reserves, *see under* foreign exchange
   reserves

securitisation, 43, 45, 47, 49–50, 57,
   94, 163–4, 171
speculation, 13, 15, 28–34, 37, 45–6,
   74, 80, 83, 95, 122, 139, 154, 158,
   160, 165
   attack, 59, 95, 117, 157, 164
   finance, 28–30, 175
   investment, 25, 156, 179
   mania, 34, 154
   motive, 22, 139
   portfolio inflows, 70
stability
   capital, 80
   economic, 56, 98, 108, 134, 144,
      156, 164, 172
   exchange rate, 68
   financial, 26, 29–30, 56, 177
   political, 80
   price, 70, 99
   see also instability
state owned enterprises, 41, 94, 109
sterilization, 7, 29, 66, 76, 96, 99–104,
   133, 135, 137, 153, 155, 170, 172,
   178–9
stock exchange market, 44, 47–8, 58,
   96, 138, 155
   capitalization, 3, 123–4, 129, 177
supply-push, 3, 38–40, 47–56, 63,
   133, 152, 154, 157, 162, 170

Taiwan, 109, 116, 169, 176
tariffs, 66, 77, 84, 108
telecommunications, 105, 173
  see also information
Tesobonos, 73, 79–81, 141, 148, 155
three routes, 6, 46, 122, 152
trade, 27, 32, 35, 41, 45, 56, 59,
    59–64, 129, 143, 174, 178
  Brazil, 84, 86–7, 94
  Korea, 105, 111–3
  liberalisation, 8, 59–61, 66, 74, 133,
    141, 169
  Mexico, 67–8, 77, 82
  terms of, 52, 68, 171
  USA, 37
transparency, 45, 62, 117, 122, 138,
    173

UK, 40, 44, 48, 165
unemployment, 16, 21, 32

USA
  Dollar, 39, 42, 48, 49, 67, 71, 72–80,
    87–89, 99, 100, 107, 116, 118,
    123–4, 126, 128, 131–2, 135–7,
    140, 143, 170–1, 175, 177, 179
  interest rates, 67, 103, 165 *see also*
    interest rates USA
  Treasury bills, 53, 80, 81, 97

volatility, 1, 3, 5, 59, 61, 73, 77, 79,
    122, 125–9, 150–1, 160–3
  debt, 79
  financial, 23, 61, 146, 154, 156
  geopolitical, 108
  inflow, 146, 150, 156, 165–6
  investment, 156
  price, 43, 61, 138, 145

World Bank (WB), 12, 61–2, 119, 169,
    177